MODERN BODY ARMOUR

MODERN BODY ARMOUR

MARTIN J. BRAYLEY

THE CROWOOD PRESS

First published in 2011 by
The Crowood Press Ltd
Ramsbury, Marlborough
Wiltshire SN8 2HR

www.crowood.com

© Martin J. Brayley 2011

All rights reserved. No part of this publication may be reproduced or transmitted in any form or by any means, electronic or mechanical, including photocopy, recording, or any information storage and retrieval system, without permission in writing from the publishers.

British Library Cataloguing-in-Publication Data
A catalogue record for this book is available from the British Library.

ISBN 978 1 84797 248 4

Frontispiece: The frontispiece is a pre-production photograph of NATICK developed aircrew armour and ballistic flight helmet, from December 1970. (US National Archives)

NB. Weights in pounds (lb) and ounces (oz) are imperial British unless suffixed by (US) in which case they are in US measurement.

Within this work the term 'body armour' refers to the complete ensemble of outer fabric cover, inner ballistic filler and SAPI plates where fitted.

'Our armed forces have seen a lot of combat in recent years, in the Gulf War, the Balkans, Sierra Leone, Iraq and Afghanistan. Improvements in body armour and vehicles have meant that many injuries that were once fatal are now survivable.'
Surg Lt Cdr B Tamayo RN

Designed and typeset by Focus Publishing, Sevenoaks, Kent

Printed and bound in China by Everbest Printing Co Ltd

Acknowledgements

I am wholly indebted to a number of individual collectors and interested parties for their invaluable assistance with this work and without whom it would never have come to print. An alphabetical listing of contributors is an inadequate thank you as I am grateful to each and every individual who assisted with this book and without whom it would not be quite the work that it is. I would, however, like to highlight the contributions made by John Bodsworth for access to material from his series of magazine articles on British body armour. Andy and the team at Eastwestrading Group have provided support for a couple of my recent titles and are always more than happy to assist with items for photography. Ed Storey has once again provided much of the material in the Canadian section, and I must also thank my son Toby for his input, and an excellent knowledge of current military uniforms and equipment.

From the UK:
Julian Atwood
John Bodsworth
Toby Brayley
Shane Coyne, 3 Para
Brett Emblin and Simon of VietnamGear.com
Mike Glover of Beaufort
Andy Stevens of UCAP
Richard Ingram of Sabre Sales
Rob Jose
Loz Moynihan, Royal Marines Fleet Protection Group
Richard Sanders, Hampshire Police
Vincenzo Sidoni
Solo International
Surgeon Lieutenant Commander Brando Tamayo, Royal Navy
Andy and Killa of Eastwestrading Group, ew-trading.com
Andy Wooders, Hampshire Police

From overseas:
Walter H Bradford, US Army Center of Military History, USA
Jack Carrico, author of Vietnam Ironclads, USA
Michael Ferretti, USA
Dave De Ridder, Belgium
Jennifer Robinson, BAE Systems, USA
Michaela Hahn, Mehler Vario System GmbH, Germany
Luther Hanson, Quartermaster Corps Museum, USA
Elias Jones, USA
Ljubisa Kovacevic, Serbia
Thomas Kuehnlein, Mehler Vario System GmbH, Germany
Adrian Li, Australia
Sarah Parke, National Museum of the US Air Force, USA
Victor Shestakov, Russia
Bruce Siemon, USAREUR
www.soviet.com.pl Poland
Mike Stelzel, USA
Ed Storey, Canada
Jared Sweet, USA
Lars Wigren, USA
United States Department of Defense
US National Archives

Contents

	Introduction	6
1.	United States of America	16
2.	Great Britain	76
3.	Other Nations: A Visual Summary	126
	Belgium	126
	Canada	128
	Denmark	131
	France	132
	Germany	135
	Iraq	141
	Israel	143
	Italy	144
	Japan	146
	Netherlands	147
	Norway	148
	Russia	149
	Serbia	153
	Slovenia	155
4.	Conclusion: The Future of Individual Body Armour	156
	Glossary	157
	Bibliography	159
	Index	160

Introduction

Body armour epitomized by the protective suit worn by a medieval knight. The areas of the body that required protection would be readily recognized by modern armour developers. While the armour could defeat sword blows, it required a considerable layer of padding, in the form of bulky undergarments, to reduce blunt-trauma injury. Inevitably, it was often the combined effects of exhaustion and blunt-trauma injury that led to the eventual incapacitation of any combatant wearing this heavy armour.

Iron body armour, on display on the warship *Success*, of the type worn by Australian bushranger Ned Kelly and his gang. Its weight, 92lb, has been painted on the armour. This set was certainly heavy and would have been exceptionally clumsy in wear. Additionally, blunt-trauma injury could have been quite severe. The provenance of this particular armour is not known. (US Library of Congress)

Modern ballistic body armour

Ballistic armour is usually considered a relatively modern tool in the soldier's armoury. Armour used in the 19th century, when rifle and artillery dominated the battlefield, was generally used by cavalry as a protection from lance and sword thrusts, or as a badge of office for troops who were the elite of their day. It was relatively incapable of providing any ballistic protection or preventing close range penetration from the muskets or rifles of the time. Advances in small arms and field artillery, as well as tactical considerations, soon saw armour relegated to use simply for ceremonial duties. No thought was given to providing soldiers with protection from small arms or artillery, since there was no practical protection available at that time.

While the military had not taken up the use of body armour, one historic use of ballistic protection was by the criminal gang led by Ned Kelly in Australia. Kelly used a variety of scrap metals to fabricate a heavy metal suit that covered the head, torso and abdomen. Weighing in at 96lb (44kg) it was certainly quite heavy, but did provide protection from the weapons in use with the police and military forces hunting down the Kelly gang. Ned Kelly used the armour during the Glenrowan raid of 26 June 1880 – possibly the first recorded use of individual ballistic body armour.

By the beginning of the 20th century silk fabric was being used to produce effective, but extremely expensive, ballistic vests. A Polish immigrant, Casimir Zeglen of Chicago, designed one such vest in the late 1800s. It offered limited protection from low velocity, black-powder handguns, but was ineffective against the higher velocity smokeless powder, metal-cased ammunition. In 1914 Zeglen's vests cost US$800, a figure probably close to £10,000 in the current economy. Zeglen later worked with fellow Pole Jan Szczepanik to further improve upon personal body armour. King Alfonso XIII of Spain used a heavy-duty silk vest produced by Jan Szczepanik. It was stated that the vest would stop the 8mm (0.32in) ball ammunition fired from a Mannlicher 1895 rifle. Indeed, the vest and armour cladding of the King's carriage saved him in 1902 when an assassin made an unsuccessful attempt on his life.

The value of ballistic protection was not at all alien to many of the world's leaders during the turbulent opening stages of the 20th century. Archduke Franz Ferdinand of Austria was one of those who routinely wore a silk fabric ballistic vest when in public. During a visit to Sarajevo on 28 June 1914, Franz Ferdinand was wearing his silk vest beneath his high-collared tunic. He was approached by Bosnian Serb activist Gavrilo Princip, who, at close-range, shot the Archduke with a .32 ACP pistol. The vest would probably have been more than adequate to reduce the injury from the impact of such a round. However, the round passed just above the edge of the vest, lodging in the Archduke's neck, the injury ultimately leading to his death.

Introduction

In France, around 1914, this was not quite personal body armour, but a one-man assembly nonetheless. This handcart with frontal armour was deployed by French troops during the opening stages of the Great War. The contraption was considered a portable defensive fixed-firing position, rather than a mobile offensive apparatus. While reasonably mobile on roads or hard flat ground, the entrenched warfare that was soon to dominate the conflict rapidly made this type of device all but useless. However, the idea was explored by other combatant nations. Early in the war the Admiralty produced wheeled shields for 5-15 men. Made by Vickers and Beardmore, the shields were believed to have been sent to the Dardanelles and France and also to Russia with the 15th and 17th Armoured Car Squadrons. The 6th Infantry Division used wheeled shields in France, during 1915, designed by Lt Smith of the RN Armoured Car Service. Quite unbelievably, a programme to develop a man-portable mobile shield was initiated by the USA during September 1943. The research resulted in the production of the 'T1E2 Mobile Shield', but the project was soon scrapped because it encountered the same problems and restrictions as had been found during the Great War. ('Horsepower' KRH Museum)

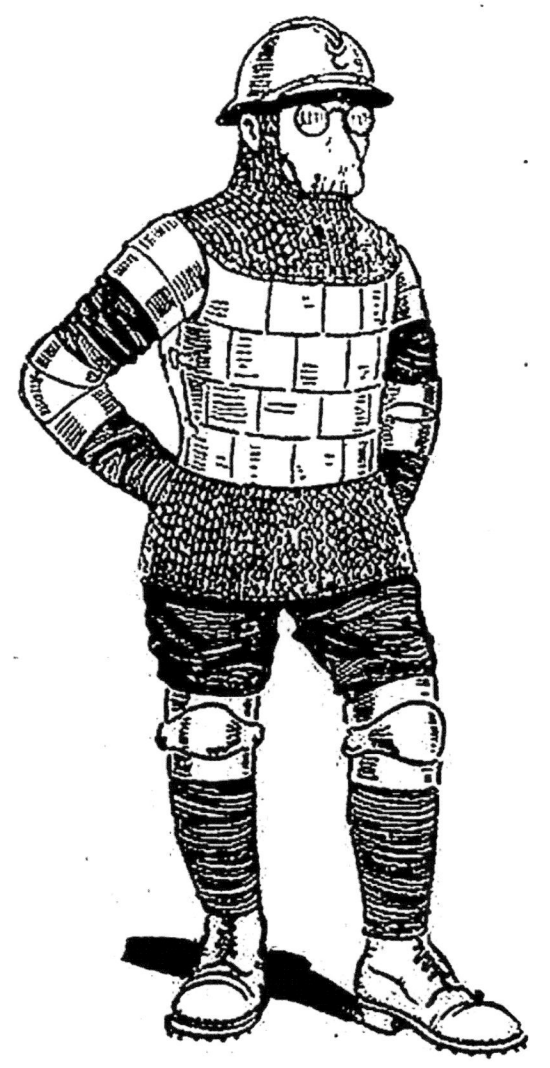

A comical sketch from a 1917 magazine shows the lengths to which armour could have been developed to provide ballistic protection in the trenches. This was a derisory comment on serious efforts to reduce casualties with the use of individual armour.

Introduction

A vest type body armour is demonstrated to civic dignitaries and members of the police force in the USA, around 1923. Such tests left little doubt among the observers as to an armour's effectiveness. However, in truth, such commercial displays were of limited value, since results could be engineered, for example by using ammunition modified to reduce impact velocities and thus 'improve' a product's value. Regardless, high confidence in one's demonstration partner was an essential attribute. (US Library of Congress)

Body armour requirements

Body armour is required to provide ballistic protection to the wearer, while still allowing them to undertake their prescribed duties. This means that the wearer must be able to move unhindered, to sit, stand, lie prone or adopt a number of different body positions as required; use any personal weapons or weapon systems without detrimental effect upon the accuracy or efficiency of the weapons; and be readily able to use any optical, communications or other equipment – a tall order indeed.

The levels of ballistic protection and body coverage both determine the weight of the armour, and thus have a great effect on the ease of movement. The body coverage itself also affects ease of movement, thus the heavier the armour and the greater the body coverage, the greater the restriction on movement. The knock-on effect results in a degree of hindrance. A basic example is the difficulty of adopting a comfortable prone firing position when using the majority of armour sets that provide any degree of neck protection. Typically any set of armour is a compromize, based upon a careful assessment of the levels of ballistic protection and degree of body coverage, weighed against ease of use of equipment and freedom of movement.

Body armour is required to provide protection from penetrative and blunt-trauma impacts from small arms and blast fragments. Vital body areas that should be protected are the major body organs, heart, lungs, kidneys, etc. Additional protection, in varying degrees, is often provided for the neck, groin, lower abdomen and shoulders.

Blunt-trauma injury can be reduced by having an adequate 'standoff'. This is the gap between the wearer's body and armour vest. In most soft armours this requirement is ignored to reduce weight and bulk. However, small arms protective insert (SAPI) plates often have an anti-trauma backing as standard, since they allow some protection from high velocity impacts, with their inherently increased risks of blunt-trauma injury, by providing the necessary standoff. As an example, with a heavy armour plate designed to protect against .5in (12.7-mm) impacts, the standoff required is no less than 1in (2.5cm) and the backing material must have a dynamic pressure of around 20psi (139kPa) to absorb the impact. Even then, a hit from such a high-energy projectile would be most debilitating, since the transmission of impact pressure waves could not be completely prevented and there would still be a resulting high risk of bradycardia or other blunt-trauma injuries.

Soft Armour

Modern soft armour consists of multiple layers of woven ballistic fabric such as nylon, Kevlar, Dyneema, Spectra or Twaron. Missiles striking the armour vest usually penetrate any outer cover and impact the ballistic filler. The individual fibres and successive layers serve to reduce the missiles' impact velocity by dissipating and absorbing the kinetic (impact) energy throughout the fibres and layers of the vest, with each layer acting in series to slow and then stop the bullet. A great degree of the surface area of fabric is used in defeating the impact and reducing blunt-trauma injury.

Dependant upon the missile's velocity and mass, and the ballistic rating of the armour filler, the vest will defeat the projectile if impact parameters are within the protection standards of the vest. However, the impact will usually result in a degree of indentation of the vest filler against the wearer's body, causing some bruising. In more severe impacts there may also be blunt-trauma injury where

A USAF airman of the 31st Security Forces Squadron, provides perimeter security at Aviano Air Base, Italy, during 2007. The airman wears an Army Combat Helmet (ACH) and the basic Interceptor OTV vest. While most vests provide reasonable cover to the front of the body, firing positions (such as the kneeling position shown here) present a side-on aspect to the enemy. Equally, the fragmentation weapons used in combat tend to have a 360° blast arc and can fall at any point around a soldier, resulting in all areas of the body being vulnerable. The areas shaded in red are those that are highly vulnerable to injury, even when wearing a ballistic helmet and body armour, since vital organs lay beneath these areas. The axillary region was dangerously exposed in most of the vests used during the 20th century, but additional protection is now offered by modern vests, such as the OTV and Osprey, in the form of axillary and/or deltoid protector panels. If the additional OTV axillary and deltoid panels had been fitted to the vest worn here, it would have left only the head and face exposed, dramatically increasing the protection offered. (US DoD)

A Navy Hospital Corpsman treats a wounded Marine from 6th Marine Regiment, following the explosion of an IED initiated by the patrolling Marines. This Marine has suffered injury from fragmentation and flash burn to the neck and face, but his MTV armour may have helped prevent serious wounds to his upper body. (US Marine Corps)

Introduction

the body itself has absorbed some of the impact energy. However, impacts close to the edge of the fabric, although they can still be defeated, are often the cause of increased blunt-trauma injury, since less of the energy is absorbed by the vest and more by the wearer's body. Upon impact the bullet itself absorbs energy and changes shape upon contact with the ballistic fibres, the usual bullet form deforming into a mushroom shape. The degree of deformation of the fabric is linked to the instances of injury to wearers.

The acceptable individual levels of impact depression (back face deformation) vary with nation of manufacture and end user. The American National Institute of Justice (NIJ) standards allow for 44mm (1.75in) of impact depression. However, military users often require indentation of 20mm (0.75in) or less to help reduce incapacitation from blunt-trauma injury. The NIJ standard of depression in soft armour is quite a deep impact. Such a figure would allow for quite severe blunt-trauma injury, particularly over the sternum, since soft armour deforms readily under impact and transfers the kinetic force of the fragment or bullet strike directly to the wearer's body through the armour. In addition to immediate blunt-trauma injury the greater the amount of energy absorbed by the body, rather than the vest, the greater is the wearer's level of incapacity immediate post impact. The ability of a wearer to recover and react quickly after any strike on their armour is vitally important in preventing further injury from additional impacts, the threat of which is extremely great in both close-quarter battle (CQB) combat and policing situations.

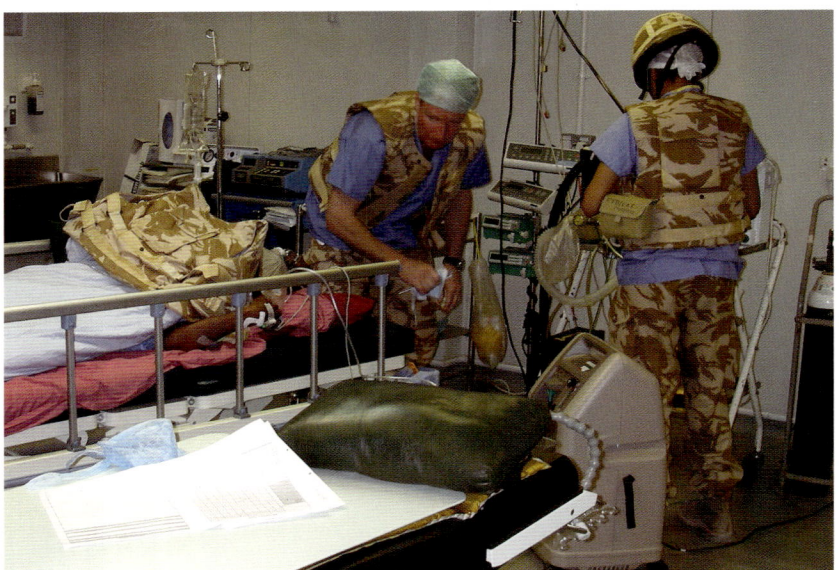

At British surgical facility at Camp Bastion, Afghanistan, in 2008, a post-operative patient is covered with an ECBA vest. The medical team also wear ECBA armour, a necessity in an environment where mortar and RPG attacks come without warning and show no respect for hospitals. (Surg. Lt Cdr B Tamayo, RN)

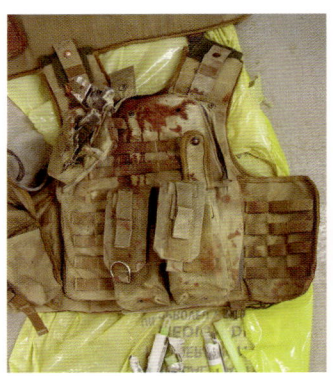 
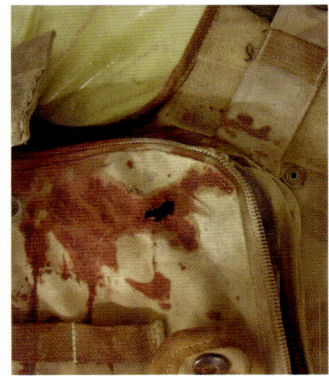 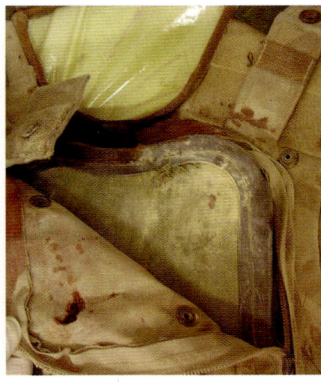

The reality of service in Afghanistan: This Body Armour, Osprey, DPM Desert vest was being worn by a rifleman positioned behind the cover of a low wall. The wall directly in front of him was struck by an RPG round, causing blast and fragmentation injury, but the soldier's life was undoubtedly saved by the Osprey armour. In this composite image the damaged front section of the vest is shown at top left; at top right is a detail of the smashed radio; at bottom left is shown the (top right) corner of the SAPI plate pocket, showing an entry mark left by a fragment penetration; and at bottom right the cover is opened to show the point of impact on the upper edge of the SAPI plate which had defeated the missile. (Surg. Lt Cdr B Tamayo, RN)

Introduction

Stab Resistance

Ballistic vests do not necessarily offer protection from edged weapons or spikes. A pointed bayonet or knife tip thrust against a Kevlar vest will generally part the fibres of the ballistic layers and allow the blade to penetrate. Specialized fabrics with extremely close knit weave, or resin-impregnated fibres forming sheets of pointed-object defeating cloth are required to prevent stab wounds. While such layers are not normally included in military vests they are standard in most police vests, which usually offer protection from fragmentation, pistol rounds and stabbing weapons. Many armour vests are produced for particular usage where a ballistic vest is not a requirement but stab protection is vital. Such vests are commonly used by nightclub doormen and other personnel at risk from stabbing. NIJ standards are applied to the stab protection value of a vest. The NIJ basic standard 0115.00 allows a maximum blade/spike penetration of 7mm (0.28in). This is insufficient to cause anything but minor injury and is unlikely to be incapacitating.

As well as woven soft armour, a number of companies produce ballistic-resistant rigid polyethylene panels (such as Spectra Shield). Ballistic-resistant polyethylene armour is made from woven ECPE (extended chain polyethylene) fibres injected with polyethylene resins, silicones, urethanes or vinyls, and then hydraulic hot pressed into rigid sheets of ballistic-resistant armour. The ballistic-resistant polyethylene is frequently used in vehicle and other applications, seeing only limited application in body armour.

Hard Armour

Hard armour works quite differently to soft armour. Hard armour is inflexible and generally heavy. It is usually made of laminated materials, such as hard metals, plastics and ultra hard ceramics, combined with high performance ballistic fabrics. In modern ceramic hard armour the SAPI plate causes immediate changes in the shape of the bullet upon impact, the energy being absorbed by shattering the SAPI's hard ceramic surface. The secondary projectiles (spall) produced by the shattering of the ceramic plate and bullet are then caught by the ballistic fabric, preventing penetration to the body. Since most hard plates are worn in conjunction with a ballistic fabric vest, this works exceptionally well. Older metal plate armours, capable of defeating bullets, were prone to the creation of spall fragments that could injure the armour wearer or those around him. The heavy plate did not absorb the energy well, the transfer of energy being achieved by shattering the bullet and sending fragments in a multitude of directions. The problems of spall were encountered with the aircrew armour used in Vietnam and were alleviated by wearing a soft armour vest (such as the M1952A) over the hard armour.

The tungsten carbide core of an armour-piercing (AP) bullet has a hardness value (HV) of 1,200–1,500 HV; the core of the AP projectile is the hardest of all small arms rounds. Ceramic armour is considerably harder than tungsten carbide, but has a much lower density and weights less than armoured steel. The different ceramic armours

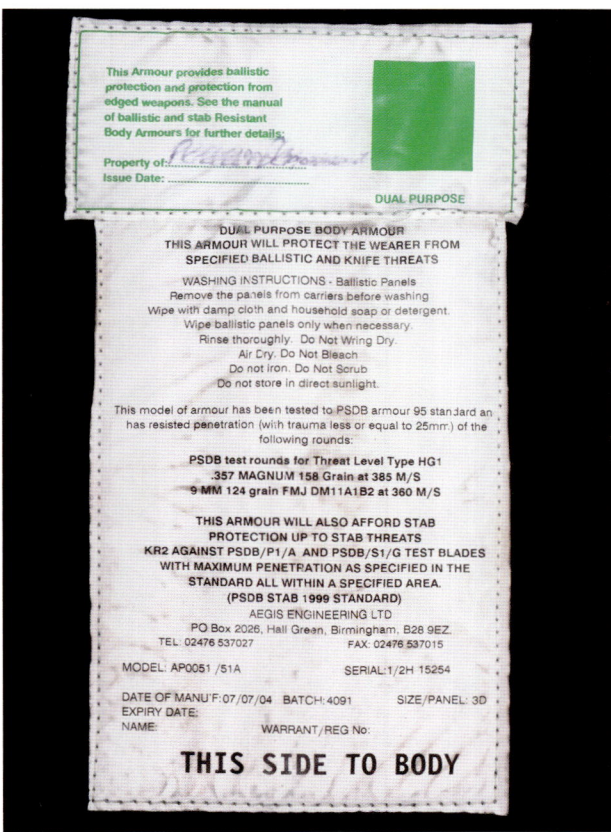

Manufacturer's label from the inner face of the ballistic panel used in the test firing (see pages 14 and 15). It shows that the panel was made by Aegis Engineering Ltd, in July 2004. It provides details of the ballistic and stab protection afforded by the vest and shows that it will protect from impacts by .357 Magnum and 9mm ammunition. The green square indicates that this vest is dual purpose, providing both ballistic and stab protection.

British standard body armour markings, showing, from top: red triangle used on stab-resistant vests, blue circle used on ballistic vests and the green square used on dual-purpose stab/ballistic protective vests.

Introduction

Typical ammunition types relevant to body armour development. Shown left to right are 7.62mm × 51 NATO Armour Piercing, 7.62mm × 51 NATO ball, 5.56mm NATO, 7.62mm × 39 Russian, .30 M1 Carbine, SPIW flechette, .357 magnum, .38 Special, .45 ACP and 9mm Parabellum. Most standard soft body armour will only defeat .38 Special, .45 ACP, and 9mm. Some standard armours have sufficient extra protection to defeat M1 carbine and .357 Magnum. However, ceramic or composite ballistic SAPI plates will defeat 7.62mm × 51 NATO Armour Piercing, 7.62mm × 51 NATO ball, 5.56mm NATO and 7.62mm × 39 Russian ammunition. The Special Purpose Individual Weapon (SPIW) flechette had an exceptionally high velocity (4,690fps/1430m/s, falling to 3,379fps/1030 m/s at 1,312ft/400m compared to 2,749fps/838m/s for 7.62mm ball). It also had excellent penetration, comparable to that of 7.62mm ball ammunition, and it deformed readily upon impact with flesh, causing a rapid transfer of energy with a disproportionate wounding effect. Developed by the US during the early 1960s, to be used with a 5.56mm round, the flechette saw limited use during the Vietnam War in a special shotgun ammunition. Although the SPIW flechette retained high velocity and penetration to as far as 1,640ft (500m) it was not at all accurate and thus soon fell out of favour during the 1970s.

have hardness values as follows: alumina 1,500–1,900 HV, silicon carbide 1,800–2,800 HV, titanium diboride 2,100–2,600 HV, boron carbide 2,800–3,400 HV. The properties of ceramic armour were first observed during 1918 when it was applied as a facing to steel. However, its first military application was in 1965, when it was used as armour in helicopters. During the Vietnam conflict the UH-1 'Huey' was fitted with HFC hard faced composite armour kits. This and crew armour reduced wounds by 27 per cent and fatalities by 53 per cent.

National Institute Of Justice Ballistic Performance Standards (USA)
American classification of the level of protection offered by any body armour is provided by extensive testing, resulting in the armour being graded at NIJ (standard 0101.04) levels I, IIA, II, IIIA, III and IV, with level IV providing the greatest levels of protection. Levels I to IIIA are soft armour, while levels III and IV provide the greater protection offered by additional hardened plates, typically titanium or ceramic.

Many manufacturers and nations, including Germany, allow only 20mm of depression in their national standards, less than half that required under NIJ standards.

This listing provides the basic requirements for categorisation of NIJ ballistic levels.

- Level I provides the minimum level of protection. Suitable for use against .22 (5.5mm) LR and .38 (9.7mm) ACP projectiles

- Level IIA provides the minimum level of protection. Suitable for use against .22 LR, .38 ACP, and 9mm (0.35in) and .40 (10mm) Smith & Wesson (S&W) projectiles

- Level II provides improved level of protection. Suitable for use against .22 LR, .38 ACP, 9mm and .40 S&W, and .357 magnum projectiles

- Level IIIA provides maximum levels of protection against the majority of handgun-calibre ammunition, including .22 LR, .38 ACP, 9mm and .40 S&W, .357 magnum, and high velocity 9mm and .44 (11mm) magnum projectiles

- Level III provides protection against all handgun-calibre ammunition, including .22 LR, .38 ACP, 9mm and .40 S&W, .357 and high velocity 9mm and .44 magnum projectiles. Its increased protection levels also provide protection from 7.62mm (0.3in) (NATO) rifle-calibre rounds

- Level IV provides protection against all handgun-calibre ammunition, including .22 LR, .38 ACP, 9mm and .40 S&W, .357 and high velocity 9mm and .44 magnum,

Introduction

Members of the US Air Force's 380th Expeditionary Logistics Readiness Squadron (ELRS) process racks of body armour and SAPI plates during an operational readiness exercise held during 2009. (US Air Force)

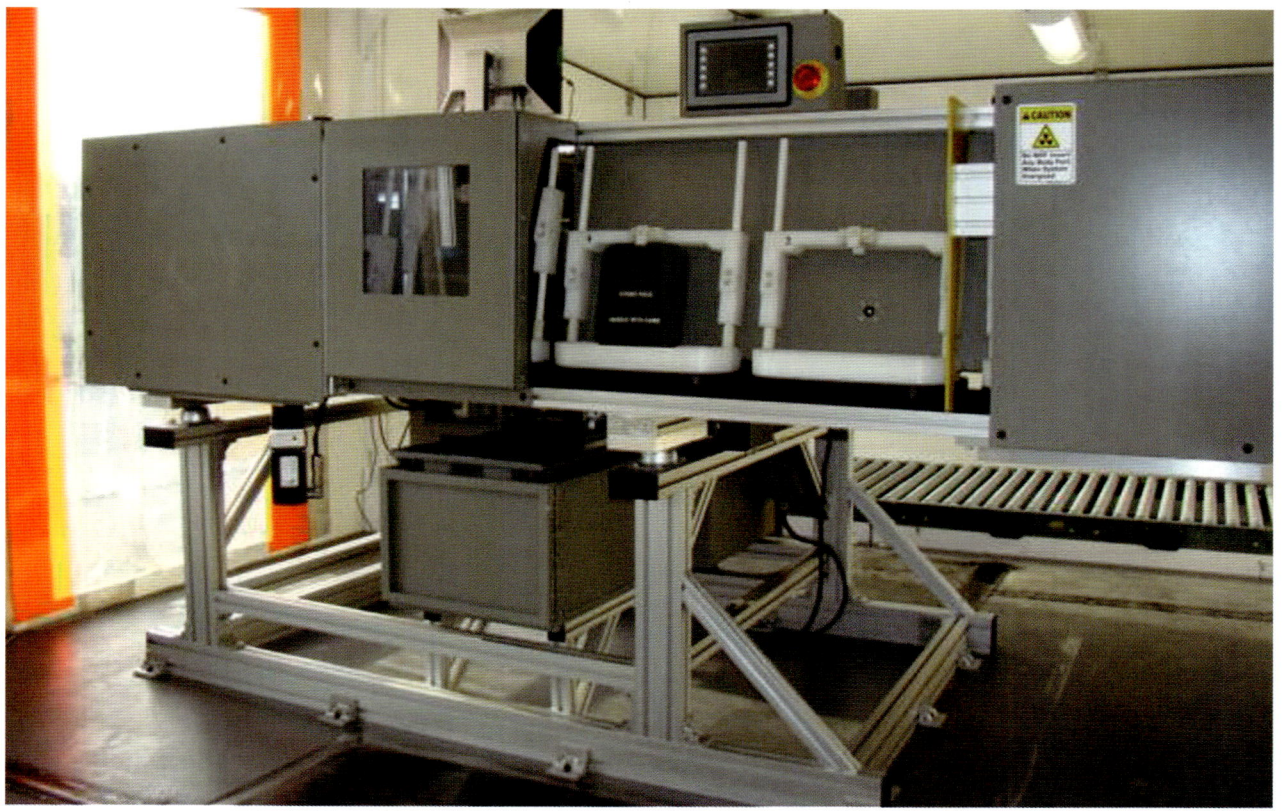

The non-destructive test equipment (NDTE) used by US units in operational theatres uses digital X-ray to detect any physical or structural defects in the SAPI. A plate can be seen fitted to the frame in the centre of the picture. The unit enables defective plates to be spotted and discarded, and thus reduces the risk of faulty plates being used by frontline troops. NDTE is a portable, deployable, self-contained system that can scan a plate in 15 seconds or less, or as many as 240 in an hour. (US DoD)

Introduction

7.62mm (NATO) rifle calibre rounds and 30-calibre (0.3in; 7.62mm) armour-piercing rifle ammunition

International Standards of Ballistic Protection

Police Scientific Development Branch and Home Office Scientific Development Branch Standards

Introduced in 1995, the Police Scientific Development Branch (PSDB) ballistic body armour test standard provided updated benchmarks for the measurements of levels of protection offered by UK police body armour. The PSDB have been revised as the Home Office Scientific Development Branch (HOSDB) 2003 standards. Levels of protection range from HG1/A, HG1 and HG 2, protecting against 9mm and .357 magnum rounds at velocities from 1,180 to 1,475 fps (360 to 450m/s), and with back-face deformation of 25 to 44mm (1 to 1.7in); through SG1, which protects against a 28.4 grain, 12-gauge shotgun; to RF1 and RF2 which provide protection from standard 7.62mm ball.

Russia-GOST R 50744-95 Ballistic Standard

Russian ballistic standards have six classes. The basic level 1 provides protection against the 7.62mm Nagant and 9mm Makarov pistol rounds at 870 to 935fps (265 and 285m/s). Level 3 protects against the standard 7.62mm AKM and 5.45mm (0.21in) AK-74 rifle ammunition. Level six offers protection from a 9.6 grain, 7.62mm rifle round fired at 2,740fps (835m/s) when from an SVD (Dragunov) sniper rifle. Acceptable back face deformation is 17mm (0.67in) in all classes, the most protective of any international standard.

Other standards

Other important international armour standards include the European CEN prEN ISO 14876 Body Armour Standards (2000-2002), the standard for bullet resistance and knife stab resistance of body armour developed by the European Committee for Standardization (or Comité de Normalisation, CEN).

In Germany the Schutzklassen Technical Guidelines are a standard for bullet resistance of Schutzwesten Deutsche Polizei (German police body armour) developed by the Police Command and Staff Academy. The classification is also used for military armour. Classes within it are Schutzklassen (SK) L and SK 1 through SK 4. SK L and SK 1 protect against 9mm fire; SK 2 from .357 Magnum; and SK 3 and SK 4 protect against 5.56 and 7.62mm. Acceptable back face deformation is 18–22mm (0.70–0.87in) in all Schutzklassen.

A Hampshire Constabulary firearms instructor takes aim at a ballistic panel, from the front section of a police issue vest, with a 9mm Heckler & Koch MP5 sub-machine gun (SMG). Three sets of ballistic tests were undertaken using standard police-issue ammunition in three weapon types: 9mm MP5 SMG, 9mm SIG Pro pistol and (the now obsolete) .38 Special revolver. While in no way a scientific test, and not to national standards, this allowed the vest's ballistic properties to be witnessed first hand by the author. (Martin J. Brayley)

Introduction

A police-issue MP5 SMG and the ballistic panel from a police-issue vest, after having been used for the test firing. The black tape was used to fix a compressible backing to the panel to simulate the panel resting against a human body and to allow for controlled compression (back face signature) of the vest upon impact. This panel is from the front of the vest. (Martin J. Brayley)

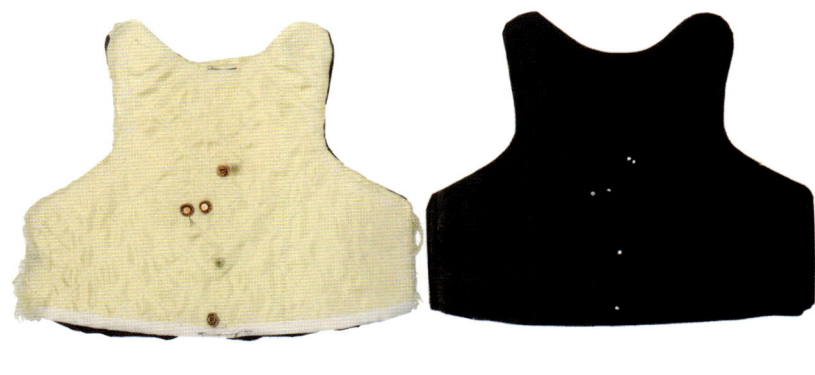

Here the ballistic panel has been removed from the water-impermeable Pertex outer cover (at right). It is laid over the stab-proof panel that is still retained in its own separate water-impermeable cover, the two normally being sealed in the outer cover in use. (Martin J. Brayley)

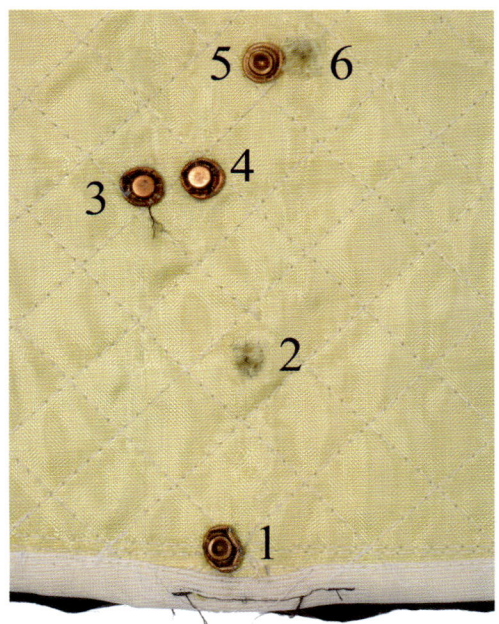

Close up of the ballistic panel showing that four of the six rounds fired at the vest have passed through the outer cover, but have been stopped by the first layer of fabric. Two rounds passed through the outer layers of ballistic fabric and lodged between ballistic layers without damaging the stab proof layers beneath. The rounds were fired in order from the following weapons: One and two, 9mm (95-grain jacketed soft point (JSP)) MP5; three and four, .38 special (125-grain JSP) revolver; five and six, 9mm (95-grain JSP) SIG pistol. Although round number one struck the edge of the armour and was defeated by the first layer of fabric, the lack of surrounding fabric to absorb the full impact caused marked compression damage to the underlying stab-proof layers and would have resulted in considerable blunt-trauma injuries to any vest user. (Martin J. Brayley)

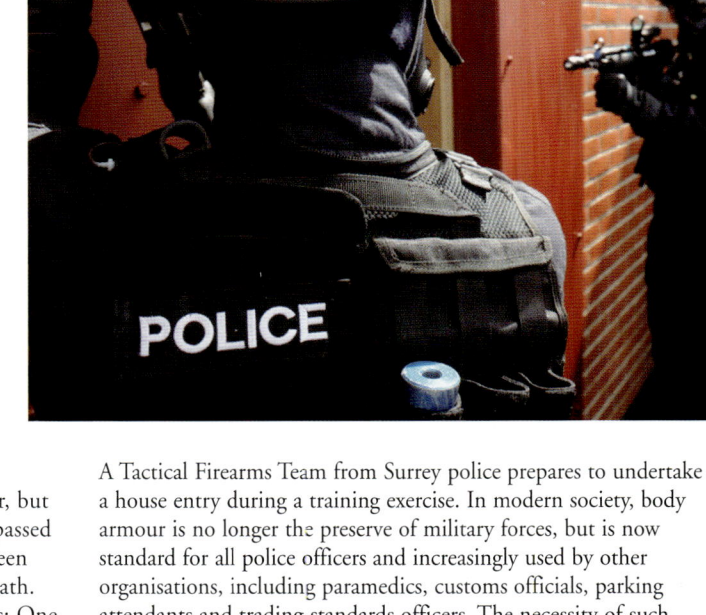

A Tactical Firearms Team from Surrey police prepares to undertake a house entry during a training exercise. In modern society, body armour is no longer the preserve of military forces, but is now standard for all police officers and increasingly used by other organisations, including paramedics, customs officials, parking attendants and trading standards officers. The necessity of such protection in daily use and the effect on public perception is undoubtedly open to debate. (Martin J. Brayley)

Chapter 1 United States of America

World War I

The 'Sentinels' armour was based upon the design of the German 'Infanterie panzer' armour and was rapidly developed during February 1918. It offered some improvements over the German original, including rubber padding at pressure points to aid in the distribution of weight, but it only protected the front of the wearer. However, trials with rear echelon troops in France produced unfavourable comment regarding its use. The soldiers declared that it was unwieldy and excessively heavy causing fatigue and difficulty in the operation of weapons. It was also noisy in use. It did resist penetration by German MG (machine-gun) fire at 300 yards (275m). Despite the lack of enthusiasm from troops using the armour, the US Army recommended that it was issued to machine-gun detachments, but with the addition of a back plate. The Sentinels armour was but one of a number of armour patterns manufactured during the war, but few saw any widespread use.

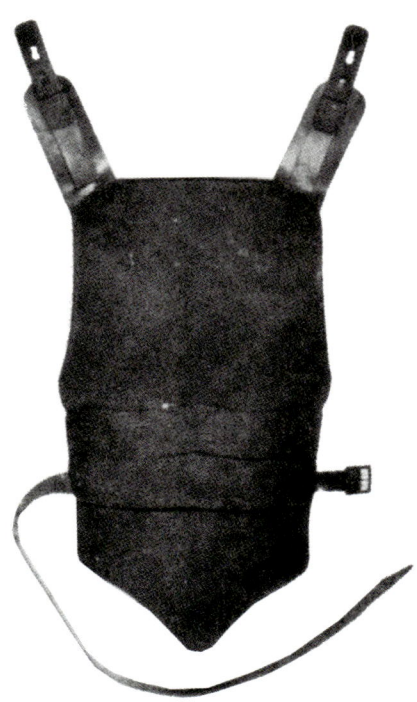

The back plate of the experimental lightweight armour developed by the Engineer Division. The manganese steel used in the armour was between .036 and .040 inches in thickness and was able to withstand impacts from service revolver ammunition, shrapnel and shell fragments. Both the back and front panels were made up of four articulated sections providing chest, back and abdominal protection.

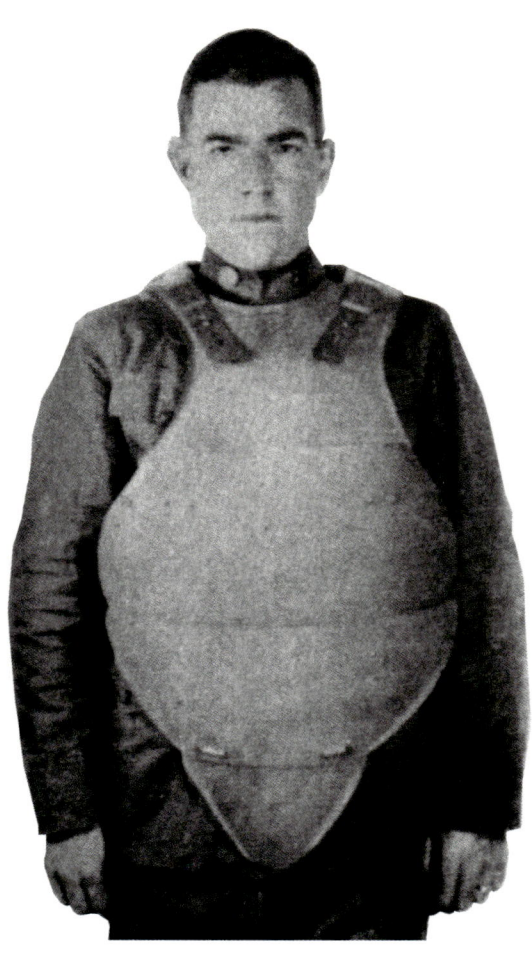

An experimental lightweight armour developed by the US Army's Engineer Division of the Ordnance Department. The weight of the armour is not known, but trials with British armour resulted in a specified maximum weight of 8lb. The outer surfaces were covered in khaki canvass, while the interior was provided with rubber cushioning.

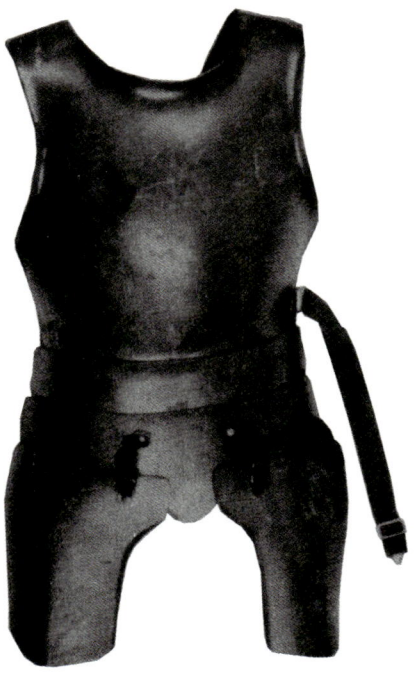

The heavyweight Sentinels armour owed much to the features found on captured German 'Infanterie panzer' armour. The Sentinels armour weighed in at some 27lb (12.25kg). The complete ensemble consisted of a breastplate, two abdominal plates and two thigh plates. It rested on the shoulders in the same manner as the German armour, but benefited from a robust waist-strap that steadied the armour in use.

United States of America

Fort de la Peigney, Langres, France, around 1918. This image shows the results of an Army Ordnance Department body armour test. The heavyweight Sentinels armour shows the effects of pistol, rifle and machine-gun fire against the all-metal vests – donned post impact. The chest and two abdominal plates remain intact on all three examples, but only one thigh plate (left) has remained attached. The thick rubber shoulder padding is readily visible on the two soldiers at left.

RIGHT: 'Wisbrod' armoured vest showing the front of the vest with blue fabric cover. The vest had no rear protection and consisted solely of the front panel. The Wisbrod Armoured Vest Company was based in California and produced vests for military and police applications. This vest dates to the 1930s and has an integral groin protector. (Michael Ferretti)

FAR RIGHT: Interior view of the Wisbrod vest, showing the neck and waist support straps. Most of the vest's weight would have been taken by the neck, which would have caused discomfort and strain during extended wear. (Michael Ferretti)

Manufacturer's label from the Wisbrod vest. The label shows that the vest was designed to stop the standard .38 Special ammunition and the 45-calibre round fired from a Thompson (M1928) SMG. Elliot Wisbrod was granted a number of patents in the design of body armour. As a method of promoting sales, Wisbrod regularly gave demonstrations of his vests' capabilities by wearing body armour while allowing an assistant to fire at him. (Michael Ferretti)

United States of America

World War II

As early as October 1941, prior to the US entry into the war, a single set of the British Medical Research Council (MRC) developmental lightweight body armour had been supplied to the American Embassy in London. It is not known what the Americans thought of the armour, nor whether any further research was done with this single example. However, during the early stages of American involvement in World War II, both the US Army Quartermaster and Ordnance Corps were undertaking active research into the development of body armour for ground troops. A number of vest types were explored, including further examples of the MRC armour manufactured for trails by the British War Office (WO). The US War Office had experimented with several types of armour, the requirement for such protection being highlighted by the campaign in North Africa. A number of protective armour vests were field tested by the British, but the materials available at that time, and the designs, resulted in the vest being too heavy and cumbersome for use by infantrymen. American Office of the Quartermaster General (OQMG) efforts into developing body armour for ground troops provided the same results. It was just too heavy and cumbersome, restricting the movement and endurance of troops wearing it. Then, on 8 March 1943 the US Army sent a secret cipher message to the British War Office requesting details of British body armour development including scales of issue, reason for adoption and user trials. Although the MRC armour was seriously considered for issue and extensively evaluated by the US Army, it felt that at 3.13 per cent body coverage it provided inadequate protection. 'Infantry Board Report 1501' of July 1943 rejected any further consideration of the adoption of the British MRC armour for US troops.

Flyers' Armour

An October 1942 analysis of wounds received by 303 United States Army Air Force (USAAF) airmen in combat highlighted some interesting facts. Some 70 per cent of wounds received in aerial combat were from low velocity missiles. Of this figure it was estimated that 38 per cent were from flak (Fliegerabwehrkanone), 39 per cent from 20mm cannon shell fragments, 15 per cent from small calibre bullets (typically 7.92mm/0.31in), and 8 per cent from secondary missiles (this figure encompassed all other objects that had caused wounds, usually aircraft debris from explosions or other impacts). A second much larger survey of 1,293 airmen

In England, probably during 1943, 1st Lieutenant J. T. Lundy, at left, wears the pre-production version of the bombardier/navigator flak vest (later designated M1), with its broad lower apron (later designated M4), while the pilot of B-17 Oklahoma Okie, 1st Lieutenant Cos wears the pilot's flak vest (later M1) with curved apron (later M3). The vest worn by pilots and co-pilots had no armoured back, since they had armour-plated seats. 'Oklahoma Okie' was from the 324th Bomb Squadron, 91st Bomb Group, Eighth Air Force. It was shot down on 31 December 1943, following a raid against submarine pens in Bordeaux, with the loss of five of the ten-man crew. (National Museum of the US Air Force)

British made flyers' armour. A full set consisted of a back section, a front section and an apron that fitted to the front section. Above is the rear section of the Armor, Flyer's, Vest M1. Below is the Armor, Flyer's, Vest M1 fitted with the Armor, Flyer's, Apron M3.

casualties showed similar results and extended the research into defining the areas of the body most susceptible to fatal and non-fatal wounds. The results of the work suggested that some form of protection for the high-risk areas of the body, the head, chest and abdomen, would save a considerable number of lives. The Surgeon of the Eighth Air Force (8th AF) at this time was Colonel Malcolm C. Grow, and it was at his insistence that it was decided to examine the feasibility of the production of specialist armour for combat aircrews in the European Theatre of Operations (ETO). Since the 8th AF was stationed in England, Colonel Grow looked to the British for assistance with his requirements. British developers had already found that Hadfield manganese steel plates as thin as 1mm were capable of resisting penetration by the standard British .303 (7.7mm) ball round at a velocity of 1,250fps (380m/s). This provided a reasonable benchmark for continued research, since the standard German 7.92mm ball round had similar performance characteristics to the British ammunition. In association with the Wilkinson Sword Company, Colonel Grow had a protective vest made from overlapping 2in- (50mm-) square plates of Hadfield manganese steel. The plates were held in small fabric pockets allowing for a consistent overlap so that minimum protection was 2mm (0.08in) of steel at all points. The small size of the plates allowed for a greater degree of articulation, although flexibility was nonetheless quite restricted. Provisional experimentation with the product proved favourable, therefore. In October 1942, Wilkinson made up ten sets of test and development armour under the authority of Lieutenant General Carl Spaatz, commander 8th Air Force. The experimental sets of armour were well received and the initial research was extended in March 1943 with the acquisition of sufficient armour for issue to the crews of twelve B-17s.

In April 1943 the US Army Ordnance Department despatched a written communiqué to the HQ Army Air Forces advising that further research into body armour for ground troops had concluded and that the requirement had been rejected on the grounds of loss of mobility, adding that it was felt that applications should be considered by the USAAF for the use of armour as fittings in aircraft (ballistic panels or curtains) or individual personnel armour. However, by this time the use of experimental armour in the 8th AF was providing positive information as to the benefits of armour to operational aircrew. Analysis of the data led to a decision to adopt protective armour suits for the crews of all heavy bombers operating with the 8th AF and orders were placed for armour to be produced in England. It was also recommended that armour suits be provided for all heavy bomber units stationed outside of the UK but destined for the 8th Air Force. The manganese steel used in the production of the vests was a critical war material and in limited supply. It was required for many applications and the drain upon limited British resources was already high. A total of 600 suits were produced in the UK, but it was soon apparent that production needed to be moved to the USA where manpower and materiel were under less pressure and there was less competition for such limited resources. In July 1943, examples of the British-made armour were received by the US Army Ordnance Department, which then took on the task of sourcing manufacturers for large-scale production, and researching improvements and modifications highlighted by operational use. An order for procurement was also made at that time requesting 25,000 armour assemblies, of the four patterns being produced in England, with 25 per cent of that figure to be available at ports of embarkation by 5 August. The necessary procurement contracts and appointment of three contractors was rapidly executed, with letters of intent being placed with manufacturers within 24 hours of the request being received. New design specifications were issued on 12 July and by 12 August slightly more than 25 per cent of the contract figure had been delivered to the port of Newark.

An example of the Hadfield steel plate used in the overlapping armour of M1 flak vests and accoutrements. The 0.039in (1mm) thick 2in (50mm) square plates were normally flat, but curved plates were used in some armour, such as the T44 neck shield. Plates were arranged so that minimum protection throughout the armour was at least two plates, or 0.078in (2mm) of protection.

United States of America

An image showing B-17 waist gunners Technical Sergeant Everett and Staff Sergeant Furmanek. Furmanek wears the M1 flak vest with M3 apron directly over the 'Suit, Flying, Electric Heated, F1', or 'Bunny Suit', suggesting a posed photograph. Interestingly, the M1/M3 vest combination has been modified by the removal of the waist belt and quick release pull, and the integral shoulder release cords that allow rapid doffing of the vest. Both men wear the M3 flak helmet, essentially an M1 helmet with hinged side extensions to protect the cheek area. (National Museum of the US Air Force)

The Ordnance Department of the Metropolitan Museum of Art in New York took on the role of researching the further development of 'Flyers' Armor', having gained considerable experience of body armour production during the Great War. On 6 July 1943 the Air Force Materiel Command at Wright Field, Ohio, which had previously been involved in researching Flyers' Armor, was required to relinquish its previous role to the Army Ordnance Department.

American production of armour was based upon the standard British designs, but the basic ensemble was rapidly expanded and by the end of hostilities some twenty-three types of Flyers' Armor had been developed. The British armour had been covered in brown cotton duck (canvas) but American production switched to OD (Olive Drab shade No.7 was the recently standardized colour for US army uniforms and equipment) cotton duck, and then a change to nylon duck from the end of 1943. The nylon slightly improved the ballistic qualities of the armour, was harder wearing than the cotton and moisture resistant.

Flyers' Armor Components

The 'Armor, Flyers' Vest M1' was the base for the aviators' armour system. It consisted of two sections, front and rear, connected at the shoulders by 'lift the dot' (LTD) fasteners and at the waist by an adjustable waist belt closing with LTD fasteners. The waist closure was fitted with a red pull-release tag and backing section. The waist belt attached to the backing section with two LTD fasteners; two ripcords fitted to the upper section passed through a metal grommet in the front of the vest and ran through the interior of the vest, exiting at the shoulder section where they were fixed between the shoulder LTD fasteners. A sharp pull on the red pull-release tag separated the LTD fasteners at the waist belt section and, via the internal cords, also released the LTD fasteners at each shoulder. Once released in this manner, the two sections of the vest fell away from the wearer. The Armor, Flyers' Vest M1 provided ballistic protection to the anterior and posterior thorax, covering an area of protection of 3.8sq ft (0.4m2). It was designed for use by mobile crewmen such as gunners, navigators,

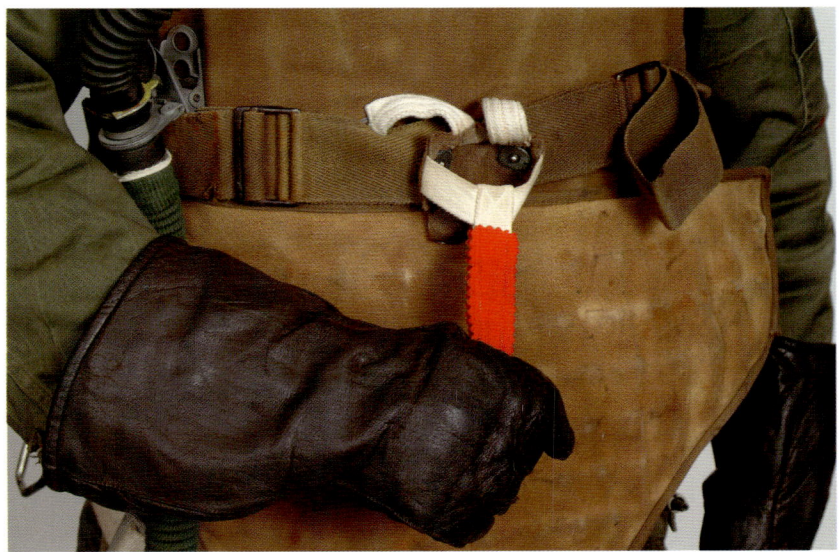

The red pull-release tag was an integral part of the M1 vest front section. It was permanently fitted to the release cords that ran through the front of the vest to the shoulders, where a pull of the cords would release the shoulder 'lift-the-dot' (LTD) fasteners. The tag was also connected to the M1 rear vest waist belt via two LTD fasteners. Pulling the tag also released the waist-belt fasteners, at the same time as the shoulder fasteners, allowing the M1 vest and M3 (or M4) apron combination to fall away in two sections.

bombardiers, and radio operators, who were required to move around the aircraft. The two components of the M1 vest weighed 17lb 6oz (7.88kg). Between August 1943 and August 1945, 338,780 M1 vests were manufactured.

Seated crew, such as pilots and co-pilots, did not require protection for the back as the posterior dorsal region was protected by their armoured seat back. The 'Armor, Flyer's Vest, M2' therefore consisted of an armoured front section identical to that of the Armor, Flyers' Vest M1 and an un-armoured back section based on the back section of the M1, but with no ballistic inserts. Later production front sections for the M1 and M2 vests were standardized as the 'Armor, Flyers' Vest M1 & M2', the same panel serving as the front section to the M1 or M2 rear sections. The armoured front section of the M2 vest (essentially the front section of the M1) weighed 7lb and 2oz (3.23kg) and provided protective coverage of 1.45sq ft (0.13m2). Between August 1943 and July 1945, 95,919 M2 vests were manufactured.

Research continued into improving the protective coverage of the vests, and decreasing the weight. Little headway was made initially, since the materials then available made a decrease in weight and a corresponding increase in coverage almost impossible. However, by 1945 the use of Hadfield steel in Flyers' Armor had been superseded by aluminium. This gave designers the opportunity to reduce the weight of armour and thus increase protective coverage. The 'Armor, Flyers' Vest M6' was virtually identical to the M1 vest, but utilized aluminium ballistic plates and a ballistic nylon backing cloth. At 14lb and 9oz (6.61kg) the M6 vest was some 2lb 14oz (1.30kg) lighter than the M1 vest. It also provided an area of protective coverage up by 0.27sq ft (0.03m2), giving a total cover of 4.09sq ft (0.38m2). The standardisation of the M6 vest in July 1945 made the M1 a limited standard item, to be issued until stocks were exhausted; 1,075 M6 vests were manufactured in 1945. Aluminium was also used to provide ballistic protection in the replacement for the M2 vest. Like the M2, the 'Armor, Flyers' Vest M7' had an armoured front panel and un-armoured rear panel. It weighed 7lb 13oz (3.54kg) and provided 1.82sq ft (0.17m2) of protective coverage.

ABOVE, RIGHT: Armor, Flyer's Vest, M2. The M2 assembly was designed for use by personnel using armoured seats, such as pilots and navigators. The armoured seat negated the need for the body armour to have an armoured back section. This is an American-made M2 vest, readily identifiable as being of American manufacture by the green nylon cover.

RIGHT: Printed weight statistics and manufacturer's label in the armoured front section of the American-made Armor, Flyer's Vest, M1 & M2. Both seated and mobile crewmen used the front section. The label at right reads:

Armor, Flyer's Vest, M1 & M2
Front Piece, Spec. Axs-1025
Mfg. By Crawford Mfg. Co., Inc.
Contract W-36-034-Ord-113
Lot 75

A 1945 photo showing a B-17 waist gunner jettisoning body armour. The M1 vest front section and attached M3 apron have fallen away separate from the M1 vest rear section (dropped behind the gunner). This image clearly illustrates the confined area in which bomber gunners were required to operate. (National Museum of the US Air Force)

United States of America

A B-17 waist gunner stands amid a heap of empty 50-calibre cases. He wears the Armor, Flyer's, Vest M1 fragmentation 'flak' vest, with the Armor, Flyer's, Apron M4.

Further research into Flyers' Armor saw the development of the 'T5' armour, using larger ballistic plates held firmly within the vest by the use of elasticated webbing. Research had shown that larger plates were more effective ballistically, but increased plate size also reduced the flexibility of the panels. Nevertheless, it was considered that the loss of flexibility was not disproportionate and larger plates should be used where possible. The 'T37' test armour had seen the use of 2-inch square, 0.13-inch thick Doron plates as a possible replacement for steel in Flyers' Armor. Curved plates with increased thickness were also tested. Doron was found to be superior to any other plastic-laminate armour, but aluminium proved to be a better choice and the research into the use of Doron for Flyers' Armor was soon discontinued.

The lower front face of the M1 vest was also fitted with three short straps, each bearing the male, post section of an LTD fastener. These married with three female LTD fastener sections fitted to the 'Armor, Flyers' Apron M3'. The apron provided additional protection to the lower abdomen and pelvic region. The M3 apron was contoured to allow use by seated personnel, or those working in confined spaces. It weighed 4lb 14oz (4.88kg) and had an area of protection of 1.15sq ft (0.11m2). The 'Armor, Flyers' Apron M4' was similar to the M3, but had a rectangular shape, providing a greater area of protection for crewmen who were required to stand, such as waist gunners. It weighed 7lb 2oz (3.23kg) and provided an area of protection of 1.66sq ft (0.15m2).

The M6 and M7 vests were modified to produce the 'Armor, Flyers' Vest M6A1' and 'M7A1', respectively. The modified armour allowed better fitting over back-type parachutes. The M6A1 weighed 16lb 15oz (7.68kg), and the M7A1 7lb 1oz (3.20kg). The vests gave 5.88 and 2.08sq ft (0.55 and 0.19m2) of protective coverage, respectively.

Pilots and co-pilots, or other seated personnel, were unable to easily use the M3 apron with any comfort, since it was poorly articulated. The M4 was even less suited to their requirements. Many seated crewmen therefore discarded the apron and this left the thighs and lower

Picture showing the main identifying features that differentiate between British-made armour components and American-made items. The two sets of armour apron shown here are both Armor, Flyer's, Apron M3, dubbed the 'nut protector'. Above is a British-made plate showing the front face at left and the inner face at right. The front is covered with heavy-duty brown canvas. The inner face has a soft, white, velvet-type fabric cover and the edge is bound with brown tape. Below is an American-made panel. The outer covering of this panel is Olive Drab canvas, with a white velvet fabric inner face. The edge is bound with green tape. While the British example is void of any markings, the American panel has a small fabric label in the top left corner giving stock number and manufacturer's details. Just visible on the lower part of the inner face is a bold black printed WT. 4 LB. 12 OZ.

abdomen wholly unprotected; even with the apron the thighs were unprotected. To rectify this deficiency the 'Armor, Flyers' Groin, T12' was developed during 1943 to test the application of such armour. This contoured armour covered the lower abdomen and thighs, and provided enhanced protection when compared to the M3 apron. The T12 would have been instantly recognisable as armour by any medieval soldier, and would not have been out of place in the fourteenth century. It consisted of ten contoured and articulated steel plates, two over each thigh, and six over the abdomen and groin, weighing a total of 10lb (4.54kg) and giving a protective coverage of 1.63sq ft (0.15m2). Further research and development led to the creation, in January 1944, of the 'Armor, Flyers' Groin, T13'. The T13 discarded the large steel plate structure of the T12 and utilized the tried and tested multiple small steel plates as used in the M1 and subsequent armours. The plates were fitted into three large panels that sat over the thighs, across the abdomen and between the wearer's legs, where a 'diaper' extension provided protection to the inguinal region. The T13 was somewhat heavier than the T12 at 14lb (6.35kg), but provided similar protective coverage. In March 1944 the T13 was further modified and then standardized as the 'Armor, Flyers' Groin, M5'. As with the M3 and M4 aprons, the M5 armour fitted to the lower edge of the M2 vest. The M5 weighed 15lb 4oz (6.92kg) and gave an area of protective coverage of 3.7sq ft (0.34m2). During 1944 and 1945, 109,901 sets of Armor, Flyers' Groin, M5 were manufactured.

The subsequent 'Armor, Flyers' Apron M8' and 'Armor, Flyers' Apron M9' were standardized in July 1945 to be used with the Armor, Flyers' Vest M6 and M7. The aluminium-armoured, nylon-backed M8 weighed 4lb 11oz (2.13kg), while the M9 weighed 6lb 8oz (2.95kg). The M8 and M9 aprons gave 1.23 and 1.89sq ft (0.11 and 0.18m2) of protective coverage, respectively. The 'Armor, Flyers' Apron, M8A1' was developed to be used in conjunction with the M6A1 vest. It weighed 4lb 4oz (1.93kg) and gave 1.23sq ft of protective coverage. The similar 'Armor, Flyers' Apron, M9A1' was produced to attach to the M7A1 vest. It weighed 5lb 12oz (2.61kg) and gave 1.89sq ft of protective coverage.

In July 1945 the 'Armor, Flyers' Groin, M10' was standardized. It was made of a ballistic nylon cover with aluminium armour and was to be used with the new aluminium-armoured M6 vest then being introduced. It weighed 13lb 11oz (6.21kg) and provided 3.62sq ft (0.34m2) of protective coverage. The M10 was superseded by the improved and lighter M10A1, which, at 12lb 5oz (5.58 kg) also gave 3.62sq ft of protective coverage.

Flyers' Armor in Use
The body armour with attached apron or groin armour provided a high degree of coverage to the body. While the anterior pelvic region remained unprotected it was at best impractical to provide coverage for the buttocks as it would interfere with sitting while at rest, and increase weight borne, thus affecting mobility, increasing stress and reducing the wearer's ability to perform his duties over extended periods in a hostile environment. In any case, pilots and co-

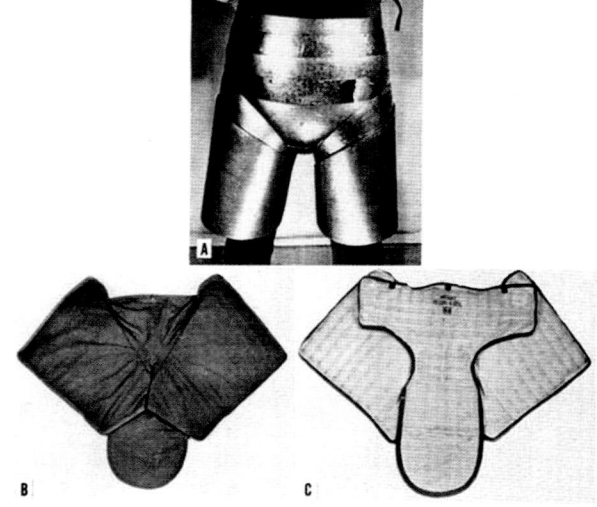

Flyers groin armour as illustrated in a wartime publication. Above is the T12 experimental armour. The T12 was not adopted in this form, but was modified as the T13, which later became standardized as the M5 armour. Below is the production pattern Armor, Flyer's, Apron M5 showing the outer (left) and inner (right) views of the articulated abdominal and thigh protective armour for seated personnel.

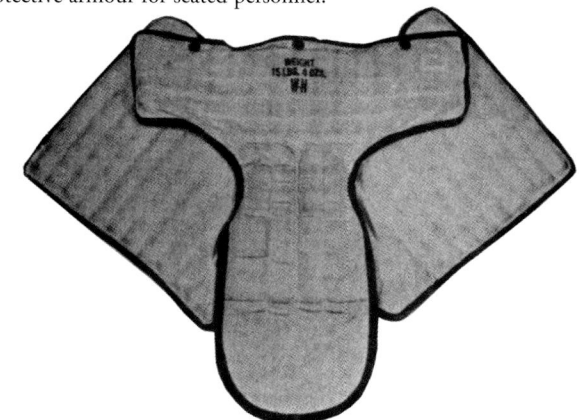

Detail of the inner face of the Armor, Flyer's, Apron M5. It is stamped with the weight, WT. 15 LBS. 4 OZS. The large central flap was drawn up between the wearer's thighs to provide protection to the groin and buttocks. The two large side flaps gave protection to the thighs.

A 1944-dated image of a USAAF B-17 crewman wearing the Armor, Flyer's, Vest M1 with the Armor, Flyer's, Apron M5. The bulk of the armoured aprons meant that they were only suited to pilots and co-pilots, or similarly seated crewmen.

United States of America

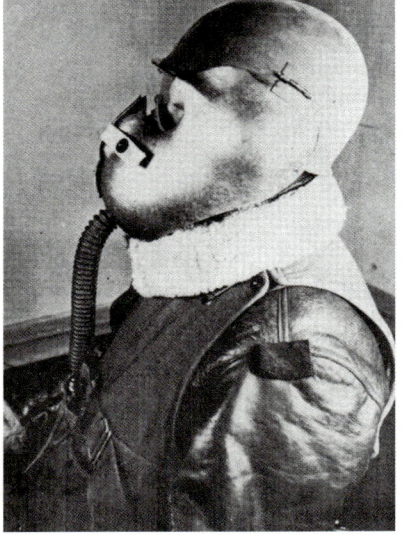

Armour, Flyer's, Neck, T44. This view shows the inner face with its fabric covering. The obverse of this example was of soft leather, but OD canvas was also used in the trials. The two leather straps were used to attach the armour to the M4 helmet. Development of the T44 was discontinued in June 1945 when it was decided to replace the Hadfield steel with aluminium armour and a nylon-duck cover, and develop the T59 series of armour.

The two-piece experimental T59E1 armour was designed in conjunction with the M5 helmet and T46 vest. The aluminium armour T59 series (T59, T59E1 and T59E2) proved effective and the experimental T59E2 neck armour was eventually standardized as the Armour, Flyer's, Neck, M13 in September 1945. The ensemble weighed 4lb 8oz (2.01kg) and provided an area of 1.3sq ft (0.12m2) of protection.

Following a project initiated in October 1943, the development of face armour and flak hoods was undertaken by the USAAF. Shown here is the face armour T6E1. Made of two steel sections that replaced the hinged side flaps of the M3 helmet, the armour fitted around the oxygen mask and goggles. Research into facial armour was discontinued in July 1944.

pilots had armoured seats, while the M10 groin armour offered inguinal protection; a steel helmet adequately protected the head. The area of the body that was still highly vulnerable was the neck and face. Neck wounds could easily be fatal, the close proximity of major arteries and the spinal column to the neck's outer surface left them most vulnerable. The face was equally at risk from penetrating wounds – missiles could enter the brain or damage the major arteries or spine following impact to the face. However, relatively slight facial injuries, which elsewhere on the body would be of little consequence, could be severely incapacitating mentally, and even minor facial disfigurement was often emotionally devastating. Methods for protecting the whole head, face and neck were examined in great detail by the Ordnance Department. Protecting the face was highly impractical; facial armour would interfere with communications equipment, oxygen masks and goggles.

The greatest degree of additional protection could be provided by neck armour, covering the gap between the flyer's armour vest and the helmet. The 'Armor, Flyers' Neck, T44' was an attempt at providing protection to the neck. Of a similar construction to the M1 vest, it was made up from slightly curved 2-inch square Hadfield steel plates fitted into overlapping pockets. The front was faced with leather or canvas. The armour rested on the shoulders and was fastened at the front of the throat by an LTD fastener. Two leather tabs at the top edge held female LTD fasteners that connected with male LTD fasteners fitted to M4 helmets. Development of T44 was discontinued in June 1945 with

the change from Hadfield steel to aluminium as the ballistic component of Flyers' Armor. The T44 neck armour weighed 3lb 3oz (1.45kg) and provided 1.33sq ft (0.12m2) of coverage. During the first half of 1945, 10,969 were manufactured before production was terminated in favour of the 'Armor, Flyers' Neck, T59'. This provided decreased lateral protection, but increased comfort in wear. The armoured side sections of the M3, M4A1 and M5 helmets offset the decrease in lateral protection. The similar 'T59E1' armour was briefly tested before the 'T59E2' version was finally standardized as the 'Armor, Flyers' Neck, M13' in September 1945. It is believed that fewer than 100 examples of the M13 were manufactured before the cessation of hostilities eventually brought manufacture to a halt.

The ballistic plates and fabric covering of Flyers' Armor developed during the war saw each subsequent pattern of armour being lighter and providing better protection than preceding examples. Cotton duck covering and 0.045in (1mm) Hadfield manganese steel ballistic panels were used on the M1 and M2 vests, M3 and M4 aprons, and the M5 groin armour. Improved 7-ply, 19oz nylon duck and 0.102in (2.6mm) 24 ST aluminium were used in the production of the M6 and M7 vests, M8 and M9 aprons, and the M10 groin armour. Further improvements saw the use of 6-ply, 13oz nylon duck and 0.102in 75 ST aluminium used in the production of the M6A1 and M7A1 vests, M8A1 and M9A1 aprons, and the M10A1 groin armour.

The Flyers' Armor was a fully integrated system. Individual armour components provided cover to the posterior and anterior thorax, abdomen, anterior pelvic region, groin, thighs, neck, face and head. While the items that provided protection have been discussed in detail, the helmets used with the system are essentially outside the scope of this work. However, since they were integral to the system as a whole, a brief description of them is warranted. All GI's were provided with the standard 'Helmet, Steel, M1'. Bomber and transport crews soon realized the advantages of using the helmet on missions and thus the M1 helmet was pressed into service as the first component of Flyers' Armor. The helmet did not sit readily over flying helmets and earphones, however. A number of modifications were thus made at unit level, from using the shell without a liner, to widening the shell to fit over earphones, or cutting away the sides. The first helmet especially designated for use by flyers was the 'Helmet, Steel, M3'. This resembled the standard M1 shell but it had an integral cradle, rather than a liner helmet, and large hinged ear sections that protected the side of the head. The M3 was soon replaced by the 'Helmet, Steel, M4'. The M4 was a leather-covered helmet without side protection. It was soon modified as the 'M4A1' and then the 'M4A2' versions that incorporated protective flaps at the side and a fabric rather than leather cover. The last purpose-designed flyer's helmet of World War II was the 'Helmet, Steel, M5'. This was a development of the M4, but was better contoured to fit over flying helmets and communications headsets. It also had larger side protection flaps.

Wound Ballistics Studies

The introduction of flyer's armour for aircrews also saw the introduction of routine surveys of users and wound studies. The results showed an overwhelmingly positive reduction in fatal wounds incurred in areas protected by the armour. The total number of wounds received, as well as the number of fatal wounds received to the thoracoabdominal region showed a marked decrease. The results of surveys conducted prior to the issue of Flyers' Armor and similar surveys conducted after widespread issues, left little doubt as to the effectiveness of armour. Between March and September 1943, surveys of non-armoured crews were conducted. During this six-month period 137,130 combat crewmembers went on bombing missions. Of these, some 746 were wounded, receiving a total of 896 individual wounds, with some crew receiving multiple wounds. This level of casualties produced a casualty rate of 5.44 men wounded, with 6.53 wounds per 1,000 crewmen who had flown combat missions, giving a wounds received/crew member mission ratio of 0.646 per cent.

The surveys of crews using armour were conducted from November 1943 to May 1944. During this six-month period 684,350 aircrew were sent on combat missions. Of these men, 1,567 became casualties with 1,766 wounds between them. This provided a casualty rate of 2.29 casualties and 2.58 wounds per 1,000 crewmen who had flown combat missions. The resulting casualty rate for wounds received/crew member missions was 0.248 per cent. These figures represented a reduction of 58 per cent in persons receiving wounds and 60 per cent in total number of wounds received per 1,000 crewmen/missions ('Body Armor, Air Surgeons Bulletin, 2:8-10, January 1945').

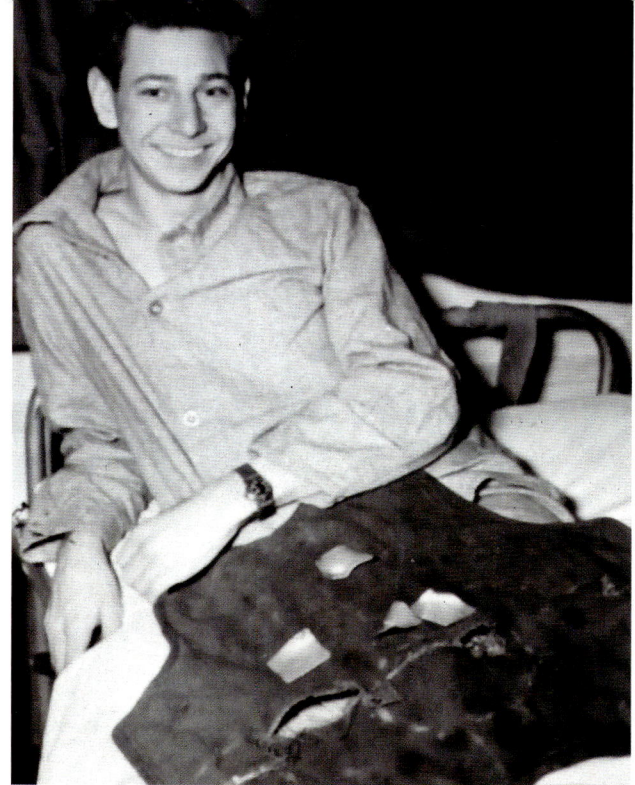

USAAF Technical Sergeant James W. Bothwell was a radio operator with the 333rd Bomb Squadron, 94th Bomb Group, 8th Air Force. On 11 November 1943, during a bombing mission, Bothwell was struck in the back by a 20mm cannon shell, which exploded on impact. He was thrown to the floor by the blast but suffered only superficial lacerations and bruising. Squadron Surgeon Earl H. Koepke, who later treated Bothwell, stated that the armour vest saved him from fatal injury, since the shell would undoubtedly have penetrated his body and exploded within the chest cavity. Here Tech Sgt Bothwell recuperates in the station hospital, displaying the damaged vest that saved his life.

Reconstruction of a World War II USAAF airman, circa 1945. He is wearing the Armor, Flyer's, Vest M1 with the Armor, Flyer's, Apron M3. Also shown is the Helmet, M4A2. The protective body coverage of the M1 vest and M3 apron combination is clearly shown here. However, the M3 apron offered little lateral protection and the crewman's rear was unprotected below the kidney area. Equally, axillary protection was also limited. Aircrew were susceptible to injury from blasts in a full 360° arc, including from below their crew position. It was not unknown for airmen to acquire additional armour upon which they stood or sat.

United States of America

The figure for the decrease in wounds received could not be taken in isolation, however. Before the effectiveness of individual Flyers' Armor could be assessed, many other factors had to be taken into account, such as changes in tactics, both Allied and enemy. Such considerations included changes in formations, fighter cover, targets, enemy aircraft and flak concentrations, as well as changes in enemy attack procedures and methods of air defence. To balance the apparently excellent results in the reduction of casualties through the use of Flyers' Armor, surveys of aircraft battle damage were also undertaken. It was found that between March and September 1943, as many as 26.46 per cent of aircraft that returned to their bases having completed or been engaged in bombing missions over enemy territory had received some form of combat damage. The period after the issue of Flyers' Armor, November 1943 to May 1944, saw a reduction in the number of aircraft returning to base with battle damage. During this period only 21.47 per cent of aircraft returning to their bases had received battle damage. This indicated a decrease in aircraft battle damage of 18 per cent compared to a concomitant casualty reduction of 60 per cent for the same period, following the issue of armour. The reduction in aircraft damage indicated that an associated reduction in casualties was to be expected, due in part to factors other than the use of Flyers' Armor. However, the greater percentage of the reduction in battle casualties was undoubtedly due to the use of armour by aircrews.

A study of wound types and anatomical locations was also conducted during the two survey periods of March to September 1943 and November 1943 to May 1944. The results of these surveys were less affected by any changes in tactics, since they recorded actual wounds or bodily impacts. The issue of Flyers' Armor resulted in a clear reduction in wounding, typically a reduction of 14 per cent to wounds to the head and neck (protected by a helmet, but still leaving a large area exposed and vulnerable), a remarkable 58 per cent reduction in wounds to the thorax (well protected by the body armour) and a reduction of 36 per cent in wounds of the abdomen (also protected by the body armour, but only at the anterior aspect, leaving the posterior unprotected and accounting for the lesser reduction in wounds when compared to the thorax). The incidents of fatal wounds received to the thoracoabdominal region dropped markedly after the introduction of armour. Prior to the use of armour, 36 per cent of thoracic and 39 per cent of abdominal wounds were fatal wounds. Following the issue of armour the fatality rates for thoracoabdominal wounding dropped dramatically to 8 per cent for abdominal and 7 per cent for thoracic wounds. The figures represented a reduction in fatal wounds by 77.1 per cent for wounds to the thorax and 82.8 per cent for wounds to the abdomen. Overall, the use of body armour prevented 74 per cent of wounds to the region of the body actually protected by the armour, a testament to the effectiveness of the Flyers' Armor.

Post-war studies of overall wartime casualty figures for fatalities from thoracic and abdominal wounds showed slightly differing results to those of the short duration ETO-based wartime surveys. These peacetime studies showed that 34.9 per cent of thoracic and 32.5 per cent of abdominal wounds had been fatal for those not wearing armour. For those using body armour the fatality rate fell to 15.3 per cent for thoracic wounds and 15.7 per cent for abdominal wounds.

The Flyers' Armor was further developed and improved upon post-war. By 1948 the Armor, Flyers' Vest M1 and M2; the Armor, Flyers' Apron, M3 and M4; and the Armor, Flyers' Groin, M4 and M5 had all been declared limited standard (to be issued until stocks were exhausted). They had been replaced by new standardized items: Armor, Flyers' Vest M6A1 and M7A1; Armor, Flyers' Apron, M8A1 and M9A1; and Armor, Flyers' Groin, M10A1.

Ground Troops' Armour
The Flyers' Armor saw some limited use beyond the confines of aircraft. Combat Engineers of the 2nd Infantry Division routinely used the M1 vest and M3 apron combination for special operations such as bulldozer work, land mine removal and when working under enemy fire. The use of armour by engineers was illustrated in The Times of 15 November 1944. In an official report, Major General Gavin of the 82nd Airborne Division stated that while aircraft and glider crews were equipped with body armour, the airborne troops they carried were not provided with any protection. Glider crews discarded their 'flak suits' (Flyers' Armor) once on the ground and despite their weight these were then readily liberated by the airborne troops, for their own use. The 102nd Infantry Division also procured the flak suit, during the breakthrough of the Siegfried Line in November 1944. It is believed that the ensembles were issued to stretcher-bearers, who had suffered high casualties resulting in the evacuation of wounded becoming bogged down for lack of manpower. In October 1943 the US Navy's Motor Torpedo Boat Squadron Twenty Five had expressed an interest in the Flyers' Armor, with consideration for its modification to suit the needs of exposed crews on the decks of motor torpedo boats (MTBs). The Cavalry Board, based at Fort Riley in Kansas, also expressed an interest in the possible modification of the Flyers' Armor for mechanized cavalry troops, but it is not known how this interest from the Navy and Cavalry was progressed.

While the steel plate construction used in the aircrew armour proved highly effective, the armour was too heavy for general issue to ground troops. In June 1944 the Army Service Forces requested that armour be issued to protect soldiers from antipersonnel mines, an increasingly prevalent cause of casualties in Normandy. The results of analysis of the use of armour in the USAAF and the consequential reduction in battle casualties resulted in the OQMG undertaking further research into protective armour for ground troops. While it was fully appreciated that steel was too heavy and cumbersome, alternative lightweight armour was becoming an increasingly realistic proposition. The Quartermaster General Research and Development Branch had previously experimented with a number of fabrics and products. Aluminium stood out as being a possible candidate for use in ground troops' armour, as did woven glass-fibre plastic laminates. The

United States of America

An unidentified experimental pattern of Doron armour vest produced by the US QMC during World War II. This is a simple garment with basic font fastening and adjustment using the metal star-type buttons found on HBT (herringbone twill) work wear and camouflage clothing. (US Army Quartermaster Museum)

This unusual jacket with combined 'coat tail' was produced by the QMC during the latter part of World War II. It has lightweight Doron panel inserts designed to protect the wearer not from grenade or mortar fragmentation, but from native Indian arrows. It was produced to fulfil a requirement to provide protection from poisonous arrows for engineers and oil prospectors working in the Columbian jungle. The prospectors were frequently targeted by Indians unhappy at the intrusion into their lands. (US Army Quartermaster Museum)

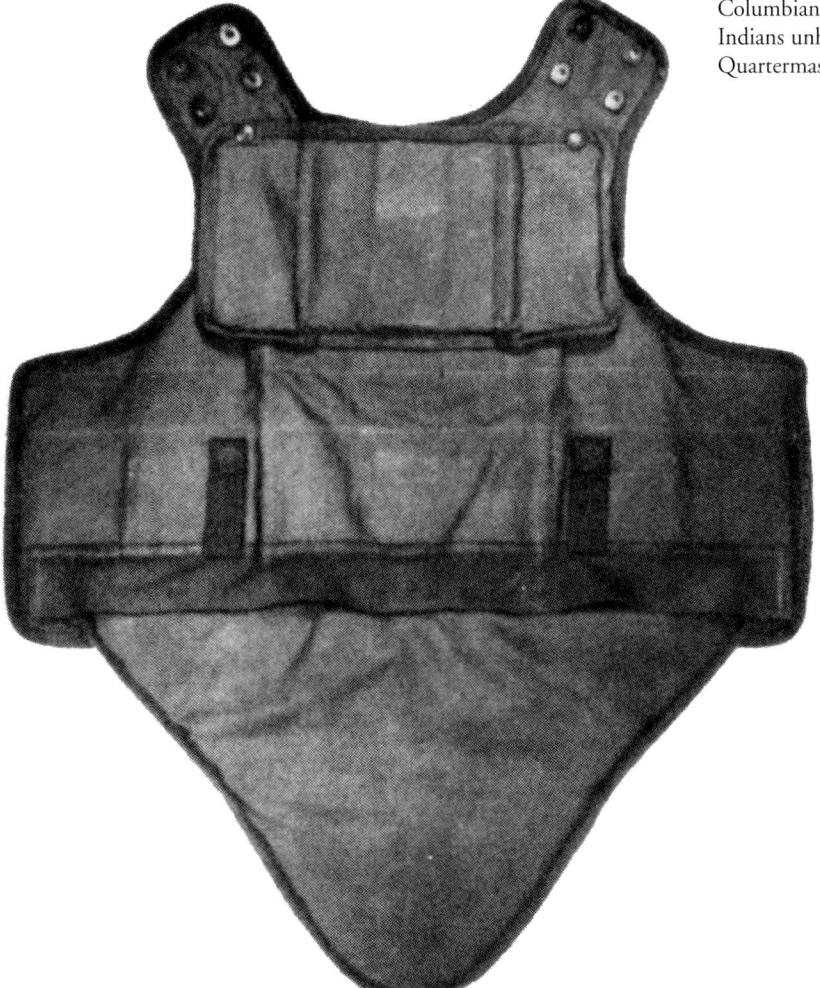

In August 1945 the developmental T65 armour was standardized for troop issue as the Armour, Vest, M12. However, the end of hostilities between the US and Japan saw interest in body armour waning and production was soon halted. The M12 is shown here fitted with the Apron, T65.

United States of America

OQMG had coordinated its work with the US Navy Research Laboratory, which was undertaking research into lightweight armour for aircraft, to replace the heavy manganese steel then in use. The commercial plastics industries were encouraged to assist with the research, having been approached by Edwin Hobson, chief of the Plastics Section in the QMG Research and Development Branch. The industry had already undertaken work in developing bonded plastics and had found them to be a particularly strong form of laminate. By May 1943 the Dow Chemical Company had produced a methacrylate resin, laminated glass-fibre fabric that, as well as being light, had excellent ballistic properties. The new fabric was called Doron, after Lieutenant Colonel (later Brigadier General) Georges Doriot, a naturalized Frenchman, who was then chief of the Research and Development Branch. Doron was such a promising fabric that a number of projects were set in motion with the industry in order to establish the best production and development methods, fabrics and weaves, bonding resins and glass fibre filaments, to provide the best fabrics for use in armour. Among the companies that were to pool their efforts for the war effort were American Cyanamid, Bakelite, Continental Diamond, Dow Chemical, Firestone, Formica, General Electric, Hercules Powder, Monsanto, United States Rubber and Westinghouse.

To improve the coordination of effort, the elements of the armed forces formed a joint committee, set up by the US Defense Department, to oversee development of non-metallic armour. Under the control of the OQMG the committee included the Naval Research Laboratory, Bureau of Ships, Army Ordnance Corps, the Bureau of Medicine and Surgery, and the Bureau of Aeronautics.

Doron plates were also used in the fabrication of an armoured life vest designed by the OQMG's Edwin Hobson and Dr Irwin of the Naval Research laboratory. The vest was demonstrated to interested parties at the Marine Barracks Camp Lejeune, Quantico, and to the FBI. Two officers from the Bureau of Medicine and Surgery, Lieutenant Commander Andrew Paul Webster and Lieutenant Commander Lyman Corey, US Naval Reserve (USNR), undertook the demonstrations, with Webster firing a Colt .45 at Corey, who wore the vest. The US Marine Corps (USMC) was impressed by the properties of the ballistic vest and undertook the manufacture of 1,000 USMC HBT (herringbone twill) utility jackets with Doron plates stitched into internal pockets. These items were intended for use by assault troops during the invasion of Okinawa in 1944, however it is believed that the marine division that they were issued to did not then take part in the assault. Recommendations were also made that the US Navy should procure 300,000 kapok life jackets that had been externally fitted with Doron panels in fabric pockets. Both the HBT jacket and the life jacket used 4lb (1.81kg) of Doron armour plates, providing a coverage of 3sq ft (0.23m2).

Armor, Vest, T62E1; Armor, Vest, T64; Armor, Apron, T65; and Armor, Vest, M12

A number of ground troops' armour patterns were produced for research and development during World War II. Among these were the 'T34', 'T39', 'T62', 'T64' and 'T65' series. The T34 armour was developed from designs and observations submitted by, among others, Lt Col I. Ridgeway Trimble, MC, then chief of the surgical service at the 118th General Hospital, Sydney, Australia, following examination of Japanese body armour captured in the South West Pacific theatre of operations. Its protection was provided by 0.684in (17mm) thick carbon steel plates and it was thus too heavy to be considered seriously and research was discontinued. The T36 armour was based upon a World War I design, but this was again considered unsatisfactory. The T39 was yet another example of armour that did not receive any practical recommendations. It

The M12 armour was the first to be provided with its own carriage/storage bag. The 'Bag Armor, C 7162233' was a small 15in (38cm) square bag with drawstring top closure. Surprisingly, the M12 armour could be folded small enough to fit into this bag.

September 1952 and a soldier of 'L' Company, 38th Infantry Regiment, 2nd Infantry Division, wears the M12 armour during operations in Korea. The M12 did not see issue during World War II, but stocks were provided for use in the Korean conflict. (US National Archives)

consisted of overlapping ballistic metal plates on a fabric backing, and research into the T39 was soon discontinued.

The 'T62E1' vest was the most promising of the patterns developed. Protection consisted of 24 overlapping 0.102in (2.6mm) thick aluminium plates with a backing of 5-ply nylon fabric. Additional protection was provided to the region of the heart, with a total protected area of 3.45ft (0.32m2). Weighing in at 9lb 10oz (4.37kg), it was a two-part vest, the front and back sections being joined at the shoulder with quick-release fasteners. Some 4,100 T62E1 vests were manufactured during June 1945. The T62E1 vest was modified and further enhanced by the addition of increased armour protection and an OD inner face, replacing the white inner, the modifications producing the T64 vest. In August 1945 the T64 was standardized for issue as the 'Armor, Vest, M12'. Its 75 0.125in (3.175mm) ballistic aluminium plates were thicker than those used on the T62E1, and the backing was 8-ply, 13oz nylon duck. Somewhat heavier than the T62E1, the M12's additional armour brought the weight of the vest to 12lb 3oz (5.53kg). The M12 had greatly increased protection when compared to the T62E1, with improved coverage of the axillary anterior thorax and axillary regions. However, despite the improved cover, the axillary region and the neck remained relatively unprotected and were to prove a weak point during combat use of the vest in the Korean War.

Additional protection for the M12 vest was offered by the 'Armour, Apron, T65', which had originally been designed to be fitted to the T62E1 vest. Using quick release fasteners, the apron was attached to the lower front edge of the M12 vest to provide cover to the lower abdomen and pelvic region. Consisting of 21-ply, 13oz nylon duck fabric in a canvas cover, and weighing only 1lb 9oz (0.71kg), it gave an additional 0.66sq ft (0.06m2) of ballistic protection. During June 1945, 8,060 T65 aprons were produced, and 53,352 M12 vests were manufactured in the period June to August 1945. Production and further development of the T65 apron was terminated in January 1946 with the available stock to be used for further trials in general armour development. The T62E1, T64 and M12 armour were all provided with a small storage bag that also took the T65 apron.

A large quantity of the armour produced was destined for field trials in the Pacific and during July 1945 some 1,000 T62E1 vests, 1,200 T65 aprons and 1,200 T64 vests were despatched to theatre. Observer Team 12, consisting of medical, infantry and ordnance ranks, was to observe and report on the use of this armour. However, the cessation of hostilities in August 1945 prevented any combat trial taking place.

Armor, Crotch, T64

During World War II, crotch armour had been developed for use by flyers and one of the designs was used as the basis of the 'Armor, Crotch, T64E4' crotch armour for ground troops. The design consisted of a small crotch section of overlapping manganese steel plates within a nylon cover that covered the genitals, the upper thighs and the buttocks, providing 1.15sq ft (0.14m2) of protection and weighing 3 lb 6oz (1.53kg). The cartridge or pistol belt, being attached to the belts' lower equipment eyelets using four straps and spring hooks, supported the armour. Some 12,220 sets were made between January and June 1945. The 'Armor, Crotch, T16E6' was similar in design but was lighter and provided reduced protection to the rear and thighs, but increased protection to the groin and genitals.

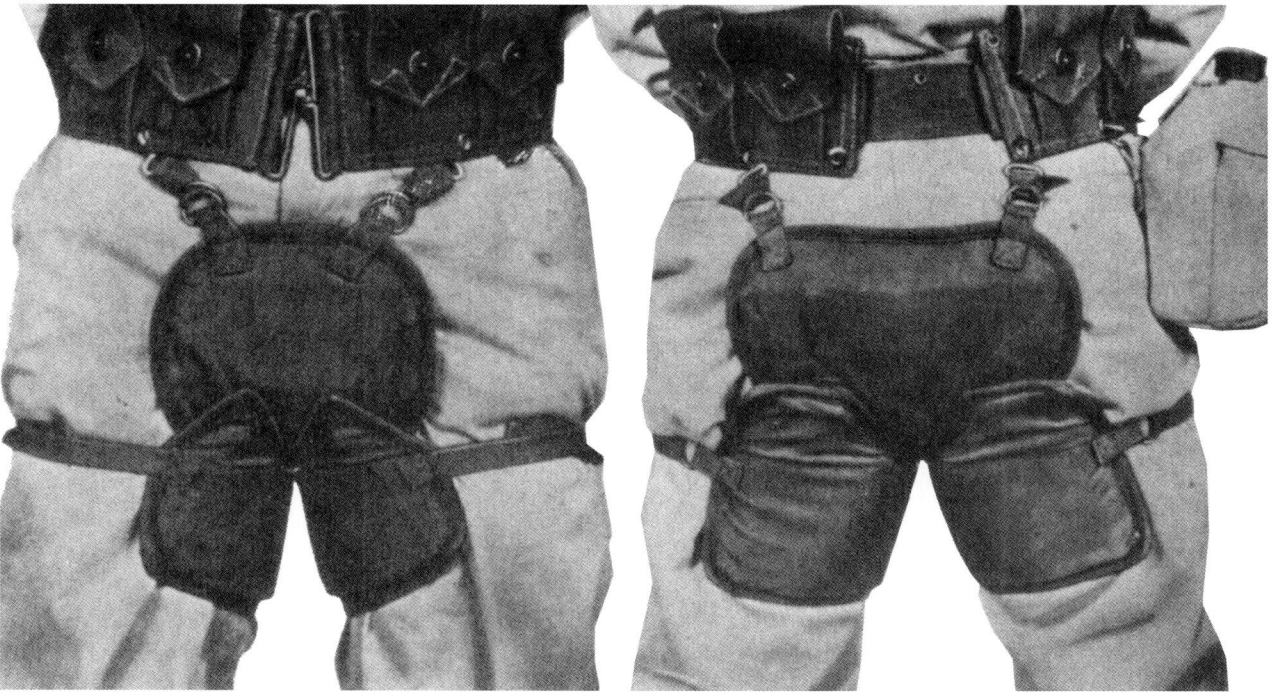

Groin armour had originally been designed around the requirements of aircrew, but the design was adapted for use by ground troops and developed under the T64 and T16 designations. Shown here is the experimental Armor, Crotch, T64E4 that provided protection to the vulnerable groin and inner thigh areas, and particularly to the femoral artery. The armour did not progress beyond the trials stage.

United States of America

Armor, Eye, T45

It was the French who first undertook development of eye protection towards the end of World War II. The US Army took on the concept and experimented with a series of helmet-mounted visors and goggles, which resulted in the T45 series. The developmental 'Armor, Eye, T45E4' and 'Armor, Eye, T45E6' used steel plates mounted in standard M1944 rubber goggle frames. The E4 and E6 differed in the arrangement of their vision slits. The 7oz (198g) 'Armor, Eye, T45E6' was standardized as 'Armor, Eye, M14' in January 1946, to be issued for use in mine clearance. Some 100 pairs of goggles had been produced during September 1945, but it is not believed that the armour entered full-scale production.

Korean War

USMC Vests, Armored, M1951; Armor, Vest, Nylon T52; USMC Armor, Body, Fragmentation, Protective, Vest Type, M1952; Armor, Body, Fragmentation, Protective, Upper Torso, M1952A; USMC Armor, Body, Fragmentation Protective, Lower Torso, M1953

In June 1947, responsibility for the development and research into individual armoured protective equipment was assigned to the Army Quartermaster Corps (AQMC). The AQMC thus became responsible for the development of combat helmets, body armour and other protective items. Having recently been victorious in a world war, its initial requirement was limited, and funding restricted by post-war re-development and reconstruction. However, one legacy of the war was an urgent requirement for the removal and disposal of countless items of explosive ordnance, work that was undertaken by engineers who required some form of protection from blast. Research and development into the provision of armour for engineers working on the removal of mines and similar smaller explosive ordnance was thus the primary concern at this time, with only limited interest in other ground troops. In 1949 the Operations Research Office of the Department of the Army issued a report into the benefits of armour for use by troops engaged in ground combat. It repeated the conclusions of previous reports and research, and confirmed that the currently available materials precluded any extensive use by ground troops, since the levels of protection required were incompatible with the weight burden and increased inflexibility and restrictiveness in use (similar conclusions had previously been reached during the exhaustive ballistic testing undertaken at the Watertown Arsenal during World War II). However, the report was a little premature. The AQMC had already begun development of a far older method of providing ballistic protection, that of using soft fabrics rather than hard ballistic plates. The concept of using plates was necessary for many reasons, cost as well as lack of suitable fibres being primary considerations. Silk had been proven to be a superior fibre, but it was expensive and had a limited life under military usage or combat conditions. However, nylon had proven itself to be a suitable fabric when woven into tight, high-twist multi-layer sheets. The ballistic nylon was found to readily arrest low velocity fragments, such as those produced by grenade or mortar blasts – the most common cause of battlefield casualties. The US Army Ordnance Corps undertook extensive testing of the ballistic nylon and found that it was considerably better as a ballistic fabric than steel, on a weight for weight basis. By 1948 the AQMC had produced a set of body armour manufactured from laminated nylon fabric. The ensemble consisted of a two-piece vest with a groin apron, similar to the USAAF M1 vest and M3 apron. Continued development led to the groin apron being discarded and the laminated nylon was replaced by spot laminating to provide a greater degree of flexibility in the trials vests.

The outbreak of the Korean War in June 1950 brought about a renewed and urgent requisite for the protection of ground troops engaged in combat. This requirement was initially filled by the issue of the World War II M12 vest, pending the production and issue of a replacement. Initial combat casualty statistics showed that 92 per cent of wounds were caused by fragmentation of all types, mainly from shell fire, mortars and grenades, with only 7.2 per cent caused by small arms, suggesting that ballistic vests capable of preventing the penetration of low velocity fragments were essential in restricting the number of casualties. These results were the conclusions of extensive battlefield studies by the Battle Casualty Survey Team that were conducted between November 1950 and May 1951. Of the wounds studied some 4,600 were for men wounded in action (WIA), with an additional study of 1,500 casualties killed (KIA) in action. The 4,600 WIA suffered 7,773 wounds. Of these 16.4 per cent were to the head and neck; 7.9 per cent to the thorax; 6.2 per cent to the abdomen and 69.5 per cent to the extremities (including 0.8 per cent to the genitals). Injury from shell fragmentation accounted for more than 84 per cent of the total number of wounds in the WIA examined. In stark contrast, the survey for the KIA showed that 63 per cent were killed by small arms fire, with 29.9 per cent from shell fragments; 2.8 per cent to mortars; 2 per cent to mines; 0.7 per cent to grenades; 0.5 per cent to artillery fire and 4.1 per cent to miscellaneous injury. It was further concluded that wounds from shell fragments usually occurred within 8m (26ft) of the blast and that wounds from small arms were usually within 100 to 200m (328 to 656ft).

The AQMC continued development and research of body armour apace. Typically, the Department of the Navy was undertaking independent research into the development of combat body armour, and had considered Doron to be the best option. In 1950 the AQMC and Department of the Navy pooled their expertise and began joint research into the use of both nylon and Doron. The combined effort resulted in the production of a combined Doron plate and nylon fabric armour. The vest components were provided by the AQMC (including Doron plates, nylon fabric and webbing) and the USMC made up the vests. Weighing only 6lb 2 oz (2.78kg), the slip-over design used inflexible overlapping curved Doron plates over the torso and flexible nylon fabric over the shoulder areas.

United States of America

The nylon/Doron slip-over vest manufactured by the USMC for joint Army/Navy trials. The vest was field tested in Korea between 14 June and 13 October 1951. It consisted of 16 overlapping Doron ballistic plates, with a ballistic nylon cover. The vest weighed 6lb 2oz (2.77kg), but it was found that it readily absorbed water, which added as much as 2lb (0.91kg) to its weight. Its design did not meet approval, but resulted in further development and the issue of the much modified USMC Vest, Armored, M1951.

PFC Jackson, Company 'L', 6th Regimental Combat Team, US 8th Army, wearing an early production USMC Vest, Armored, M1951 Doron vest with zip front and no fly front flap. Of general interest is the special magazine clip that holds three 30-round .30 M2 carbine magazines and the rubber feed covers. (US National Archives)

Members of the 443rd Quartermaster Group, US 8th Army, model types of armour used in Korea, in August 1953. From left to right they are the Armor, Flyer's, Vest M1, the Armor, Vest, Nylon T52-3 and the Vest, Armored, M1951. (US National Archives)

The experimental Armor, Vest, Nylon T52-2 had two adjustment straps at each side and two chest pockets. It was tested in Korea and led to the production of the Armor, Vest, Nylon T52-3, which was standardized as the Armor, Body, Fragmentation, Protective, Upper Torso, M1952A.

United States of America

In June 1951 a batch of fifty of the nylon/Doron slip-over vests were despatched to Korea via Japan, with a joint AQMC/USMC body armour field test mission to oversee its use. Between the team's arrival in Korea in July and its departure in September, the fifty sets of armour were worn by 6,000 men as the team rotated between the 5th Marine Regiment (1st Marine Division), and the 23rd and 38th Infantry regiments (2nd Infantry Division).

The mission found that the prototype vests were well received, but that concerns were raised at the weight gain, as much as 2lb (0.91kg), when the vest was exposed to moisture, although this could be overcome by using a waterproof cover. The pattern was to undergo further development and extended field testing, however, the urgent need for vests in-theatre led to the continued field testing being shelved and a modified pattern being standardized for issue to the USMC as the 'Vest, Armored, M1951', commonly called the 'Marine vest'. By July 1952 some 9,772 Vests, Armored, M1951 were available to the USMC's 1st Division in the Korean theatre. A variant of the vest was later produced as the 'Armor, Body, Fragmentation, Protective, Vest Type, M52'. The USMC M52 used aluminium plates rather than Doron. Early M51 vests had a plain zip front, but this was soon provided with a snap-closure fly front, that as well as protecting the zip allowed a secondary method of securing the vest if the zip failed. The fly front crossed left to right on the M52 vest and right to left on the M51 vest, which was otherwise identical.

While the USMC introduced the Doron/nylon pattern Vest, Armored, M1951, the Army remained convinced that nylon was superior to Doron; it was more flexible and had less serious physiological issues than Doron, which caused problems if it was drawn into a penetrating wound (such as when a rifle round passed through a plate and into the body). However, Doron, unlike nylon, did provide protection against a bayonet thrust and it also provided greater protection from blunt-trauma impact. Using the results of the joint AQMC/USMC body armour mission field test, the Army produced an all-nylon armour vest for tests, the 'Armor, Vest, Nylon T52-1'. Ballistic protection was afforded by twelve layers of basket weave, spot-laminated nylon, within a lightweight 6oz (170g) waterproof nylon cover. An under layer of rubber added blunt-trauma protection to the ribs and shoulder area. The vest came in two sizes, '42', weighing 7lb 12oz (3.52kg) and with 6.7sq ft (0.62m2) of protection; and '46', weighing 8lb 4oz (3.74kg) and with 7.4sq ft (0.69m2) of protection. Army body armour test team field trials under the codename Operation Boar were conducted in Korea between February and July 1952, providing a total of 400,000 man hours of wear by 15,000 troops on which to draw test conclusions. Tests were extensive and the armour vests were field tested by men of the 2nd, 3rd, 7th, 25th, 40th and 45th Infantry Divisions. Additionally, vests were used to some extent by Colombian, Ethiopian, French, Philippine and Republic of Korea troops. During this period, 1,400 T52-1 vests had been sent to Korea with minor modifications being added to production vests as feedback from the tests filtered back to the USA. The test team originally departed the US with only 48 vests, but a constant flow of vests was despatched between February and May, as they became available. The vests were well received by the troops using them, so much so that in August 1952, Far East Command requested the immediate issue of armour vests, expressing a preference for the Army pattern vest, but conceding that an issue of USMC vests would be acceptable. An immediate procurement of 31,017 USMC Vests, Armored, M1951 was shipped to Far East Command with an urgent order placed for 5,000 of the non-standardized 'Armor, Vest, Nylon T52-2' variant (a front zipper closing vest with web adjustment straps at each side), and an additional 20,000 'Armor, Vest, Nylon T52-3' to be delivered between January and May 1953 at a unit cost of $39.04 (the T52-3 was similar to the T52-2, but with side laces that provided size adjustment and were easily cut to remove the vest from a casualty). Both the T52-2 and the T52-3 were made in three sizes: small, medium and large. The T52-2 provided an area of 5.5sq ft (0.51 m2) of protective coverage and the T52-3 gave 6sq ft (0.56m2) of protection.

The results of combat testing of the T52 armour were impressive; 67.9 per cent of all impacts were defeated, 75.8 per cent of fragment impacts were defeated, 24.4 per cent of small arms impacts were defeated, and the incidence of chest and upper abdomen wounds were reduced by 60 to 70 per cent, with a reduction of 25 to 35 per cent in severity of wound. Marine PFC Lee Ward provided comment on the use of body armour

> I had an enemy mortar shell land about ten feet away from me. I picked five pieces of shell fragments out of my vest. Didn't bother me. Another guy on the same patrol stopped six burp-gun slugs with his jacket. All he got out of it was a couple of bruises...

An unidentified corporal, believed to be from a quartermaster unit, poses with a .30 M1 carbine and the experimental Armor, Vest, Nylon T52-1 during service in Korea. This view clearly shows the three LTD fasteners that secure the front of the vest, and the loop and LTD fasteners that provided support for the equipment belt. (US Army Quartermaster Museum)

United States of America

The issue of the USMC Vest, Armored, M1951 and the standardisation of the trials pattern T52-3 as the 'Armor, Body, Fragmentation, Protective, Upper Torso, M1952A' saw the old M12 vests passed on to UN and Republic of Korea troops.

During field trials of the T52 series armour it had been found that some troops had taken to using an extra armour vest as protection for the lower abdomen and groin (soldiers had even been observed to wrap a vest around their heads). Protection for the groin had been previously provided with the M1 Flyers' Vests in the form of aprons and a similar item, the T65 apron, had been tested with the T62E1 and T64 (M12) vests. The 'Armour, Crotch, T16E4' had also been given serious consideration, but no item had actually been standardized for ground troops before the end of World War II. During the Korean War the Army's QMC nevertheless developed an armour to be used with the T52-3 vest. This lower torso armour resembled a pair of boxing shorts and had twelve layers of nylon encased in waterproof vinyl, with a hard wearing outer cover of water resistant green nylon. The armour had lace fastenings at both sides and was supported by suspenders (braces) worn under the armour vest. While the Army did not proceed with lower torso armour, the USMC felt that there were sound reasons for producing such an item. The USMC 'Armor, Body, Fragmentation Protective, Lower Torso, M1953' was designed to be used in conjunction with the USMC Armor, Body, Fragmentation, Protective, Vest Type, M1952. It resembled the pattern developed by the Army, but had elasticated side sections, a zip fastener at the left side and a waist draw cord for adjustment. The 'Flak Diaper', as the lower torso armour was dubbed, was not well received by ground troops. It was field tested by the 1st Marine Division during early 1953 and was standardized on 18 June 1953. Weighing some 3lb (1.36kg), it was to see only limited service.

Research into the use of body armour in Korea, published in February 1953 (Army Operational Research Group Memo No. 5), concluded that approximately one in every eight men receiving non-fatal wounds would not have been wounded at all if they had been wearing body armour. Of every ten men KIA, two would have survived if they had been wearing body armour, one unharmed and one non-fatally wounded, suggesting a reduction in KIA figures of 20 per cent for those wearing body armour.

USMC Armor, Body, Fragmentation, Protective, Vest Type, M52. This vest is a variant of the M51 and uses aluminium plates rather than Doron. The fly front also crosses left to right, whereas it was right to left on the standard M51 vest. The two vests were otherwise identical in construction.

The experimental Armor, Vest, Nylon T52-3 was standardized as the M52, or to give it its full designation, Armor, Body, Fragmentation, Protective, Upper Torso, M1952A. This was probably the first modern body armour to receive extensive issue and provided the base for body armour development for the next three decades.

Armor, Body, Fragmentation, Protective, Vest Type, M52. Detail of one of the eighteen ballistic aluminium plates used in the M1952 vest. Each plate measures roughly 5in (12.7cm) square.

United States of America

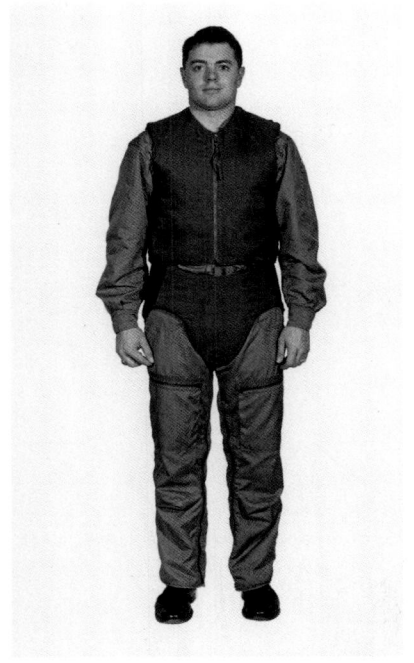

This Armor, Flyer's, Protective, developed for use by aircrew, was photographed in May 1952. The image shows the full ensemble being worn by a USAF Staff Sergeant. The armour is worn over the parachute harness and like the World War II M1 ensemble, it has a pull cord at the waist, attached via cords to LTD fasteners at the shoulders and sides, which when tugged separated and released the panels from the wearer. The torso, abdomen, groin and thighs are well protected. The axillary regions are unusually well protected. However, the restriction in the armpits and across the chest may have caused excessive strain leading to exhaustion in extended use. (National Museum of the US Air Force)

The Armor, Flyer's, Protective laid out to show the component parts. In the upper part of the image is the back pad, connected via quick releasable shoulder straps to the front armour with its fitted groin and thigh plates and four axillary plates. The outer cover appears to be OD nylon. While the material used in the armour is not known, it is probable that it was Aluminium. (National Museum of the US Air Force)

A second pattern of Korean War period experimental armour tested by the USAF, the 'Aircrew Body Armor, Layer Cloth Type, WADC-1-WCUPP-1'. This image dates to 1954, and the armour was undoubtedly the predecessor of the standardized 'Vest, Flak Protective (BuAer (US Navy Bureau of Aeronautics))' and the 'Groin Protector, Flak Protective (BuAer)' from which it differs only in detail. (National Museum of the US Air Force)

At Hook Ridge in November 1952, US Marines held back 800 North Koreans using mass human wave assaults against their lines. Here one of the many Marine casualties is given aid while awaiting evacuation to the rear. All of these Marines wear the USMC Vest, Armored, M1951.

United States of America

Korea, around 1952, and Lieutenant Rodney M. Brigg (right), of the Quartermaster Corps body armour team, points to a bruise on the back of Lieutenant Frank H. Bassett of Company 'G', 160th Infantry Regiment, 40th Infantry Division. The Armor, Vest, Nylon T52-1 worn by Lt Bassett defeated two hand grenade fragments, the impact marks being circled in white. The 40th Infantry Division deployed into combat in February 1952 and was involved in the battles of Sandbag Castle and The Punchbowl. The division suffered 1,180 casualties in Korea, including 358 killed or died of wounds. Of the 1,400 T52-1 vests used in field trials, 254 received hits while worn in combat. (US Army Quartermaster Museum)

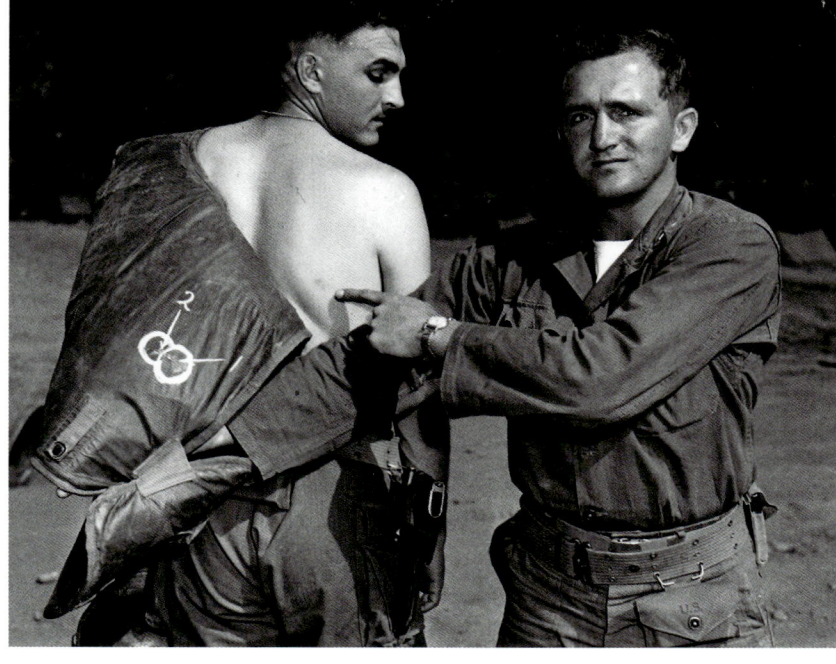

LEFT: The commercially produced 'Model P' armour vest manufactured by Federal Spooner of Saltsburg Pennsylvania. This is an exceptionally heavy vest. Weighing just short of 20lb (9.07kg) this bulky vest uses ballistic steel plates with a ballistic nylon cover. It has a groin protector and wrap around side sections that provide good overall cover and protection levels.

A feature printed in the February 1949 edition of *Mechanix Illustrated* magazine, showing 58-year old Leo Krouse demonstrating the protective power of a 14lb (6.35kg) 'Federal Spooner' armoured vest, a predecessor of the 'Model P'. According to the feature Krouse had been demonstrating armoured vests for 30 years.

Both the US Army and the USMC experimented with lower torso armour, but only the USMC actually standardized a design for use by ground troops. The Armor, Body, Fragmentation Protective, Lower Torso, M1953 was standardized in June 1953, following field combat testing by the 1st Marine Division in Korea. The 'Flak Diapers' as they soon became known, were to be worn in conjunction with the armour vest.

United States of America

Vietnam

The conflict in Vietnam saw the issue of body armour on a large scale. Stocks of Armor, Body, Fragmentation, Protective, Upper Torso, M1952A were issued alongside the USMC armour and newer variants developed during the conflict. While USMC troops were usually to be seen wearing armour at all times, Army personnel were somewhat reticent to don armour in the oppressive heat and it was usually only worn by troops on static duties.

Armor, Body, Fragmentation Protective, Upper Torso, (with collar M1955)

The USMC 'Armor, Body, Fragmentation Protective, Upper Torso, (with collar M1955)' was the standard 'A' armour vest in use with the Marines and Navy. It was essentially a Korean War design using 23 overlapping ⅛in (3.2mm) thick, 5in (12.7cm) square Doron plates in a nylon outer. Protection across the shoulders was provided by thirteen layers of ballistic nylon, with a total protection area of between 5.35 and 6.03sq ft (0.50 and 0.56m2). The M1955 vest was issued in three sizes, medium, large and extra large, weighing 10lb 3oz (4.62kg), 11lb 8oz (5.22kg) and 12lb 8oz (5.67kg), respectively. It was also issued in three distinct variants. The first version had a rope ridge on the right shoulder and a small open-top pocket on the left breast. It was closed by a zip, with a covering flap using four press snaps. Equipment hanging eyelets were positioned along the lower edge of the vest and allowed attachment of equipment using the standard M1910 hanger. The second pattern vest saw the addition of two large button flap pockets at each lower front. The third pattern vest, fielded in 1968, included the second pattern's pockets and added a second rope ridge on the left shoulder. The M1955 vest was still being produced a decade after the Vietnam War and last saw operational use with the 800 Marines of the 32nd Marine Amphibious Unit who landed in Beirut in August 1982. The unit cost was listed as $47 in the June 1971 publication Personnel Armor Handbook.

The Armor, Body, Fragmentation, Protective, Upper Torso, M1952A in use with UH-1 'Huey' helicopter air cavalry troopers of the 1st Cavalry Division (Airmobile) during the Vietnam War. This vest was soon augmented by specialist aircrew armour vests, although the M1952A was frequently worn over the aircrew armour vests to reduce impact 'spall'. (US Army Quartermaster Museum)

Operation *Pitt*, 12 miles north of Da Nang, December 1967. Marine Private Jones of the mortar section, 2nd Battalion, 7th Marines, looks battle weary as he takes a break from offensive operations. Jones typifies the image of a Vietnam conflict Marine and, typically, wears his Armor, Body, Fragmentation Protective, Upper Torso, (With Collar), M1955 open fronted.

United States of America

Armor, Body, Fragmentation Protective, Upper Torso (With Collar), M1955. This armour was issued to the USMC, which has always preferred to use its own pattern of equipment rather than use standard Army patterns. The evolution from the Korean War Vest, Armored, M1951 is evident in the general design. Improvements include a short collar, a snap-closed front flap over the zip, M1910 eyelets along the lower edge and a cord stop around the right shoulder to hold the rifle butt secure when aiming. This also served to help prevent the rifle sling slipping when the weapon was slung. The vest used 23 Doron plates as ballistic protection. (VietnamGear.com)

Armor, Body, Fragmentation Protective, Upper Torso, (With Collar), M1955. This was the third and final variant of the USMC M1955 vest. The vest has rope rifle stops at each shoulder and the two pockets have button through flaps; these modifications were incorporated during initial production. The vest contained 23 Doron plates below the shoulder area, which was protected by six-ply ballistic nylon. (Jack Carrico)

Vest, Flak Protective (BuAer). This vest was made, under a June 1957 contract, by L. W. Foster Sportswear Company Incorporated, a well known manufacturer of vest outer covers. It was used by US Navy and USMC aircrew during the early stages of the Vietnam War. The vest was worn with the Groin Protector, Flak Protective (BuAer), later re-designated for all-services issue as the Armor, Body, Fragmentation Protective (For the Groin). (J. Sweet)

The joint Army/Navy specification Armor, Body, Fragmentation Protective (For the Groin). Based on the USMC Armor, Body, Fragmentation Protective, Lower Torso, M1953, this pattern had a front zip and a groin strap with a brass ring that looped over a snap fastener below the zipper for quick and easy release. It was made up of two imposed sections of eight layers of ballistic fabric providing a total of sixteen layers of protection. The M1953 had a fixed strap, elasticated side sections and an adjustment cord that allowed for a far better fit and greater comfort than this pattern provided. Originally costing $19.10 each, the groin armour was used by aircrew and was provided in eight sizes at an average weight of 4lb (1.81kg). This item was originally classified as the US Navy Groin Protector, Flak Protective (BuAer).

United States of America

Armor, Body, Fragmentation Protective for Neck and Torso, Composite T61-5

The 'Armor, Body, Fragmentation Protective for Neck and Torso, Composite T61-5' was a standard 'B' issue vest. It was also designated 'Armor, Body, Fragmentation Protective, Titanium Nylon Composite (T61-5)'. It provided the same degree of protective area cover as the Armor, Body, Fragmentation, with Collar. Fragmentation protection was provided by six layers of ballistic nylon at the neck and four layers of ballistic nylon across the torso. Complete additional coverage was provided by between 125 and 150 (dependant on size) overlapping 0.032in (0.813mm) thick titanium plates. Ballistic protection was slightly better than the Armour, Body, Fragmentation Protective, with Collar vest and it was also designed to defeat the Special Purpose Individual Weapon (SPIW) small arms flechette. Articulated shoulder pads were incorporated into the design along with two front pockets and grenade hanging loops. Elastic laces at the sides allowed for size adjustment. The front closure was a 2in (5cm) wide section of Velcro. The outer nylon shell had drainage holes along the lower edge to allow for water drainage. The Armor, Body, Fragmentation Protective, Titanium Nylon Composite (T61-5) was provided for limited issue to US Army personnel and members of the US Navy SEALs in sizes small (weighing 7lb 14oz/3.57kg), medium (8lb 11oz; 3.94kg) and large, which weighed 9lb 9oz (4.34kg). This vest was somewhat expensive, costing $174 each. It was still under development in 1971 when technical report TR-2574 noted that efforts were being made to reduce the weight and cost, but little advance was made. During 1969, 1,291 T61-5 vests had been issued to an Infantry Division and 1,347 issued to the 1st Cavalry Division (Airmobile) serving in Vietnam. This issue represented the full available stock of 2,638 vests. Field reports suggested that the titanium plates were the source of excessive noise, and that the weight of the vest was a problem.

Armor Vest, Felt, Lightweight T66-1

The 'Armor Vest, Felt, Lightweight T66-1' came into existence following a 1964 project A Study to Conserve the energy of Combat Infantryman (February 1964) and a letter dated 23 February 1966, from Headquarters US Army Vietnam to the Natick laboratories informing them of an urgent theatre requirement for a lightweight armour vest for issue to combat troops. Natick undertook the development of the lightweight vest to possibly replace the standard M1952A vest, which in its medium size weighed 8.5lb (3.86kg). The Armor Vest, Felt, Lightweight T66-1 was similar to the M1952A in appearance. The outer cover was from Olive Green (OG) 14oz ballistic nylon, while the inner vest was made up from a single layer of 6oz ballistic nylon felt and two layers of woven ballistic nylon encased in a polyethylene cover. Increased protection was given over the spine and heart by an additional four layers of the woven ballistic nylon. While overall ballistic protection was some 20 per cent less than the standard vest the protection offered to the vital areas was equal to it. This was balanced by a saving in weight of some lb (1.36kg), with the vest weighing a total of only 4lb 14oz (2.21kg), the reduction in weight aiding greatly in the increased combat effectiveness of soldiers wearing the lightweight vest. Production costs were estimated at less than $50 per vest, but later reduced to $30. In June 1967, the vest was rejected by the Infantry Board, since it did not provide adequate protection and had several deficiencies and fundamental shortcomings.

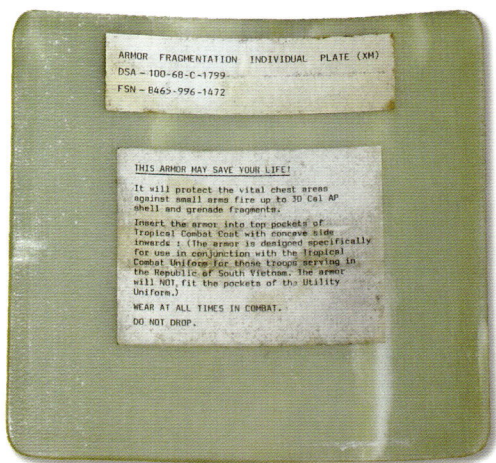

The experimental 'Armor, Fragmentation, Individual Plate (XM)' was an attempt at providing a lightweight body armour to frontline troops in Vietnam. Infantrymen had been particularly loath to wear standard body armour because of the excessive weight burden in the hot and humid weather found in most of Vietnam. The polyethylene plates were designed to fit into the pockets of the tropical combat jacket and provided protection from fragmentation and small arms up to .30in AP. (VietnamGear.com)

The Armor Vest, Felt, Lightweight T66 was developed by Natick during 1966 in an effort to field a lightweight replacement for the M1952. The filler used layers of nylon felt, the ensemble weighed just under 5lb (2.27kg), a weight saving of some 3lb (1.36kg), but with equal protection to the standard vests. It was not standardized, however, since it was found to be too hot in use. (Natick via VietnamGear.com)

Armor, Infantry Small Arms, Protective front and back with Carrier (Body Armor, Ground Troops, Variable Type, Small Arms-Fragmentation Protective – VBA)

In September 1966, 200 of the Armor Vest, Felt, Lightweight were shipped to Vietnam for field evaluation trials with the 1st Infantry Division. The following month lightweight vests were issued for evaluation to the 1st Cavalry Division (Airmobile), along with 'Armor, Infantry Small Arms, Protective front and back with Carrier'.

The results of the trial showed that the evaluation of the lightweight armour was generally unfavourable. Despite the reduced weight, the vest was considered to be too hot for use in Vietnam, it was uncomfortable and caused skin rashes due to the restricted ventilation. The lightweight vest was, however, considered as suitable for use by mounted or static units. Results for the 'Armor, Infantry Small Arms, Protective front and back with Carrier' were, surprisingly, slightly better. It was described as comfortable but heavy, but it did not restrict wearers in the performance of their duties. The official conclusion was that the lightweight armour be further evaluated and that the Armor, Infantry Small Arms, Protective front and back with Carrier be issued for troops engaged in convoy protection duties and vehicle-mounted patrols. The Armor, Infantry Small Arms, Protective front and back with Carrier went into production as the 'Body Armor, Ground Troops, Variable Type, Small Arms-Fragmentation Protective', or VBA for short. Between September and December 1968, some 2,050 sets of VBA were delivered to units in Vietnam, with an additional requirement for 46,000 sets to be procured by December 1969. They were to be issued at a level to equip 50 per cent of personnel for infantry units, 20 per cent for artillery and 10 per cent for truck companies. It is believed that no more than 28,000 sets of VBA were actually delivered to theatre. The VBA was based on the armour developed by Natick for use by aircrews – the 'Armor, Small Arms Protective, Aircrewman's'. It was a nylon felt vest that provided standard protection against fragmentation. It was also provided with ceramic/fibreglass SAPI plates that provided protection from small arms fire up to 30-calibre ball ammunition with a velocity of 2,850fps (869m/s) at a range of 100 yards (91m). The SAPI could be inserted into the vest or worn independently using the integral harness fitted to the SAPI. The VBA vest system weighed between 5lb 4oz (2.38kg) and 22lb 3oz (5.53kg) depending on protection levels, and cost $385 per complete unit, $35 for the vest and $175 per SAPI.

Interestingly the VBA was a unique concept that was all too soon discarded. It was not to be resurrected for some forty years, until both the UK and US started issuing plate carriers and scaleable body armour.

RIGHT: Armor, Body, Fragmentation Protective for Neck and Torso, Composite T61-5. The T61-5 used composite ballistic protection in the form of ballistic Nylon and Titanium plates. Unlike nylon the Titanium plates were able to defeat the SPIW flechette that was being developed at the same time as the vest. The T61-5 offered increased protection over contemporary US vests and introduced the concept of articulated shoulder sections. (Jack Carrico)

Body Armor, Ground Troops, Variable Type, Small Arms or Variable Body Armour (VBA). The VBA was an attempt at upgrading the armour worn by ground troops. A development of the Armor, Small Arms Protective, Aircrewman's, it used SAPI plates front and rear, the first use of such plates by ground troops, but a passing phase in armour development that was not be standardized for a couple of decades. Its weight meant that it was only suited for use by troops in static positions or vehicle mounted. However, the vest could be worn with or without the plates and the plates could also be worn independently of the vest. (Dave De Ridder)

United States of America

Armor, Body, Fragmentation Protective with Collar; Armor, Body, Fragmentation Protective with Collar (M69); and Armor, Body, Fragmentation Protective, Vietnamese Forces

By the close of the war in Vietnam the 'Armor, Body, Fragmentation Protective with Collar' was the standard 'B' type body armour in use with the Army, Navy and Air Force. The first full design specifications were issued in 1963, but it was not until 1968 that full-scale production was underway. This vest was the first to provide any degree of neck protection (albeit somewhat limited). Its inner consisted of a ballistic nylon vest using 12 plies as standard over the front and upper back, ten plies across the lower back and two additional plies, 6in (15cm) wide across the spine. The collar used six plies of nylon. Later production vests incorporated plastic stiffeners inserted under the fifth layer of nylon. The stiffeners helped reduced bunching of the inner ballistic vest within the outer shell. The front of the vest was closed using a zip fastener and Velcro. On late versions the zip was deleted and closure was effected by a wide Velcro strip. The front of the vest had two pockets and grenade hangers. At each side of the vest were elastic adjustment laces. The vest was issued in small, medium, large and extra large sizes. It had three distinct versions, zip closing front with no stiffeners, zip closing front with plastic stiffeners and Velcro closing front with plastic stiffeners. This later version with Velcro fastening and no zip was introduced in 1969. It included a new style of large instructional label stitched into the inner rear face of the vest. The label had an open top that allowed storage of the user manual that accompanied each vest. This pattern was the first to be designated 'Armor, Body, Fragmentation Protective with Collar (M69)' although all three variants of vest with collar are now often erroneously referred to as the M69. The weight of the vest was increased with the introduction of the stiffeners. The early zip-front vests without stiffeners weighed 7lb 13oz (3.54kg), 8lb 10oz (3.91kg), 9lb 5oz (4.68kg) and 10lb 2oz (4.59kg), respectively, while the later zip-fronted vests with stiffeners and the Velcro-only closure vests both weighed the same at 8lb 5oz (3.77kg), 9lb 2oz (4.14kg), 9lb 13oz (4.45kg) and 10lb 11oz (4.85kg), respectively, for small, medium, large and extra large vests. The unit cost was $35.

A copy of the Armor, Body, Fragmentation Protective with Collar (M69) was manufactured for Vietnamese forces. The standard US-issue vests were excessively large for the smaller southeast-Asian physique and thus the 8470-144-5797-series 'Armor, Body, Fragmentation Protective, Vietnamese Forces' was introduced. The Vietnamese vests had a Velcro front fastening, lace side adjustment, two bellows pockets and a three-loop grenade carrier at each chest. They were noticeably smaller than US vests, and although supplied in a similar size range, the designated sizes were smaller than US vests. The Vietnamese vests were provided in small, weighing 7lb 10oz (7.63kg); medium, 8lb 2oz (3.69kg) and large, 8lb 13oz (4kg). At an individual cost of $24, they were $11 cheaper than the larger US vests. Ballistic protection was equal to the US M69 vest.

Armor, Body, Fragmentation Protective, with Collar, the classic Vietnam body armour that typified the US 'grunt'. A development of the M1952A vest, it has a small collar, flapped pockets and grenade loops. It has a zip-and-snap front fastening and unlike the M1952A there were no shoulder straps. Made by The Martin Lane Co., Inc in 1968.

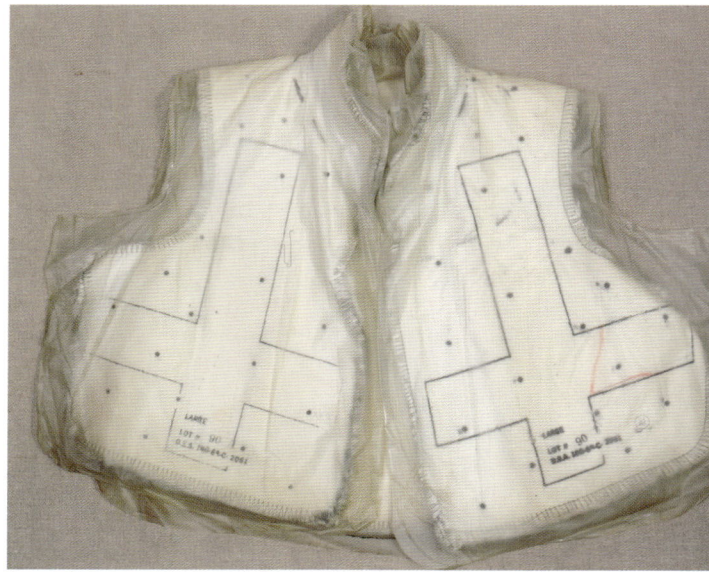

Armor, Body, Fragmentation Protective, with Collar. This ballistic inner vest came from a 1969-manufacture body armour. This inner is the type with plastic re-enforcements. The position of the plastic is marked by the inverted black cross outline. The plastic reinforcements greatly reduced bunching of the ballistic fabric. In earlier, un-stiffened patterns, the oversize clear polyethylene waterproof covering did not help in the prevention of bunching since the vest slipped around within this cover. To further exacerbate the problem, the whole ensemble moved within the outer nylon OD cover. Despite the added stiffeners, this issue of bunching was not fully resolved until the issue of the PASGT vest.

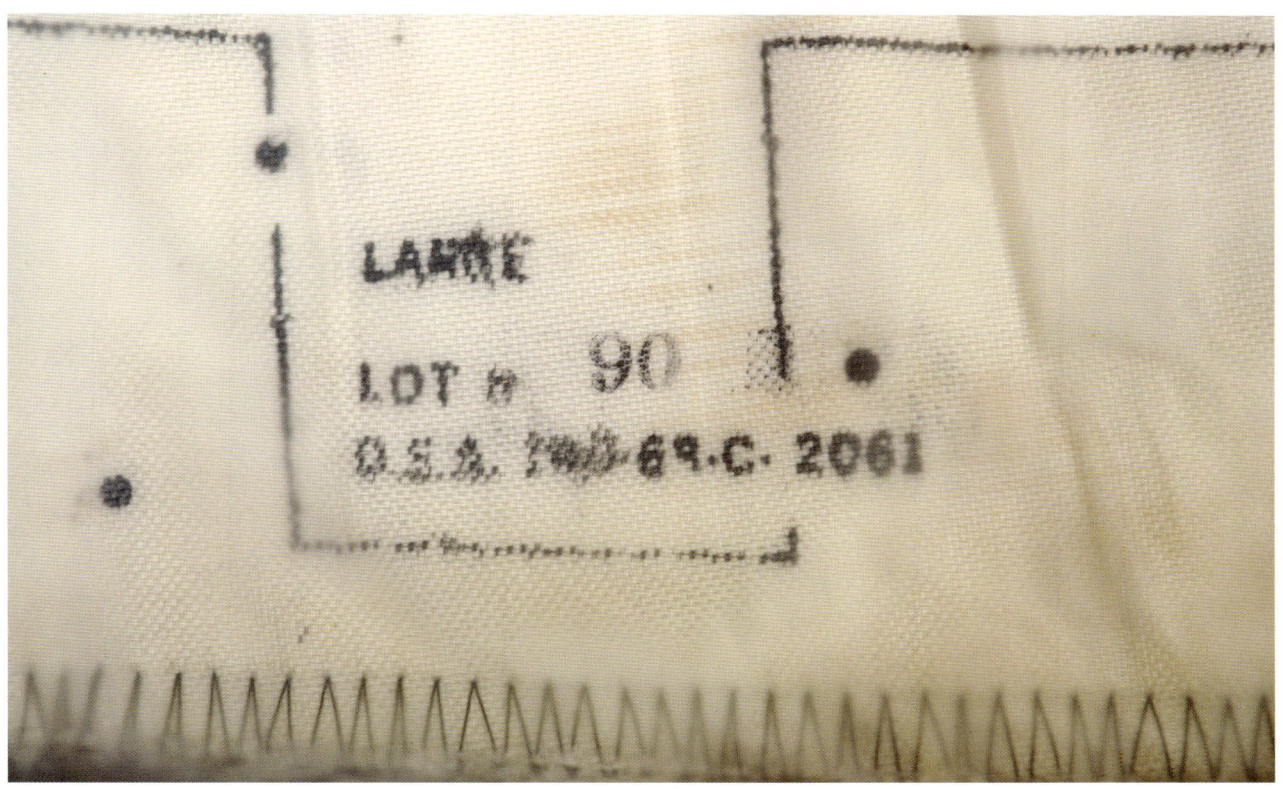

Armor, Body, Fragmentation Protective, with Collar. The markings show the size, 'LARGE', the fabric lot number '90', and the Defense Supply Agency (DSA) marking D.S.A. 100.69.C.2062. The '69' indicates the year of manufacture as 1969.

Germany, 1986, and Jack Carrico, wearing open-fronted Armor, Body, Fragmentation Protective, with Collar (M69), stands at the rear left of this group. PFC Joe Arenas, right, wears the woodland Body Armor, Fragmentation Protective Vest, Ground Troops (PASGT) vest. The other two soldiers are French. (Jack Carrico)

The standard Armor, Body, Fragmentation Protective with Collar was modified in 1969. The zipper and snaps were replaced by a broad Velcro fastening and the grenade loop holder was shortened (although it still retained three loops). The modified vest was standardized as the Armor, Body, Fragmentation Protective with Collar (M69), although the term M69 is often wrongly applied to both standard and modified patterns. On the M69 vest the designation label formed a pocket in which the user manual was stored.

Although this vest is marked Armor, Body, Fragmentation Protective, with Collar this pattern was for issue to Vietnamese forces and is often referred to as the Armor, Body, Fragmentation Protective, Vietnamese Forces. It differs only in minor detail to the late pattern Armor, Body, Fragmentation Protective, with Collar (M69), retaining the Velcro fastening front of the US issue M69 vest the Vietnamese item is smaller within each size range and has a three loop grenade carrier on each breast. Produced in small, medium and large sizes the vests weighed 7.65 lbs, 8.10 lbs and 8.88 lbs (US) respectively and cost $24 each. (Dave De Ridder)

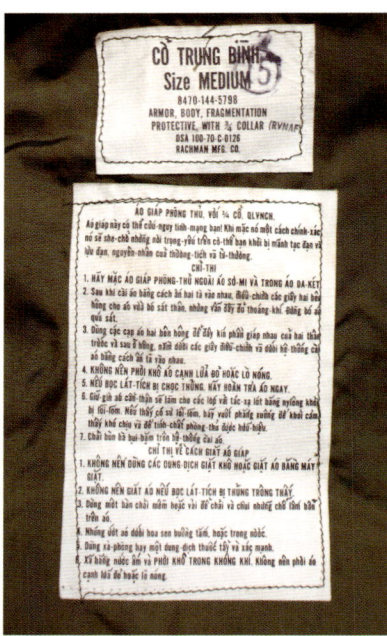

A 1970 manufacture's label from a vest Armor, Body, Fragmentation Protective, Vietnamese Forces. The manufacturer's designation label shows the vest size in Vietnamese and English, with the type, stock and contract numbers and manufacturer's details (Rachman Manufacturing Company) only in English. The designation has an additional ink stamp added, 'RVNAF', indicating that this vest was for issue to the Republic of Vietnam Air Force. The instruction label gives the vest designation and user instructions in Vietnamese. (Dave De Ridder)

Ho Chi Minh trail, Laos, February 1971 and Republic of Vietnam (RVN) troops remove North Vietnamese Army (NVA) stores from a bunker complex that had been used for storage of essential supplies including uniforms, weapons and fuel. The RVN trooper in the bunker appears to be wearing the Armor, Body, Fragmentation Protective, Vietnamese Forces.

United States of America

Body Armor, Lightweight, Fragmentation Protective Vest with Collar M71-N

The 'Body Armor, Lightweight, Fragmentation Protective Vest with Collar M71-N' was a lightweight development of the standard 'Armor, Body, Fragmentation Protective with Collar (M69)' to which it was very similar. The filler was 8oz, water repellent treated ballistic Nylon 128, within a nylon outer cover. The waterproofing of the nylon filler meant that a plastic filler cover, standard on the M69 and earlier fillers, was not required. The cover had two pockets and two three section grenade loops with a full length Velcro front closure. The medium size M71 vest weighed only 6lb (2.72kg) compared to 9lb 2oz (4.14kg) for the medium size M69 vest, a considerable reduction in weight. However, the reduction in ballistic protection resulted in a considerably poorer vest.

Experimental Body Armor, Lightweight, Fragmentation Protective Vest with Collar M71-N manufactured using lightweight Nylon 128. On this example the filler has been held in place by added heavy stitching at the neck, shoulders and down each side of the chest (running over the grenade loops). The rear has a single stitched line across the lower back. This was to prevent bunching, which was quite severe with the lightweight filler used in this vest.

Rear of the Body Armor, Lightweight, Fragmentation Protective Vest with Collar M71-N showing large paint-stamped marking 'FOR TRAINING USE ONLY – NOT FOR ACTIVE OPERATIONS VEST SERIAL NO.59'

United States of America

Aircrew armour

Armor, Aircrewmen, Small Arms Protective, Front and Back, with Carrier (Armor, Small Arms Protective, Aircrewman's) and Armor, Small Arms Protective, Aircrewman's Front Plate Carrier for Pilot and Co-Pilot

The need for individual armour for aircrew had been identified during World War II. By 1962, a Doron shield had been developed. A simple device, it rested on the aircrewman's thighs and afforded protection to the torso. The Transportation Research and Engineering Command (TRECOM) pilots' shield weighed 17lb 8oz (7.94kg) and by January 1963 it had been decided to included the shields as a standard equipment component on UH-1 and H-21 helicopters in Vietnam, and 150 sets were deployed to theatre. The shield was soon improved by the use of hard face composite (HFC) plates. However, the HFC chest protectors suffered the same problems as the earlier shields; they were uncomfortable to wear, since their weight was taken solely by the thighs. They also interfered with aircraft operation. Other shields were developed and discarded, but the 'T62-1 Small Arms Protective, Torso Armor Carrier' was a major step in the right direction. The T62-1 was a nylon/cotton fabric carrier that allowed comfortable wear of the ballistic plates with weight distributed evenly on the body and shoulders. Developed by Natick in 1962, the T62-1 had single large pockets to the front and rear allowing for a single plate to be carried in the front pocket by seated aircrew (with armoured seats), or plates at front and rear for mobile crewmen such as gunners, who were fully exposed. The HFC plates were modified and 500 T62-1 style carriers were produced in-theatre to maximize use of the new design. Further development saw the production of the T65-2 vest that in early 1966 was standardized as the 'Armor, Aircrewmen, Small Arms Protective, Front and Back, with Carrier'. The aircrew armour was called the 'Chicken Plate' by aircrewmen, but its functionality was confirmed by a 1967 report that showed that of 72 aircrewmen injured in action between July 1966 and June 1967, only 3.6 per cent had received injuries to the chest or back. However, it was also reported that many aircrew felt that their armour was insufficient when worn alone and that the M1952A vest was worn in conjunction with it by as many as 30.5 per cent of airmen. Following modification and development, the Armor Aircrewmen, Small Arms Protective, Front and Back, with Carrier was redesignated as the 'Armor, Small Arms Protective, Aircrewman's'.

The developmental 'Body Armor, Fragmentation - Small Arms Protective, Aircrewman, M70A' was standardized as the Armor, Small Arms Protective, Aircrewman's in 1971. It was available in two patterns, for seated crew (pilot/co-pilot) and mobile crew (gunners/crew chiefs). Its crew-pattern Nomex carrier had ballistic nylon filler and pockets at front and rear for two ceramic aluminium oxide, glass-reinforced plastic- (GRP) faced SAPI plates, while the pilot's variant, 'Armor, Small Arms Protective, Aircrewman's Front Plate Carrier for Pilot and Co-Pilot' had a single pocket at the front and an open mesh back section. Snap fasteners and Velcro allowed for quick release and easy donning of the vest. The Army version of the aircrew vest weighed 34lb (15.42kg) and cost $195. The pilots' version weighed between 13 and 16lb 8oz (5.90 and 7.48kg) and cost between $83 and $101. Variants of the vests were used by the Navy, USMC and USAF. These services used lighter and more expensive silicon carbide or boron carbide SAPI plates.

While the Armor, Small Arms Protective, Aircrewman's was a great improvement over the TRECOM shields, it was not without problems. It was found that spall and secondary projectile injuries were causing many casualties among aircrew in Vietnam. Ball rounds striking the SAPI plates were breaking up and their lead cores and copper jackets were impacting unprotected areas of the body and often causing severe wounds, particularly when impacting the face. A remedy was found in the Armor, Vest, M1952A. When worn over the Armor, Small Arms Protective, Aircrewman's, the collarless M1952A provided the perfect spall cover. Other vests were unsuitable because of their collars, which interfered with the aircrew helmet.

In Vietnam it was normal practice for vehicle-mounted troops to wear their amour when mounted. It provided good protection from rocket-propelled grenade (RPG) strikes and a degree of protection from mine blasts. Armour was used routinely in fire bases and its use was often mandatory at night. However, armour was rarely used by the Army during patrol work because of its weight and general discomfort. Conversely the USMC tended to use armour at all times and stated that after a time, Marines got used to the weight and discomfort. The Army noted that the Marines often moved at a pace 'similar to tortoises', but there is no doubting the USMC's fighting efficiency.

Armor, Small Arms Protective, Aircrewman's. This armour was standardized from the T65-2 trials armour. It was designed to provide superior ballistic protection to aircrews and had large SAPI plates at front and rear. The small pocket at the front held miscellaneous items close at hand. At left is the front view and at right the rear. Although heavy, the weight was not a major issue for aircrew. (Adrian Li)

United States of America

The large front SAPI plate from the Armor, Small Arms Protective, Aircrewman's. The heavy GRP faced ceramic plates used by the Army were manufactured from aluminium oxide and in combination with an M1952A vest (for spall protection) they provided excellent ballistic protection. (Adrian Li)

Developmental Body Armor, Fragmentation – Small Arms Protective, Aircrewman, M70A. This system had a standard front panel and two rear panel types. The Type I rear panel held a SAPI plate, the Type II was a ventilated mesh with no SAPI, as shown here at right. Pilots and crew in armoured seats were to wear armour Type II, other aircrew used the Type I, with front and rear SAPI. This item has Federal Stock Number 8470-177-5078. The standardized vests were stocked as 8470-450-3698 for gunners and crew chiefs, and 8470-450-3713 for the pilot and co-pilot version. (Eli Jones/Lars Wigren)

United States of America

Post-Vietnam

Personnel Armor System for Ground Troops

In April 1973 the Department of the Army set out its approval of requirements for a new armour vest, the 'Personnel Armor System for Ground Troops' or PASGT. The armour was to replace the Armor, Body, Fragmentation Protective with Collar and Armor, Body, Fragmentation Protective with Collar (M69) that were then standard. Development took some years and it was not until the early 1980s that the new vest was first issued. The vest used the new M81 woodland camouflage, it resembled the Armor, Body, Fragmentation Protective with Collar in general design, but incorporated the shoulder protection found on the Armor, Body, Fragmentation Protective for Neck and Torso, Composite T61-5, giving it a weight of around 9lb (4.08 kg). The PASGT filler consisted of 13 plies of 14oz water-repellent Kevlar fabric, the first use of this fabric in a standardized US vest. It was provided in six sizes, from extra small through to extra extra large. As with previous armour, it provided little more than fragmentation protection. However, in 1996 the 'Interim Small Arms Protective Overvest' (ISAPO) was introduced. At 16lb 8oz (7.48kg) this simple plate carrier allowed two ceramic plates to be worn over the vest, protecting the vital organs of the dorsal and anterior regions of the upper torso from small arms fire. The ISAPO saw only limited use.

The PASGT has seen widespread service with a number of nations' armed forces, including those of Afghanistan, Argentina, Australia, Belgium, Brazil, Cambodia, Canada, Colombia, Egypt, Estonia, Iraq, Israel, Italy, Jamaica, Japan, Kuwait, Malaysia, Mexico, New Zealand, Philippines, Portugal, Republic of Korea, Romania, Saudi Arabia, Singapore, Spain, Sri Lanka, Thailand, Turkey, and Venezuela. The PASGT armour was still in use with the US Navy at the time of writing (2010).

Body Armor, Fragmentation Protective Vest, Ground Troops, generally called the PASGT vest. Introduced in 1981, this was the first widespread issue replacement for the Vietnam period Armor, Body, Fragmentation Protective, with Collar (M69). Of a similar design to the M69 vest, the PASGT cover has articulated shoulder pads and is constructed of woodland-camouflage fabric.

The PASGT vest in use in Northern Iraq during 1991. (Martin J. Brayley)

United States of America

Gunnery Sgt Mike Stelzel wears the PASGT vest during the invasion of Grenada, in October 1983. Stelzel was serving with 'H' Battery, 3rd Battalion, 10th Marine Regiment, part of the 22nd Marine Amphibious Unit, when they intercepted Bernard Coard, responsible for the overthrow of the government and the murder of the prime minister. The prisoner shown here was one of his cohorts. (Mike Stelzel)

Like the Armor, Body, Fragmentation Protective, with Collar (M69), the PASGT vest had a large label stitched into the inner rear face of the cover. The label was open-topped and held the user guide, which contained basic use and care instructions. The opening paragraph of the instruction label reads:

READ, THEN KEEP THE "USE AND CARE" BOOKLET IN
THIS POCKET. THIS ARMOR MAY SAVE YOUR LIFE!!
When worn properly, this armor vest will protect YOUR vital areas against shell and grenade fragments which cause most combat casualties.

The Defense Logistics Agency (DLA) number shows that this vest was made in 1985.

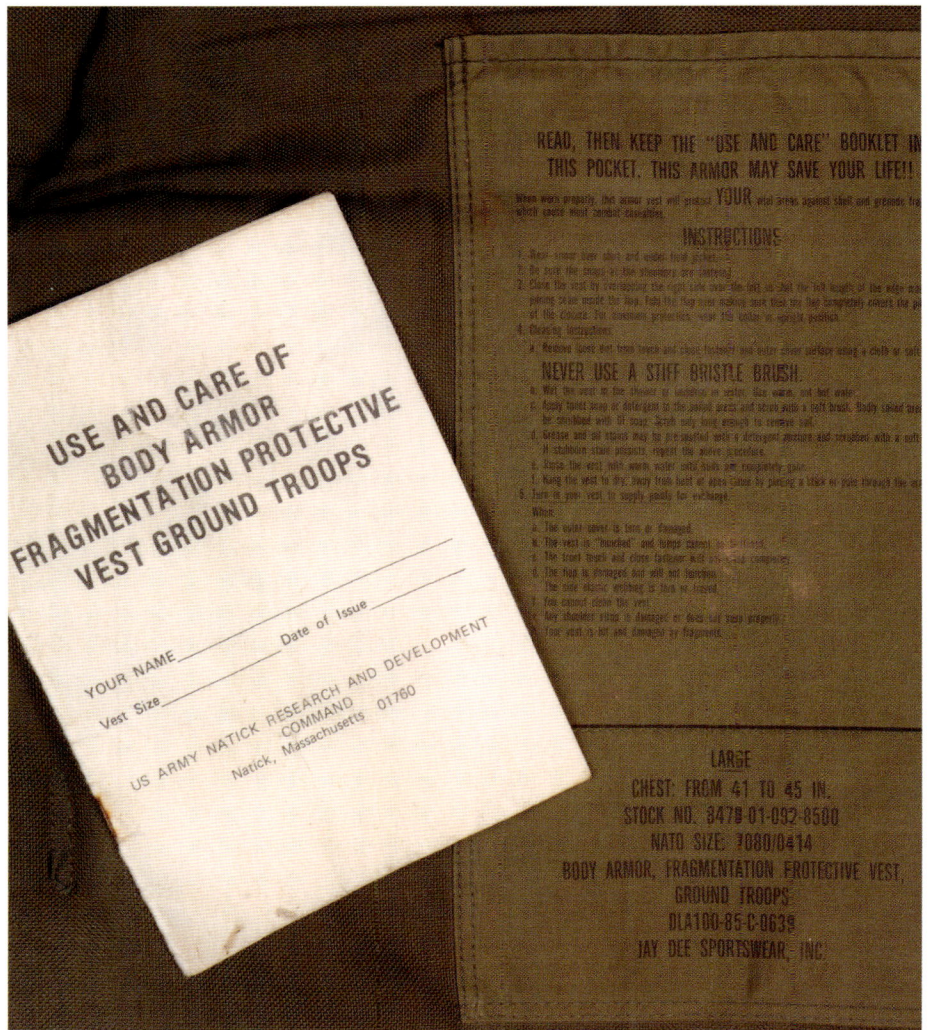

United States of America

ABOVE: Body Armor, Fragmentation Protective Vest, Ground Troops, fitted with the six-colour Desert Battle Dress Uniform (DBDU) camouflage Cover, PASGT Vest, Camouflage Pattern, Desert. The camouflage cover fitted the PASGT vest somewhat poorly.

ABOVE RIGHT: Cover, PASGT Vest, Camouflage Pattern, Desert fitted over a standard PASGT vest. Despite the change to tri-colour DCU (desert combat uniform) camouflage, the designation of this item has remained the same.

Wearing the DBDU uniform, PASGT helmet and woodland PASGT vest with desert cover, all in six-colour DBDU camouflage, a member of the 101st Airborne Division cleans his M16A2 rifle during Operation *Desert Storm* in 1990.

United States of America

American Body Armor & Equipment Incorporated 'K-55' body armour used by a US soldier during Operation *Desert Storm*. The use of commercial armour was prevalent during the opening stages of the Gulf War, but US authorities soon forbade the use of any armour other than that issued by the government.

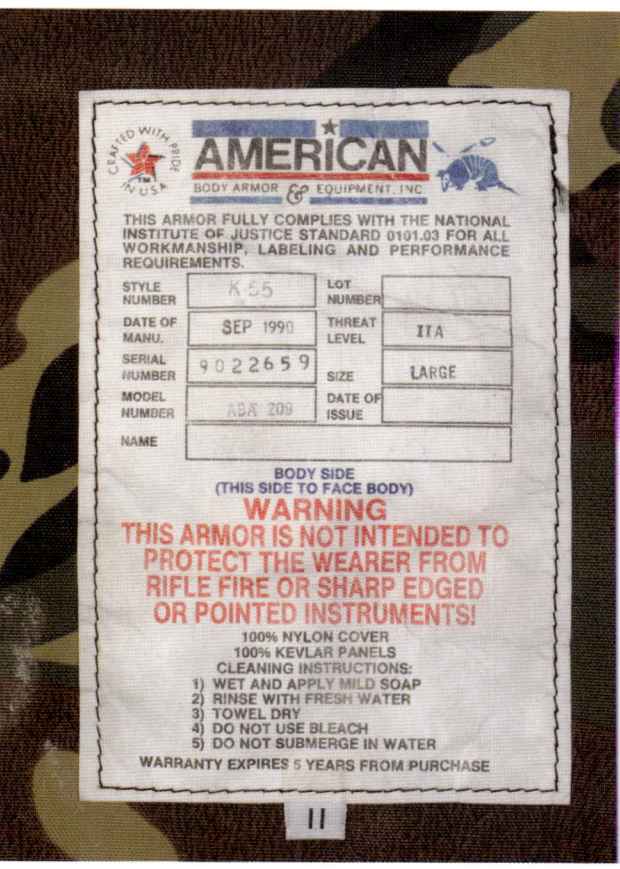

Manufacturer's and ballistic properties label in K-55 commercial vest. The label indicates that the vest complies with NIJ standard 0101.03 and provides details of cleaning, but not its ballistic properties. It does, however, advise that it does not protect against rifle fire or sharp-edged or pointed weapons and that it has a five-year warranty.

US Marines Colonel Ward, left, and Sergeant Johnson, inspect an area just to the north of Mogadishu Airport during Operation *Restore Hope* in 1993. Both men wear commercial tan camouflage flak vests and the UN beret.

United States of America

The Body Armor, Fragmentation Protective, Undergarment, Combat Vehicle Crewman's was a simple vest-type garment meant to be worn under CVC coveralls. It was an over-the-head design secured at each waist with two elasticated straps with Velcro fastening. The vest is usually referred to as CVC armour.

Body Armor, Fragmentation Protective, Undergarment, Combat Vehicle Crewman's

The close confines of armoured fighting vehicles require crewmen to be free of unnecessary encumbrances. Standard armours such as the PASGT were bulky for infantrymen, but close to unmanageable within a tank. The 'Body Armor, Fragmentation Protective, Undergarment, Combat Vehicle Crewman's' was a simple vest-type garment providing protection to the vital areas of the thorax. The vest was to be worn beneath the tanker's coverall over an undershirt. Although an armoured fighting vehicle (AFV) usually offers excellent armour protection, the problems of spallation can be quite severe. The Combat Vehicle Crewman's (CVC) body armour served to help protect the crewman from internal armour spallation following impact to the vehicle hull.

Ranger Body Armor

Designed by Natick, the 'Ranger Body Armor' (RBA) was intended to meet the operational requirements of the 75th Ranger Regiment. The design was based upon a simple vest with Kevlar ballistic filler providing protection equal to that of the PASGT vest, but with front and rear pockets for the insertion of a 10 × 12in (25 × 30cm) ceramic SAPI plate that provided protection up to 7.62mm AP for the upper torso and dorsal regions (covering the vital organs). The outer cover was of woodland camouflage fabric and was closed using a broad cummerbund with Velcro closure. The basic vest weighed approximately 8lb (3.63kg), increasing to 25lb (11.34kg) with the two SAPI plates inserted. The vests were on a limited issue, the cost of a complete vest and plates, $738 for a medium size vest, restricting widespread use. The RBA vest was procured from the Protective Materials Company in a number of variants. It was used during the mid-1990s and saw operational use on a number of missions, including Operation Uphold Democracy in Haiti and operations in the former Yugoslavia. US Army Europe (USAREUR) also requested and received 350 sets of the Ranger Body Armor. Most notably, RBA was used in Somalia.

First-pattern Ranger Body Armor, a limited procurement item issued to members of the 75th Ranger Regiment. Unlike the PASGT armour, the RBA had front and rear pockets for additional SAPI plates that provided full ballistic protection up to and including 7.62mm AP. This was a great improvement over the basic level of protection offered by the PASGT, but the area of body cover was noticeably reduced at the shoulders, neck and axillary region. The upper right corner of the front SAPI plate has a cut-away angle that allows the rifle to be held into the shoulder when aiming. (Rob Jose)

United States of America

A US officer questions a man believed to be the president of the terrorist group Revolutionary Front for Haitian Advancement and Progress (FRAPH), during Operation *Uphold Democracy* in Haiti during 1995. This officer is probably from the 75th Ranger Regiment, which was issued the Ranger Body Armour as worn here.

The fourth pattern of the Ranger Body Armor has a utility pocket added over the SAPI pocket and snap-closure shoulder straps that helped retain load-bearing equipment straps over the shoulder.

United States of America

Interceptor Body Armour/Outer Tactical Vest and Improved Outer Tactical Vest

The interceptor came into being in the late 1990s as a joint US Army/USMC development for replacement of the PASGT vest. It consisted of a cover, the 'Outer Tactical Vest' (OTV), filler (Kevlar KM2) and boron carbide ceramic SAPI plates. The OTV was a new concept. It provided not only a cover for the filler, but the pouch attachment ladder system (PALS) loops fitted to the front and rear faces allowed fixing of a multitude of ammunition and equipment pouches. The basic system included optional removable throat, neck and groin protection. This was soon enhanced by the introduction of 'Deltoid and Axillary Protection Systems' (DAPS), consisting of two ambidextrous components, a deltoid, or arm, protector and an axillary protector. In 2007 an 'Enhanced Side Ballistic Insert' (ESBI) plate was introduced as standard. The interchangeable components of the OTV allowed the soldier to dress according to the threat level and operational requirements. The ensemble was referred to as the 'Interceptor Body Armour' (IBA) or OTV interchangeably.

In early 2003 there was a shortfall of body armour; insufficient stocks were held to provide an issue to all soldiers in operational theatres, with the greatest shortage being in Iraq. On 17 April the Army Planning Board agreed that there was a requirement for 278,000 OTVs and 175,000 SAPI plates (suggesting that 103,000 OTVs would be for replacement stock or issued without plates to rear echelon troops). The repercussions of this discrepancy were soon causing problems in Central Command (CENTCOM), which was well behind the forward operational areas. Within weeks of the Army Planning Board's decision, an increase in suicide bomber and sniper activity in the rear areas brought about a reverse of the original policy and orders were issued for all troops in CENTCOM to be issued full body armour with SAPI plates. By April 2004, sufficient armour was available for all troops in Iraq and Afghanistan to be equipped with IBA.

ABOVE RIGHT: The basic Interceptor body armour Outer Tactical Vest in woodland camouflage.

RIGHT: Training prior to deployment to Iraq, a soldier from the 173rd Airborne Battalion Combat Team brings up 50-calibre ammunition. He wears standard Universal Camouflage Pattern (UCP) camouflage ACU uniform, with a PASGT helmet and Interceptor OTV vest, both in woodland camouflage. (US DoD)

United States of America

DCU tricolour camouflage version of the basic Interceptor OTV. This was the standard vest worn in Iraq and Afghanistan until the UCP camouflage version replaced it. Many DCU camouflage OTV vests have been re-issued to Iraqi units.

DCU tricolour DAPS axillary protector shown fitted inside the vest. This increases protection in the vulnerable underarm axillary region. Also shown are the two side adjustment straps and buckles.

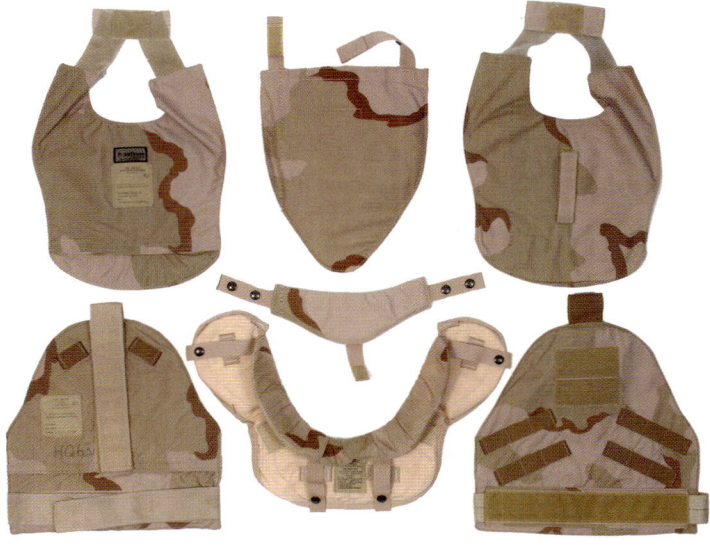

DCU tricolour ensemble showing the complete interceptor armour system, with all ancillary modules fitted to the basic OTV. The full set includes DAPS, yoke and collar, throat protector, and groin protector.

The Interceptor system had a number of ancillary items that could be fitted to the basic OTV to increase the protection offered by the ensemble. Shown here in DCU tricolour camouflage are, from top left, DAPS axillary protector inner face; groin protector; and DAPS axillary protector outer face. Below are the DAPS deltoid (arm) protector inner face; throat protector; yoke and collar; and DAPS deltoid protector outer face. The label designations on many Interceptor items can be confusing. Among the labelling variations and errors are the spelling of 'axillary', also found as 'axilliary', while DAPS can be found incorrectly printed as 'Dorsal Axillary Protection Systems' rather than 'Deltoid Axillary Protection Systems'. The yoke label in this image states 'THIS SIDE TO BODY', but, as is frequently the case, it is fitted to the side of the yoke that faces away from the body.

United States of America

Training for deployment to Iraq, troops of the 173rd Airborne Battalion Combat Team fire the 81mm mortar. The men wear the UCP camouflage ACU uniform, with DCU camouflage interceptor OTV armour, ACH helmet and Fighting Load Carrier (FLC) vest.

The shortfall of armour led to many troops purchasing their own armour from commercial sources. The use of private armour was soon curtailed, but the Department of Defense (DoD), under pressure from congress, grudgingly authorized a payment of $1,000 in 2005 to troops who had been forced to purchase their own equipment due to shortages of issue items.

The Interceptor OTV vest, in UCP camouflage. This vest differed in detail from the earlier M81 woodland and DCU camouflage vests in that the number of PALS equipment loops was increased and Velcro sections were incorporated for the fitting of rank and name insignia.

UCP camouflage OTV vest fitted with DAPS and the throat protector section. The throat protector fitted either side of the collar and a small Velcro tab secured the front to the rank patch.

The UCP version of the OTV vest, worn with the basic FLC vest. The FLC had a similar arrangement of PALS loops as the OTV, allowing equipment (magazine and grenade pouches, etc) to be carried independently of the vest; it could be removed easily while allowing the body armour to be kept on. The carrier has a large IR-absorbing 'US' stencilled on the right shoulder.

In May 2005 the standard SAPI plates were replaced with 'Enhanced Small Arms Protective Insert' (ESAPI) plates costing some $600 each, compared to $350 for the older SAPI. In June 2007 the US Army requested even greater protection and a replacement for the ESAPI. This was to come in the form of XSAPI plates, with production contracts for 120,000 being placed with Ceradyne in late 2008, for delivery in 2009.

ABOVE: OTV UCP camouflage DAPS deltoid protector, also called the arm protector. This is the right arm section fitted with a highly IR-absorbent/reflective US national flag. The DAPS were also fitted with PALS loops although it would seem that they are rarely used for the carriage of equipment.

LEFT: The UCP camouflage Interceptor system including the OTV, DAPS, yoke and collar, throat protector and groin protector.

The UCP Interceptor system in use by a soldier of the 2nd Infantry Division, on patrol in Zafaraniyah, Baghdad. The DAPS arm section, yoke, throat protector and ESBI are fitted to the OTV. The axillary section of the DAPS is not fitted, since the ESBI panel provides a similar area of coverage, but with improved protection. The Iraqi interpreter at right wears the woodland camouflage OTV. (US DoD)

By 2007, production had fully met demand and contingency requirements. The US Army operational requirement was for 154,000 OTV, ESAPI, ESBI and DAPS, against an inventory of 991,580 vests, 402,369 ESAPI, 244,192 ESBI and 243,229 DAPS available worldwide. USMC theatre requirements were for 23,000 OTV, ESAP and ESBI, and 4,600 DAPS. Available inventory stock worldwide was 198,000 OTV, 56,970 ESAPI and 50,000 ESBI. The available inventory of DAPS was 4,600, matching the theatre requirement with no allowance for spares. The 2007 Defense Appropriations Act appropriated funds for the procurement of body armour, $700 million for the Army and $25 million for the USMC. At this time a complete IBA system cost $1,585.

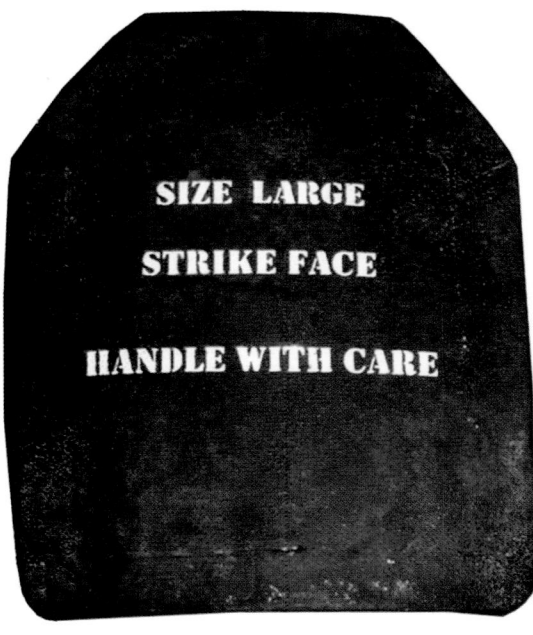 

The two Small Arms Protective Insert plates issued with the Interceptor body armour. The plates increase the level of protection over vital areas, inhibiting 7.62mm NATO ball (M80) rounds. One plate is worn in the rear and one plate in the front of the OTV. SAPI plates were progressively replaced by the improved Enhanced Small Arms Protective Insert from May 2005. (Private collection)

The Carrier, Enhanced Side Ballistic Insert. Two such carriers with side ESBI plates and trauma panels (Filler Packs) were issued retrospectively as an enhancement to the basic OTV system from 2007. The ESBI improved axillary protection, but greatly increased the weight burden.

United States of America

The OTV was designed for wear by both male and female troops. It was provided in eight sizes ranging through extra (x) small, small, medium, large, x-large, xx-large, xxx-large to xxxx-large. The corresponding SAPI plates were provided in five sizes, extra small (7¼ × 11 ½in/18.4 × 29.2cm) to extra large (11 × 14in/27.9 × 35.6cm). Typical weights of the SAPI were 2lb 13oz (1.27kg) for the extra small to 5lb 5oz (2.40kg) for the extra large. ESAPI had the same dimensions as SAPI, but were thicker and weighed slightly more at 3lb 12oz (1.70kg) for the extra small and 7lb 3oz (3.26kg) for the extra large. The 6 × 8in (15 × 20cm) ESBI was a one-size only item that weighed 2lb 5oz (1.05kg). The boron carbide SAPI had a Spectra/Dyneema fabric backing and were capable of stopping three hits from 7.62mm NATO ball ammunition having a muzzle velocity of 2,750fps (838m/s). The ESAPI provided increased protection from 7.62mm M2 armour piercing ammunition.

The Army accepted that the Interceptor OTV had a number of shortcomings and introduced a highly modified version, the Improved Outer Tactical Vest (IOTV) in 2007. The new IOTV was a side-opening vest with a cummerbund waist fastening, like that used with the USMC's MTV and various commercial designs. This image shows the complete ensemble with full ancillary protection and pouches fitted. (PEO Soldier)

Here a soldier of the 4th Infantry Division, serving in Baghdad, dons the IOTV vest, showing the side panel that pulls across and fastens to a Velcro patch at the front of the vest, which is then covered by a drop-down panel with PALS loops. (US DoD)

Photographed in Afghanistan during June 2010, this soldier wears the lower back protector at the rear edge of his IOTV.

United States of America

Complaints from troops in the field have led to the continued development of body armour. The standard OTV was upgraded as the 'Improved Outer Tactical Vest' fielded in early 2007. Similar to the OTV, it weighed less (3lb/1.36kg lighter in the medium size) but provided increased coverage. Unlike the OTV it did not have a front fastening, but was donned over the head or via the side fastening. Importantly, the IOTV had a quick release system that allowed the ensemble to be jettisoned in an emergency, allowing rapid access to wounds or the ability to discard armour in a helicopter ditching. The IOTV was available in 11 sizes and consisted of the following components: Ballistic collar, quick release assembly cord, front carrier, rear carrier, left and right ESBI carriers, groin protector, lower back protector and an elasticated cummerbund assembly. The cummerbund helped distribute the ensemble's weight from the shoulders to the waist. The lower back protector provided enhanced protection to the kidney and lower spinal area, the IOTV increasing overall protection by some 0.36sq ft (0.03m2). The IOTV was a joint venture and was produced by BAE Systems and Point Blank Body Armour.

Iraq, December 2009. Chief of Staff of the Army, General George W. Casey Jr and Commander 3rd Infantry Division, Major General Tony Cucolo, show the UCP camouflage plate carrier worn by Casey (left) and the IOTV armour used by Cucolo (right). A variety of plate carriers were tested by the US Army during 2009, resulting in a decision to field some 57,000 sets (manufactured by KDH Defense Systems Inc.) during the early part of 2010. (US DoD)

USMC coyote-brown Interceptor OTV, identical in design to the woodland and DCU camouflage vests. This vest has a metal USMC Lance Corporal rank insignia affixed, a typical Marine Corps practice.

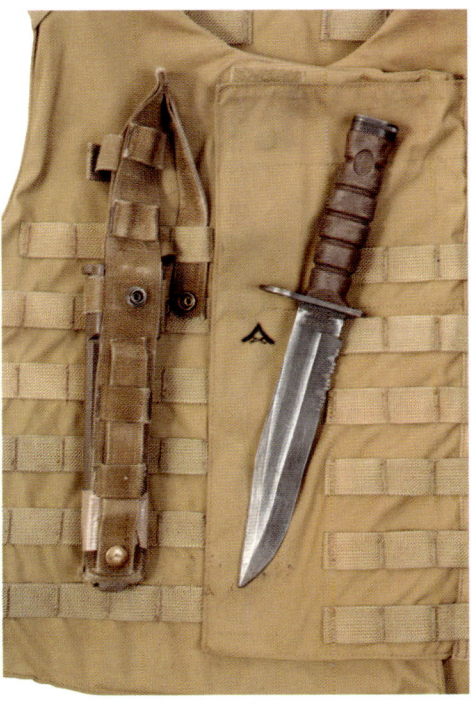

The USMC OKC3S bayonet, showing how the PALS strap and loop arrangement allows equipment to be fitted to the OTV. The strap has to pass alternately between the loops on the vest and the loops on the equipment item for it to be fitted correctly. Missing out any loops places excess pressure on those used and is the most common reason for failure of the PALS system, leading to the loops becoming detached.

United States of America

A US Marine patrol in Iraq brings in a weapons find. The Marines all wear the USMC coyote-brown Interceptor OTV with added yoke, throat and groin protectors. The vest is used with a mix of coyote and woodland camouflage pouches.

During the early stages of Operation *Iraqi Freedom*, US Marines at An Numaniyah, wear coyote-brown OTV with an interesting personal design on the rear of the cover. The artwork mirrors the USMC's use of unit stencils on clothing during World War II.

United States of America

USMC Modular Tactical Vest and Scalable Plate Carrier

The USMC was not satisfied with the OTV and set about providing Marines with a superior armour. The 'Modular Tactical Vest' (MTV) was similar in concept to the OTV and used the same SAPI, but with improved fragmentation cover to the axillary and lower back and kidney areas. Improved ballistic coverage led to an increase in weight of some 3lb. The use of deltoid protectors was confined to use in specialist roles such as turret gunner. Protective Products International was contracted to produce 84,000 sets of MTV, with issue beginning in February 2007. The US Navy requested 28,364 sets for use by naval forces in August 2008. The cost of each vest at this time was circa $1,050.

US Marines wearing woodland MARPAT MCCUU fatigues test fit newly issued coyote-brown MTVs. The vests gave considerably enhanced protection to the axillary and lower back areas when compared to the OTV, as shown by these uncluttered examples. The rifle butt stop is fitted to the outer shoulder section of the MTV, for two right-handed firers (the two left hand Marines) and for a left-handed firer (main figure at right). (US DoD)

The OTV had been unpopular with Marines and was soon replaced in USMC service by the Modular Tactical Vest, reinforcing the USMC's traditional instinct to resist using any kit issued to the Army. This image shows a layout of all of the components of the MTV, including yoke, throat protector, front and rear panels, user guide, cummerbund, groin protector, side plate carriers, the Small Arms Protective Insert and Side Ballistic Inserts, rifle butt stop and various accessories. The increased ballistic protection and coverage was deemed necessary following troop user reports from frontline units. (Corporal Robert P. Lemiszki Jr, USMC)

United States of America

While the MTV may have provided increased area of protection compared to the OTV, this was ultimately its downfall. The improved ballistic protection and coverage increased its weight and the discomfort to the wearer. Field reports from users showed that it was felt that less protection was actually needed to increase mobility and combat effectiveness. This requirement saw the introduction of the lighter USMC Scaleable Plate Carrier.

The increased weight of the MTV soon became a problem among Marines in the field, resulting in many complaints. Requests were made for lighter armour. But a loss in weight could only come with a loss in protection. Nevertheless, the rocky and steep terrain often encountered on patrols in Afghanistan rapidly drained the efficiency of Marines using heavy MTV; the solution was to reduce protection and provide a plate carrier. The USMC 'Scalable Plate Carrier' (SPC) was first fielded in late 2007 following contracts placed with Eagle Industries to produce 9,483 sets at a unit cost of $410 (excluding SAPI). The SPC was to be used as an alternative to the MTV where operational demands required a lighter load and the MTV was to be retained when maximum individual protection was paramount. While the SPC offered the same SAPI plate protection as the MTV, the soft armour (fragmentation) protection was reduced to provide ease of movement and a reduction in weight.

A USMC sergeant wears the recently fielded SPC during operations in Afghanistan, in October 2009. His body-forward position shows the degree of exposure that this type of armour allows; the neck shoulders and axillary region are considerably more exposed than with the standard MTV, however, ease of movement and weapons use is much improved. (US Marine Corps)

United States of America

USMC Staff Sergeant McMainus wears the Shirt, Combat, Desert MARPAT Camouflage, FR with the MTV armour. The rifle butt stop pad has been fitted through the shoulder PALS loops, rather than to the outer edge of the vest. Basra, Iraq, 2008. (US DoD)

Rear of the USMC Modular Tactical Vest, showing the lower back protector fitted at the rear edge of the vest. The ballistic panel improves protective coverage of the kidney area. (US Marine Corps)

A heavily loaded US Marine shoulders his kit prior to embarking on an amphibious assault ship. The SPC vest's lack of coverage to the shoulder and axillary region is clearly evident in this arms-raised view. It is interesting to see the mix of woodland and desert MARPAT camouflage and the coyote brown of the SPC. (US Marine Corps)

United States of America

Soldier Plate Carrier System
US special forces had been using plate carriers since 2002, but it was not until December 2008 that the demand for such an item came from regular US forces, when 1,500 were requested by the 1st Infantry division. The Eagle Industries Modular Body Armor Vest (MBAV) vest (already in use with special forces) was procured to fulfil this request. Program Executive Office (PEO) Soldier then took up responsibility for developing a plate carrier as a standard issue item. The result was the 'Soldier Plate Carrier System' (SPCS). While providing ballistic protection equal to the IOTV, the SPCS offers greater ease of movement and less weight, balanced against a reduction in fragmentation protection. The SPCS has a cable release system and is close fitting, has padded shoulder sections and a casualty drag strap providing functionality and comfort. The basic medium size vest weighs 5lb 14oz (2.66kg) increasing to 21lb 14oz (9.92kg) with SAPI fitted. The SPCS is issued in five sizes from x-small to x-large and provides protective coverage of 2.90sq ft (0.27m2).

A contract for 57,000 plate carriers was awarded to KDH Defense Systems at a cost of $18,600,000 with first issues taking pace in late 2009. The SPCS is produced in Universal Camouflage Pattern (UCP) camouflage and, from August 2010, MultiCam (a multi-terrain camouflage pattern), with initial issues going to the 10th Mountain and 101st Airborne Divisions.

The Soldiers Plate Carrier System in UCP camouflage was deployed to Afghanistan to provide a lighter alternative to the IOTV, where troops were working in physically demanding environments such as mountainous areas. The SPCS provides ballistic protection equal to or greater than that of the IOTV, but with considerably less coverage, while reducing the soldier's load, enhancing comfort, and optimizing mobility. (PEO Soldier)

Afghanistan 2009 and Staff Sergeant James Price of the 4th Infantry Division wears a trials pattern UCP camouflage plate carrier vest, one of a number of variants deployed to Afghanistan for trials. (US DoD)

The SPCS in Crye's 'Multicam' camouflage, which was issued to units in Afghanistan in 2010 to replace the UCP camouflage that – not surprisingly – had been deemed unsuited to operations in-theatre. Multicam has been referred to as 'Operation *Enduring Freedom* Camouflage Pattern (OCP)' in some US Army publications. (PEO Soldier)

The SPCS in use by a member of the 4th Infantry Division during PEO equipment trials. As well as the SPCS, this soldier has Multicam uniform and equipment, and is armed with a US M4 Carbine. (PEO Soldier)

United States of America

BAE Systems Ultra Lightweight Warrior

In June 2010 BAE Systems unveiled its 'Ultra Lightweight Warrior' soldier system at Farnborough. As a component of the integrated 'Ultra Lightweight Warrior (ULW) Body Armour' system, it provides a weight saving of as much as 35 per cent against comparable equipment. The quick-release armour system is scaleable and can be adapted to specific mission requirements. The armour incorporated BAE's 'Integrated Power System' (IPS). The system uses a multi-cell unit shaped like a SAPI plate and worn within the armour vest, seated over the SAPI. The cell unit weighs 12lb (5.44kg) and has the same power output as 300 AA batteries weighing some 4lb (1.81kg) more. With the ever-increasing reliance on electrically powered equipment, AA batteries add considerable weight to many soldiers' loads. The IPS can be configured to fit any vest configuration and is easily recharged via a vehicle outlet or mains electricity. The cells of the IPS are configured so that any damage to individual cells does not compromise the unit as a whole, the IPS being capable of continuing to provide power even after fragmentation impact or a bullet strike. The ULW soldier system was due to undergo field trials beginning in the summer of 2010.

The basic Ultra Lightweight Warrior armour, minus equipment pouches, with groin and neck protection and the system's light combat pack designed for use with the armour. The ULW system offers a 35 per cent saving of weight compared to similar equipment.

BAE Systems' Ultra Lightweight Warrior system, showing the ULW Advanced Combat Helmet and the ULW body armour with neck and groin protection. The power hub and connector for the Integrated Power System is fitted to the upper left side of the armour – as worn – with the power source located over the front SAPI plate beneath the cover.

The Ultra Lightweight Warrior armour configured as the ULW Plate Carrier. The armour has a quick release that allows rapid jettisoning and easier re-assembly. The ULW system has concentrated on weight reduction in five major areas, lightening the helmet, body armour, SAPI, load-bearing equipment (LBE) and the soldier's power supply.

United States of America

Specialist Armour
QuadGuard

'QuadGuard' was a full-body defensive armour designed for mounted troops, to provide a scale of protection not offered by standard body armour. The system was developed rapidly and from concept to delivery just 17 months elapsed. QuadGuard cost $1,520 per set and was designed to provide an enhancement to OTV and increased armour weight by 9lb 8oz (4.31kg). It was designed for use by vehicle crews, soldiers on sentry or checkpoint duty, security and support operations, roadside patrols, explosive ordnance reconnaissance, forward-deployed medical personnel, military operations in urban terrain, combat engineers, and aircraft crews and passengers. QuadGuard saw limited use with troops in Iraq, some 5,000 sets being issued to the USMC. Although QuadGuard gained little favour, the concept was acknowledged as providing much needed additional protection, but balanced against issues of mobility and heat. The next stage in development was the 'Body Armor, Cupola Protective Ensemble'.

QuadGuard was a full-body defensive armour introduced in 2006. Worn with the standard OTV, it was made of Dyneema and weighed some 10lb (4.54kg). It was designed to provide enhanced protection to the extremities. The blast from IEDs often left OTV users alive, but with severe trauma injuries to the arms and legs, frequently resulting in amputation. The QuadGuard was designed to reduce the number of such injuries among vehicle-mounted troops. This image shows the armour undergoing trials at Aberdeen Test Center during 2005. (US DoD)

January 2007. A Marine from Regimental Combat Team 6 dons his QuadGuard prior to a mounted patrol in Fallujah, Iraq. It is worn over a fire resistant coverall with FROG gloves and balaclava. (US DoD)

United States of America

Body Armor, Cupola Protective Ensemble
Improved Body Armor, Cupola Protective Ensemble

Operations in Iraq and Afghanistan brought with them an ever-increasing threat from roadside improvized explosive devices (IEDs). Soldiers manning crew-served weapons (the 50-cal HMG (heavy machine-gun) for example) in vehicle cupola mountings were especially vulnerable to the effect of blast and fragmentation from RPG and IED explosions. Since these were static positions, the feasibility of using improved personal armour protection was explored and as a result it was decided to issue a modified form of the armour used by IED teams. The 'Body Armor, Cupola Protective Ensemble' (CPE) consists of a blast and fragmentation protective helmet visor, trousers, jacket, front and rear blast plates, a removable explosive ordnance disposal (EOD) collar and optional neck/nape guard. The insulating effect of this heavy and bulky armour means that it requires an integral cooling system to make it wearable in hot climates. The cooling system connects to a vehicle supply and helps maintain comfortable body temperatures. The CPE is worn with the standard IOTV armour and provides additional protection to the head, neck, face and extremities. Following operational use, the CPE has been modified as a result of user feedback and an improved version is now issued as the 'Improved Body Armor, Cupola Protective Ensemble' (ICPE).

RIGHT: Body Armor, Cupola Protective Ensemble was used to provide extensive protection to soldiers manning weapons mounted in vehicle cupolas. It provided defence against RPGs and IEDs, as well as the associated flash. It had an integral cooling system that regulated the body temperature of the upper torso, but was too cumbersome to be used by dismounted troops. (PEO Soldier)

FAR RIGHT: Based on the IOTV, the Improved Body Armor, Cupola Protective Ensemble is a modular and scalable Extremity Protection System (EPS) designed for mounted and dismounted operations, such as cupola gunning and room clearing. The armour provides enhanced protection to the extremities against small arms, as well as fragmentation protection from IEDs and RPGs. The ICPE is flame resistant and available in four sizes. It is considerably less cumbersome than the CPE. (PEO Soldier)

BELOW RIGHT: Body Armour, Cupola Protective Ensemble in use by a gunner manning a cupola-mounted .50in HMG. The area of protective cover is similar to that provided by equipment issued to EOD technicians. The CPE consisted of a base jacket, sleeves with rigid composite inserts, blast plate assembly (chest and groin), rear blast plate, trousers and integrated groin protector, hand guards, collar, optional neck/nape guard and a visor system worn with the Advanced Combat Helmet. (PEO Soldier)

United States of America

Air warrior

'Air Warrior' is an integrated system of equipment for aircrew, incorporating ballistic, survival, and chemical, biological, radiological and nuclear (CBRN) protection. It includes fire resistant clothing, a survival equipment carrier (containing first aid, survival, signalling and communications kit), and body armour with SAPI plate. An important part of the system is the microclimate cooling system (a vest-like undergarment with cooling unit) that increases mission endurance by as much as 350 per cent in hot climates or when wearing CBRN clothing. The associated aircrew 'Modular Integrated Helmet' (MIH), incorporates ballistic protection, communications, laser eye protection, night-vision goggle (NVG) and, for the first time, full maxillofacial protection provided by a facial shield. By 2009, 12,000 complete systems had been provided to aircrew in theatre in Iraq (Operation *Iraqi Freedom*) and Afghanistan (Operation *Enduring Freedom*).

The first pattern Air Warrior armour in woodland camouflage. The pull strap, or 'donkey tail' at the front of the vest released the heavy SAPI plate in an emergency, such as when the aircraft was ditching. (Kevin Sullivan)

Third pattern Air Warrior armour with UCP camouflage pattern cover. (Kevin Sullivan)

A US aircrewman dressed in the complete Air Warrior ensemble, including armoured vest and Modular Integrated Helmet, and survival equipment vest. His survival equipment includes the M9, 9mm pistol; PRC 90/PRC 112/CSEL radios and aircrew survival knife. (PEO Soldier)

A Black Hawk helicopter crew from the 12th Aviation Battalion, Military District of Washington, brief before a flight. All crewmen wear the UCP flight uniform and Air Warrior armoured vest. (US DoD)

'Cobra Plus' armour issued to Kevin Sullivan, who served with 'A' Company, 5th Battalion, 158th Aviation Regiment, 12th Aviation Brigade, Geibelstadt, Germany. The armour was provided prior to the unit's deployment to Iraq. (Kevin Sullivan)

Kevin Sullivan, at left, and members of the 158th Aviation Regiment wearing a mix of 'Cobra' and PASGT armour prior to deploying to Iraq under Operation *Iraqi Freedom*. (Kevin Sullivan)

A Black Hawk of the 158th Aviation Regiment photographed during the early stages of Operation *Iraqi Freedom*. The pilot's Cobra armour is hanging on the aircraft's step ready for immediate use. (Kevin Sullivan)

United States of America

Concealable Body Armour

Although body armour is standard in combat areas, it is also required by specialist operators in the continental United States (CONUS) and other garrisons and US military bases worldwide. 'Concealable Body Armour' (CBA) provides optimum mobility, protection and comfort in a lightweight, close-fitting garment worn beneath outer clothing. It is typical of the type of concealable armour worn by military police, criminal investigators and similar personnel, who routinely face threats in the pursuance of their daily duties. The CBA offers stab and ballistic protection to 9mm, 124-grain full metal jacket (FMJ) rounds. It is provided in seven sizes, X-small, small-medium, medium, large, X-large, XX-large and XXX-large. It provides 3.99sq ft (0.37m2) of coverage for a male soldier with a 40in chest and 3.64sq ft (0.34m2) for a female soldier with a 36in bust, with the medium size armour weighing around 6lb 8oz (2.95kg). The US Army stated a requirement for 10,000 CBA, with the first 2,000 being fielded in 2010.

The Concealable Body Armour, issued to specialist operators such as military police (MP), US Department of Defense investigators, and correctional and confinement operators. The lightweight garment is worn beneath uniform or plain clothes and weighs 6lb 10oz (2.99kg) for the medium size armour. (PEO Soldier)

Army Combat Shirt and Shirt, Combat, Desert MARPAT Camouflage, FR

Unveiled in April 2007, the 'Army Combat Shirt' (ACS) was designed to be worn under the IOTV armour in hot environments, replacing both the 'Army Combat Uniform' (ACU) jacket and the moisture wicking T-shirt with a single garment. It is a flame resistant garment with a wicking body fabric that draws moisture away from the skin and dries rapidly, greatly increasing comfort. The ACS has abrasion resistant elbow and forearm sections. The garment has no seams, minimising discomfort when worn under body armour. The upper arms have large pockets with a Velcro face for attachment of insignia, and a concealable infra-red reflective tab. The right sleeve bears a name tape, rank and infra-red national flag, while the left sleeve is used to display a unit patch. Early versions of the ACS had the Army Strong logo printed on the chest; the use of this device has now been discontinued. The USMC forerunner of the ACS was the 'Shirt, Combat, Desert MARPAT Camouflage, FR'. This was the first US-issue shirt designed specifically to be worn with body armour.

Designed as a wicking, seam-free garment specifically to be worn beneath body armour, the Army Combat Shirt was introduced in 2007.

United States of America

Sgt 1st Class Sumalee Bustamante, serving with the 10th Mountain Division, at Forward Operating Base Warrior, Iraq, wears the ACS with 'Army Strong' logo. The abrasion resistant forearm and elbow sections are clearly shown.

The Shirt, Combat, Desert MARPAT Camouflage, FR was the USMC version of under armour shirt and the inspiration for the Army's ACS. It was designed to replace the MCCUU blouse for wear with body armour in hot climates.

United States of America

Hawaii, 2004 and German Shepard military working dog Arpi is dressed in body armour by his handler. Ballistic armour for military dogs has become standard where they are working in a hazardous environment, such as during explosive detection, or on foot patrols. Canine stab vest protection is also in use with many police forces. (US Navy)

A sergeant from the 25th MP Company, based at Bagram air base, works her dog during a training session. The German Shepard has DCU camouflage ballistic protection, while the handler wears a woodland camouflage Interceptor vest. (US DoD)

A khaki camouflage commercial plate carrier produced by Eagle Industries, fully loaded with magazine and ancillary pouches. This vest was typical of the type of body armour in use with many special forces operatives and security advisers in Iraq and Afghanistan. The elasticated section at the neck is a rifle sling. (Private collection)

United States of America

US Air Force special agents working in Iraq, here at Kirkuk in 2007, wear Eagle Industries MARCIRAS (MARitime Combat Integrated Releasable Armor System) plate carriers fitted with a quick release system (note the cables at each shoulder). These agents wear typical non conformist attire as used by many units operating in Iraq and Afghanistan. (US DoD)

The commercial 'PACA' body armour made by Protective Apparel Corporation of America Inc. was advertized as being the 'coolest body armour on earth'. It was used by military personnel and contractors in Iraq and Afghanistan.

The US Navy Flak Vest (NFV) has much in common with the standard PASGT vest, also used by the USN. It has no grenade loops or pockets, but has a broad elastic and Velcro adjustment at each waist, allowing 7in (18cm) of adjustment range on this, the extra-large size vest. The broad front closure allows for an additional 2in (5cm) of adjustment (a wide adjustment range was essential, since the NFV was only produced in medium and extra large). It was used, along with the US Navy Battle Helmet (NBH), by upper deck gun crews. This vest, marked 'U.S. Navy Flak Vest (MK1 Mod)' was made in 2000, to a 1998 contract. It weighs a little over 10lb (4.54kg).

A US Navy gunner mans twin .50in Browning machine-guns onboard USS Crommelin, during a 2004 maritime exercise. Both the US Navy Flak Vest and NBH are in use. (US Navy)

Pacific Ocean, February 2009. A gun crew prepare to load up 25mm rounds prior to a live-firing exercise onboard USS Preble. This image shows the PASGT vest and PASGT helmet (right) still in use with the US Navy at this time. The sailor at left wears the USMC LWH helmet. (US Navy)

US Navy gunner mans a .50 machine gun aboard the aircraft carrier USS Abraham Lincoln. The men wear woodland camouflage plate carriers with an NBH (left) and PASGT helmet (right). (US Navy)

A gunner from a USN harbour patrol vessel wears buoyant body armour as he watches Royal Malaysian Navy ship KLD Tunas Samudera enter Pearl Harbor in 2008. While providing less protection and coverage than most vests, the US Navy buoyant body armour it has a neutral buoyancy, most useful for any crewmen who may inadvertently end up in the water while wearing the armour. (US Navy)

A patrol boat from US Navy Coastal Warfare Squadron 21, operates out of Shuaybah Port, Kuwait, in 2008. The buoyant 'Tactical Maritime Body Armor System' (TMBAS) is worn by the gunner manning the patrol boat's .50in MG. The vest had a quick release mechanism for the SAPI plates and had an option for the integration of the MD3196vSO floatation device. Interestingly, this seaman wears the soft inner helmet (with communications equipment) normally used with the 'Combat Vehicle Crewman's Helmet Ballistic Shell'. (US Navy)

A Gunner's Mate of Riverine Squadron 1 fires a 7.62mm GAU-17A Minigun during live fire drills. He wears the USMC Modular Tactical Vest. (US Navy)

Chapter 2 Great Britain

World War I

A War Office document dated August 1916 discussed two principal types of armour that were of interest to the British military. The first was to give protection from shrapnel, bomb fragments, spent bullets and bayonet thrusts; the second was to protect against rifle fire and MG fire at close range. The armour consisted of three principal patterns: Metal shields, non-metallic armour, and compound metal and non-metallic shields. The metal armour included aluminium and steel, and the non-metallic armour was of vulcanized rubber, rubber, compressed paper, asbestos, woven fabrics, cotton wool and various fibres treated with resin. With the exception of woven silk fabric, none of the compounds proved to be better than steel, it being found that manganese steel with a fabric cover was the best product. The document also raised objections to the use of chain mail armour because of the problems of secondary debris being drawn into any penetrating wound. Similar objections were raised with regard to steel, although with a note that it was much less likely. Other fabrics often produced problems of damage by vermin and moisture degradation, both pertinent in trench warfare.

Manganese steel was found to offer ideal protection against shrapnel and nickel, or nickel steel, were good against close-range rifle and MG fire. Khaki Drill fabric-covered manganese steel shields with a 'woodite' layer to prevent spall, were sent to General Headquarters (GHQ) for assessment. Both 'Dayfield' and 'War Office' pattern shields were tested in France. It was found that the War Office pattern was preferred by the troops. The Dayfield was one of many commercial patterns of armour, costing 21 shillings for single (frontal protection) and 52s 6d for double protection (front and back). Sir Hiram Maxim endorsed the Dayfield in company advertisements.

As an excellent ballistic material, silk was used in a protective necklet (capable of stopping a 230-grain pistol ball at 600fps/183ms2) and silk and woven fabrics were also used in Royal Flying Corps (RFC) coats. Protective silk cushions were later developed for aviators.

The Franco-British Cuirass was one of the many less than adequate commercial products made available to the more wealthy British troops. The armour consisted of a canvas waistcoat with a frontal protection of small, interlinked metal plates – 'plate armour'. The method of joining the plates, using metal rings, allowed a slight margin of overlaying and a degree of flexibility. However, the quality and thickness of materials used ensured that this armour was less effective than the Chemico and at best it offered only one third of the level of protection of the issue Brodie helmet. This is the front face of a simple fabric waistcoat, designed to be worn beneath a tunic. (John Bodsworth)

The rear face of the simple waistcoat style Franco-British Cuirass with its waist tie tapes. This garment is a good example of the simplicity of many of the commercial designs. They were often miss-marketed, but usually promoted as affording good protection from shell splinters, spent bullets and bayonet thrusts. However, despite a slight overlap of plates, it is quite likely that a good bayonet thrust would soon have found the weak point where the plates are joined. (John Bodsworth)

Great Britain

A period advertisement for the Franco-British Cuirass, which at the time cost a small fortune at £3.15.0d. Relatively light, the weight of the garment is listed as between 6 and 7lb (2.72 and 3.18kg). Also shown in this advertisement is a steel head protector, designed to be worn under the SD (Service Dress) cap and based upon the French Secrete. (John Bodsworth)

A variant of the Franco-British Cuirass. The armour plates are the same as on the preceding example, but here they have been mounted on a heavy-duty canvas vest. Period images show this type of vest often being worn as an outer garment.

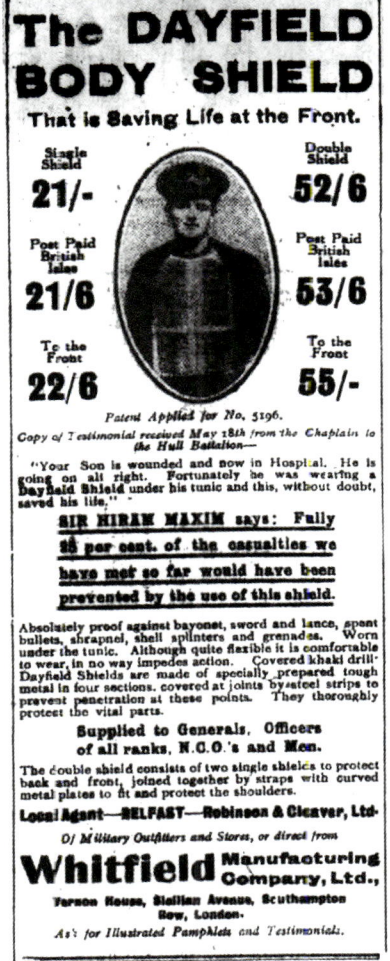

A period image of the basic 4lb (1.81kg) four-plate flexible armour version of the Dayfield Body Shield. A slightly improved pattern had an added abdominal shield. More than 20,000 sets of this type were in use on the Western Front by October 1917. (John Bodsworth)

Period advertisement for the Dayfield Body Shield, showing the purchase costs and the inclusive cost for shipping the armour to men at the front.

77

Great Britain

In January 1916, 1,000 body shields were ordered by the Ministry of Munitions, following a December 1915 request from the General Officer Commanding in Chief (GOCinC) British Armies in France. It is believed that the pattern was based upon a Japanese body armour that had been procured by the War Office and was found to be a good design to form the basis of a British-pattern of armour. Field trials in France resulted in an approval for the issue of body armour, to be in service by August 1916. Some 50,000 shields of the Japanese pattern were to be procured, being a modified version of those originally issued for trials. It was recommended that issue be at a level of 400 sets of armour per division.

One of the many commercial patterns of armour was that produced by the County Chemical Company of Birmingham. The so-called 'Chemico' body shield was advertized as protection against revolver bullets; spent rifle bullets; sword, bayonet, or lance thrusts; and shrapnel. The Chemico consisted of a waistcoat with either single frontal protection, or combined front and back protection. The vest was flexible and consisted of layers of kapok and folded phenolic resin-impregnated fabric strips, 2in (5cm) wide, apparently providing forty layers of fabric at any given point. In public demonstrations, the Chemico withstood penetration by a .45 revolver bullet at 700fps (213ms2) and in excess of a dozen full strength thrusts made with a 1907-pattern bayonet by a Private of the Dragoon Guards. But despite the advertising and public demonstrations, the Chemico was only a reasonably effective armour and at around £5.00 it was well beyond the finances of all but the richest.

The following is an interesting extract regarding the use of the Chemico body shield and its possible applications for airmen and aircraft. The text was taken from the 25 January 1917 edition of *Flight* magazine.

An Improved 'Chemico' Body Shield

It is, roughly speaking, about a year ago that the County Chemical Co., of Birmingham, brought out their 'Chemico' body shield for the protection of our troops fighting the cause of civilisation. We had occasion then to speak well of the tests through which it successfully came. Last week, the company invited inspection of an improved pattern of this valuable aid to protecting life, and again it showed enormous resisting powers against both revolver and bayonet. In the new shield the weight has been reduced, so that the full body, back and front, can now be protected at comparatively a small poundage. From evidence of users in the fighting line, the shield already has a long list of lives saved to its credit, and irrespective of its commercial possibilities it undoubtedly should have from a humane point of view a great and immediate future in the present state of world war. In regard to its application to our flying services, its value should be especially marked, as an extra pound or two is not of the same consequence on a machine as it is to an infantryman. As it appears to be only a matter of thickness for the 'shield' to resist even the highest velocity bullets, there would appear to be a chance for remarkable developments in the protection of not only the pilot and passengers of aircraft, but in the more vital parts of the machine itself. Sir Arthur Conan Doyle calculates that from 40 to 70 per cent, of the minor casualties of the war might be saved by its use. An enquiry addressed to the County Chemical Co., Bradford Street, Birmingham, upon the subject should lead to a good 'life investment' for those likely to be strafing the Hun from the air in the near future.

As well as flexible, or soft armour, plate armour was a popular, but heavier alternative. Shown here is the frontal metal shield of an early body shield made of four riveted plates, it was joined at the shoulders, by leather supporting straps, to a similar dorsal shield. Leather straps secured the shield at each waist.

World War I advertisement for the Wilkinson bulletproof jacket, often called the 'Wilkinson Jacket', since the Wilkinson Sword company produced the ballistic plate armour panels that provided protection over the chest. The text states that it will stop penetration by .455 service revolver ammunition. The jacket's actual weight depended on its size, but a figure of 9lb (4kg) is an average for such garments.

Great Britain

Parliamentary canvassing probably assisted the War Office in its efforts to develop body armour of proven ballistic capabilities, rather than accepting the claims of commercial vendors. One widely issued armour was that developed by the Munitions Development Board. The armour used three plates, dorsal, chest, and an extended abdominal/groin panel. Also worn in this illustration is the necklet. Composed of layers of silk, the necklet was heavy at 3lb (1.36kg) and somewhat expensive to produce. Although effective, it deteriorated rapidly in service. By 1917 the armour was being issued as trench stores at a figure of 400 sets per division.

The Chemico Body Shield was a popular commercially-available ballistic vest. It had a cotton cover with side button fastening and two side adjustment straps. A removable groin plate, fitted using three buttons, was secured between the legs using a narrow strap and a buckle fitted to the lower edge of the plate. Two small expanding pockets were attached to the lower front edge of the vest.

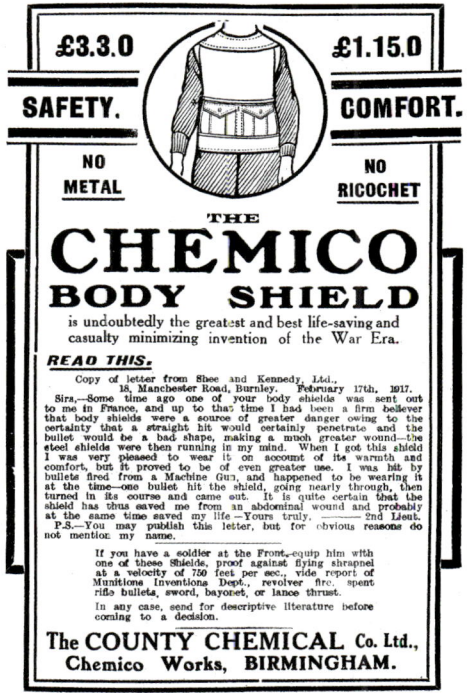

The Chemico Body Shield, manufactured by the County Chemical Company limited of Birmingham. This lightweight (about 6lb/2.72kg) armour was made from multiple layers of resin-impregnated fabric with a muslin cover. Weight-for-weight it was a reasonable compromise, but as with many of the commercial vests, it offered only limited protection.

A World War I advertisement typical of those that appeared in newspapers and periodicals of the period. It extols the virtues of the Chemico shield and includes a first-hand letter of appreciation from a lieutenant who believed the vest to have saved his life. Manufacturers' claims for the levels of protection were generally considerably greater than actual levels; letters from those buyers who discovered that the vests were inadequate were never published. (John Bodsworth)

Great Britain

World War II

A report in the Evening Standard on 30 July 1940 noted that the Prime Minister was considering the issue of body armour to British and Commonwealth forces. Studies had indicated that body armour could only be effective against fragments, and not small arms fire, because of weight restrictions and the need for troop mobility. Research also suggested that a body armour covering 30 per cent of the body would save 14 per cent of all casualties and 40 per cent of all dead. Abdominal wounds proved highly lethal, with as many as 27 per cent of all fatalities being from abdominal wounds and six of every seven abdominal wounds proving fatal.

Subsequently, an article in *The Times* dated Friday 16 August 1940 makes mention of the 'Respirator metal plate' and debate in Parliament between Sir Francis Fremantle, Chairman of the Parliamentary Medical Committee, and Kenneth Walker. It was stated that some 60 per cent of war casualties received wounds to the chest. It was suggested that an armour plate be attached to the box respirator haversack to form a shield for the chest. While some limited research was undertaken into such a form of protection, the development of body armour for issue to all troops was soon to become a serious proposition.

Medical Research Council body armour

In October 1940 the Army Council tasked the Medical Research Council (MRC) with the development of a lightweight body armour for use by the Army. By February 1941, the MRC had produced a viable pattern of lightweight armour that consisted of a thoracic and abdominal plate worn ventrally and a small dorsal plate. The metal plates were provided with a rubber edge strip and rubber buffer pads on their inner faces.

In March 1941 a signal from the War Office to Didcot stores (the army depot where body armour was kept) listed the allocation and bulk issue requirements for 5,000 sets of 'MRC armour' (also known as lightweight armour) to be provided for trials by GHQ home forces. The 5,000 sets were to be made by Briggs Motor Bodies under contract 292/B/68 Con 19.E. The armour was to be issued at a scale of 1,000 sets each to Eastern Command, South East Command and Southern Command. Northern Command was to receive 984 sets (16 sets were to be held for issue to 'interested parties'; the figure was later increased to 24 sets). Western Command and Scottish Command were each to receive 400 sets, with 200 going to London District. A requirement for 500 sets of armour to be sent to the Middle East Command (MEC) saw the totals for Southern Command reduced to 742 and Northern Command further reduced to 734 sets. This allowed for the 24 sets to be held for interested parties and 500 for MEC. Troop trials of the MRC armour were started in late May 1941 and were completed by the following November. The simple armour was made from 1mm manganese steel and weighed 2lb 12oz (1.30kg), as recommended by a report issued by the Body Protection Committee of the MRC on 27 January 1941.

The second pattern cloth-covered manganese steel, lightweight MRC body armour. At only 3lb (1.36kg) the armour was not heavy, but troops unaccustomed to wearing such an item found that it was uncomfortable in prolonged use. Around 200,000 sets of this armour were manufactured during World War II. At left is the front outer face, with the inner, padded face shown at right. (John Bodsworth)

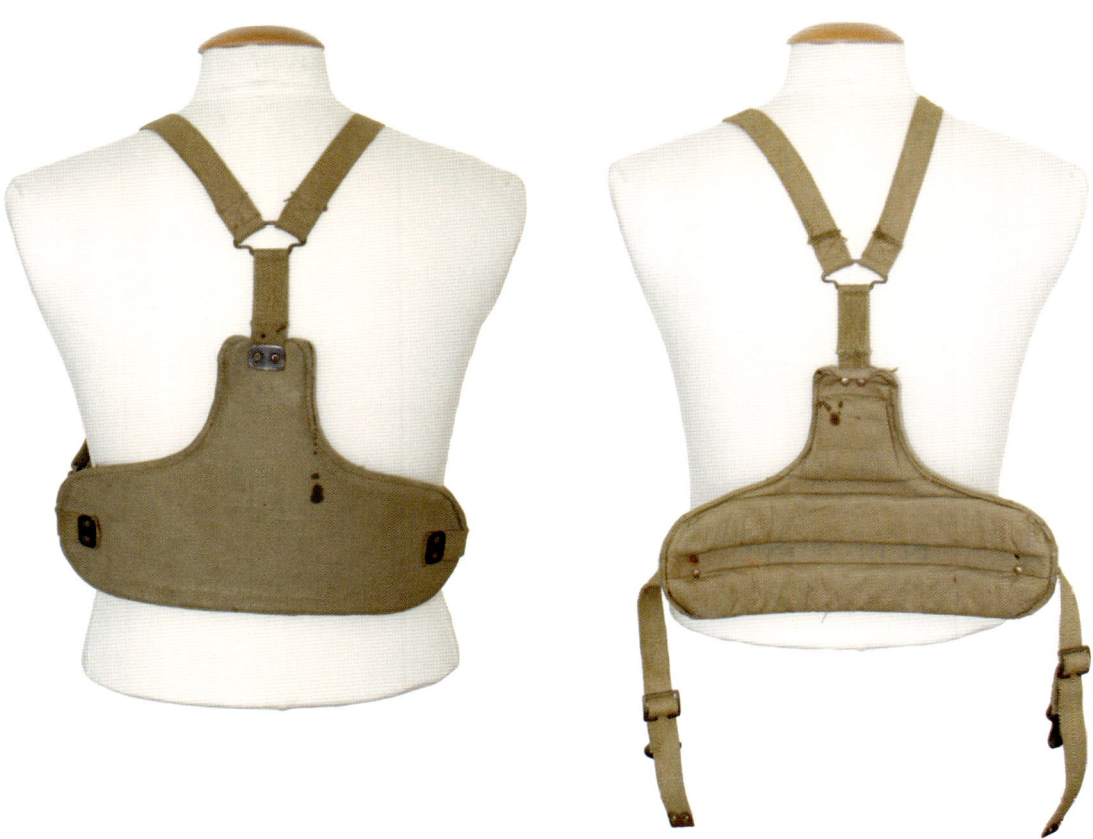

The rear face of the MRC body armour that provided protection to kidney area and lower spine. At left is the outer face and at right the padded inner. (John Bodsworth)

The MRC estimated that the use of its lightweight armour would provide casualty savings of around 5 per cent. However, these figures were later revised to 2.5–3 per cent. A letter issued by the MPRC (Military Personnel Research Committee) of the MRC in December 1941, indicated that the Army Commands trialling the armour had reported favourably on it and recommended its adoption.

No. 1 Medical Section Middle East (MSME) undertook additional testing of body armour, since it felt that the previous trials had not been extensive and lacked medical supervision. No. 1 MSME procured some 70 sets of armour that had been used in the earlier trials. Initial examination showed that many sets had been damaged in testing and that most of the sets were incorrectly assembled, with many having the abdominal and thoracic plates set too close together. A summary of the results reported by No. 1 MSME suggested that high-velocity missiles might mushroom when striking the armour and cause more extensive injury. It was stated that body armour was expensive, but that rough field experimentation had found that a thick pad of Army forms was as good as steel in the protection afforded, thus it was recommended that research into materials cheaper than Hadfield steel be undertaken. However, it was also noted that provision of armour may be cheaper than surgical treatment of wounded personnel (based upon the cost of prolonged hospitalisation), and also the cost of compensation and widows and orphans pensions. It was further stated that an investigation into which troops would benefit most from body armour would be undertaken.

In April 1942 a meeting of the Army Council accepted that body armour should be standard for all infantry and some other troops. In June 1942, an MPRC meeting declared that the body armour with rubber edges was not satisfactory and that samples with other padding should be supplemented. A felt and canvass type, designed by Briggs Motor Bodies, was recommended for mass production.

The following year, in May, it was recommended that 3,500,000 sets of MRC body armour be procured, sufficient to equip all troops (British, Indian, Colonial, Dominion and Allied) in forward areas in all theatres of war. It was envisaged that the armour would eventually be individual issue kit with an ultimate requirement for some 6,900,000 sets. In September 1943 an interim order for 500,000 sets was authorized. By August 1944 it had been decided to reduce the requirement to 150,000 sets, however, by this time contracts for 200,000 sets had already been placed (in January 1944, contracts for 100,000 sets each from Briggs Motor Bodies and Harrison Bross & Howsons had been placed). Of the 200,000 sets manufactured, only 79,000 were issued. Of these, just 15,000 were issued in response to demands from Army units, 64,000 went to the Royal Air Force (RAF) and the bulk of 121,000 remained in storage. The cost of the armour was 15s 9d in 1944 and it was listed under Army VOCAB 5261. The standardized armour that entered mass production differed in detail from the original trials sets. The exposed rubber edge strip and buffer pads were discarded and the metal plates were provided with a canvass cover and fibre buffer pads. The new pattern weighed 3.5lb (1.59kg) and was able to prevent penetration by a .38 pistol bullet fired from 5yd (4.6m), a .45 American Colt-pattern bullet at 100yd (91m) and a standard .303 rifle bullet at 700yd (640m).

Most of the armour issued to the Army went to 21st Army Group (AG). A November 1944 document stated that within the 21st AG the Canadians had received 3,100 sets of armour, Airborne forces 6,000 sets, the SAS 400, the Polish Para Brigade 2,500 (a total 12,000 sets on issue) with an additional 10,000 sets held by the WO, with 128,000 of these held on option for use by 21st AG. The Canadians issued body armour to medical units in northwest Europe, while use by British forces is best summarized by the limited number of sets used during the airborne assault on Arnhem. Airborne troops were lightly equipped. They had little tactical mobility and were generally used to secure specific objectives and hold them until relieved by units with heavier support. Thus the nature of airborne operations made body armour a desirable, if not wholly feasible, option. The Arnhem bridge assault (Operation *Market*) is a good example of where the MRC armour could have been of great tactical use to lightly equipped troops in defensive positions. However, most parachute troops dropped with a weight of some 50 per cent in excess of standard canopy limits and the gliders used in the operation were also generally heavily overloaded. Thus the use of armour by all airborne troops would have been impractical and the additional weight burden better served with ammunition or other supplies.

In August 1945 a request was made to scrap the 121,000 sets of MRC armour remaining in storage, since it was not envisaged that they would be required because of the cessation of hostilities. The MRC armour was finally declared obsolete under a General Staff Policy Statement issued in December 1945, with all remaining stocks to be disposed of, with the exception of a small general service reserve. In February 1946 the policy statement was modified and the requirement for a reserve stock was deleted. A note to the policy added that although the MRC armour was to be disposed of, research and development of body armour should continue. In March 1946 all remaining stocks of MRC body armour held in storage were finally disposed of as scrap. In April 1946, draft specifications for a new set of body armour to replace the MRC armour were actually published, but it is believed that no further action was taken in developing the specifications.

RAF Body Armour use during World War II

By early 1939, the RAF was undertaking serious testing of body armour for aircrew. In February a bulletproof waistcoat, manufactured by Wilkinson, underwent testing. It was found that the garment provided no protection from the standard .303 ammunition and was thus deemed unsuitable. In April 1939 the RAF tested chain mail armour vests manufactured by both Valentin and Firth.

Again, test results were unfavourable. Nevertheless, the RAF retained an interest in personal body armour and in July 1940 tested a Canadian armour manufactured by Laurentid Air Service Corporation and consisting of steel strips set in a canvas cover. Once again the test results were poor. In October 1940 the Army tested the 'Savelyfe Type I' and 'Type II' 'non-rebound' (spall protective) body shields that had both front and back plates. Reasonable results were obtained, but the Type I failed when tested against the standard Type 36 grenade at 3ft (0.9m). The RAF had shown an interest in the Savelyfe, but the continued failure of various equipment to provide adequate protection during testing saw the RAF's interest in personal armour wane. Interestingly, the RAF also looked into armoured life jackets. A cork pattern was tested but was excessively bulky.

Following the poor results of armour testing, there was some reticence from the Air Ministry with regard to equipping individual crew members with body armour, the official line being that aircraft losses were due to structure failure and not crew injury. The additional weight of individual armour would also reduce bomb load, with more than one official report showing a distinct requirement for maximum bomb load on target and not crew protection. It was considered that if crew casualties exceed four in 1,000 man sorties, armour should indeed be issued, but in 1943 the RAF's casualty rate was actually only 1.36 per 1,000 man sorties (interestingly, USAAF figures intermittently exceeded 30 casualties per 1,000 man missions.)

The US Armor, Flyer's, Vest M1 was reviewed by the RAF in June 1943, but it received unfavourable comments, with the Air Ministry ultimately preferring fixed crew-station armour. The Armor, Flyer's, Vest M1 and the British MRC armour were used for flying trials in the closing stages of 1943. Results were promulgated in February 1944, with the following results:

- Bomber Command (Lancaster, Stirling and Halifax): No requirement for individual armour
- Coastal Command (Sunderland and Beaufighter): No requirement for individual armour
- Allied Expeditionary Air Force, Air Defence of Great Britain (AEAF, ADGB) (Mosquito): No requirement for individual armour
- AEAF, Tactical Air Force (TAF) (Mitchell and Mosquito): It was felt that there was a requirement for individual armour within the TAF

The RAF published the trials results and the reasons for the acceptance or refusal for the issue of the Armor, Flyer's, Vest M1. These included refusal on the grounds of excessive weight, interference with movement, fatigue, and the reduction in efficiency and performance of duties. It was also felt that the use of armour would likely result in only a very small overall reduction in casualties and that the severity of some wounds would be increased because of fragments being carried into wounds. The use of armour also added greatly to the danger to low flying operations, especially over the sea, and during any bailout. It was stated that the Army's MRC type armour was completely inadequate in all respects.

Positive responses to the issue of Armor, Flyer's, Vest M1 were that it would prevent a small number casualties, but mainly those that would be otherwise be only slight or moderate, and that it would be a positive moral booster in multi-crew aircraft during fighter or flak attacks. It was noted that if the US armour were issued, it would also be wise to adopt the US A4 Mae West for those crewmen using armour. In conclusion, the RAF stated that generally the disadvantages of issuing the Armor, Flyer's, Vest M1 outweighed the advantages, in view of the small percentage of casualties that would be prevented, but that the beneficial effect on moral might outweigh the disadvantages for certain aircraft types operating during daylight, and that consideration should be given for issue to multi-engine aircraft in TAF. It was requested that armour be issued to Transport Command since the Command's aircraft had no armour, and also that Coastal Command strike squadrons should receive individual armour. Both requests were approved.

Despite the RAF's decision that MRC armour was wholly inadequate for aircrew use, the Air Ministry later requested MRC armour for ground personnel. Initially it was intended to supply MRC armour to the RAF Regiment, but it was latter requested that Servicing Commandos, RAF beach units, signallers in assault parties and combined operations personnel also be issued armour. A total of 100,000 sets of 'Army Type Light Armour' (MRC) were ordered in November 1943. Estimates showed that 29,000 sets would meet all requirements from ground units of the AEAF, South East Asia Air Command (SEAAC) and Mediterranean Air Command (MAC). These figures were revised in January 1944 with requirements as: AEAF 24,000; SEAAC 3,000; and Mediterranean Allied Air Forces (MAAF, which had assumed the responsibilities of MAC from 10 December) 12,500, giving a total requirement for 40,000 sets of MRC armour, including a 30 per cent reserve stock. However, by this time production of the MRC, which had been expected to be in excess of 50,000 weekly, was actually only 10,000 per week. This led to a reassessment of the RAF requirement and a reduction to 20,000 sets, with 10,000 going to the to 2nd TAF and 5,000 each to MAAF and SEAAC.

In March 1944 an official request, marked Most Secret, was made for 1,000 sets of the MRC armour, which was required by the Tactical Air Force to equip crews of Boston, Mitchell and Mosquito aircraft for missions to be flown during the pending Operation *Overlord*. It is interesting to note that this request was made despite the previous assertion that MRC was wholly inadequate for aircrew use.

Groin protection
During February 1945 an unusual request was made by HQ 21st Army Group in Europe. It asked that 1,000 cricketer's groin boxes be made available for field trials to assess the levels of protection that could be offered to the groin area against German Schuminen. It was noted that if the tests were successful, an armoured version of the cricketer's groin protection would be procured. It is not known how far this venture evolved, but the author has located no record of armoured groin protection being produced for British troops.

Post-World War II, Korea and beyond

Samples of Doron had been sent to the UK in March 1945 so that it could be independently tested by the British. However, it is believed that little or no progress was made with Doron. Indeed, in April 1946, Brigadier General Doriot personally requested details of what the British had achieved with his samples. Two years later, in 1948, the Ministry of Defence (MoD; Admiralty, War Office and Air Ministry) finally declared that there was no interest in body armour.

In March 1952 the Director of Weapons and Development stated that body armour research in the UK was to be limited and that primarily the United States would undertake future development and trials work to save any unnecessary duplication of effort. However, the British were to be kept fully informed of all progress, with the option of taking up production in the UK if it was found that the protection afforded by any development in lightweight body armour warranted it.

M1952A armour
The standard American vest was issued to British troops of the 1st Commonwealth Division serving in Korea with the United Nations forces. It was also issued in some quantity to allied nations. By December 1952, 1,600 sets had been supplied by the Americans and were being used by soldiers on patrols, raids and other operations in theatre. US figures show that some 15,368 sets of armour were supplied to UN forces; of these the Commonwealth Division received 4,587 units. In March 1953 it was announced in Parliament that orders had been placed for body armour to be supplied by a British manufacturer, Chemring, which was to supply 5,602 vests based on the American M1952A armour. The Chemring armour was later used by aircrew in Borneo and Aden, and also issued to British troops in Ulster in 1969.

The use of body armour by the Royal Navy
In 1953 the Royal Navy (RN) requested the supply of 2,000 body armour vests and 1,000 pants or aprons (sic). Ideally they were to be based on the vests then being issued (M1952A), but modified with a quick-release system and given added buoyancy. The request added that future armour requirements might exceed as many as 10,000 for surface warships, plus 3,400 for the Royal Marines and a further 1,000 for coastal forces units. The funding was to be added to 1954/55 sketch estimates. The request was not accepted, but a sum of £2,500 was approved under the 1954/55 estimates for the acquisition of one hundred vests and fifty pants for sea trials. The armour was duly acquired from War Department sources, as one hundred M1952A and fifty Armor, Body, Fragmentation Protective, Lower Torso, M1953 (the War Department had drawn the armour from stocks provided by the US Army under the Military

Great Britain

Aid Program; the Army had declined to even consider use of the lower torso armour). The Navy's tests showed that at 8lb 8 oz (3.86kg) the US vest was buoyant. The pants and vest were tested at the Amphibious School to ascertain their suitability for use by landing craft crews, while the armour was further tested by aircrew in fixed- and rotary-wing aircraft. It was found to be wholly unsuited to use in fixed-wing aircraft because of great discomfort under high g forces, the degree of equipment already worn in the confines of a cockpit and because its wear resulted in excessive sweating. However, it was felt that it could be of benefit to helicopter crews. In May 1955, one hundred vests were made available for testing with the Navy's Home and Mediterranean Fleets. By September 1955 a report on the armour had been issued. It stated that it was felt that the use of armour was generally not justified by the RN for many reasons, including shortage of stowage space on warships, and that it was also unlikely to be used, adding: 'The unfortunate sailor [already has] tin hats, gas masks, lifebelts, first aid outfits, torches, ant-flash clothing, electrically heated suits, or cold weather clothing, and survival suits [to encumber him]'. Armour was, however, recommended for issue to the crews of coastal forces' fast patrol boats and helicopter crewmen. It is not known what further progress was made with the provision of armour to the Navy, but a 1959 memo from the Navy's Director of Armament Supply stated that one hundred nylon armour vests and 1,200 Wilkinson Grow vests were held by the Director Armament Stores at Priddy's Hard, for coastal forces' use (this note suggests that the one hundred M9152A vests originally obtained from Army stocks were still in storage at that time and no further examples had been obtained). It was further noted that they had many unsatisfactory features. The 1,200 Wilkinson Grow vests referred to were actually the USAAF Armor, Flyer's, Vest M1, two hundred of which were also held on 'repairable charge' (unserviceable, but repairable). A request was made to confirm if the retention of the armour was still required. In April 1960 a confirmation of the requirement to retain the armour was made.

The subject of armour was raised again in 1966, when the Royal Navy requested the issue of new armour vests of the type then in use with US forces in Vietnam. The vests were to be used by exposed personnel working on upper decks. The request added that the pattern-249819 vests had been in use for almost ten years (it is probable that these were the Grow-type vests). The following year, in 1967, a 'Bullet proof' vest (sic) of the American pattern was supplied for evaluation to HMS Excellent, the Royal Naval School of Gunnery Training. At this time, UK holdings of body armour were limited and little interest had been shown in replacing the old stock, or developing new armour. The Army still had several thousand M1952A vests, plus fifty heavyweight Wilkinson vests that had been procured in 1959. Also suggested in 1967 was a requirement for aircrew armour based on the armour being issued to US aircrew. Little further action was taken. Armour was heavy and still deemed unsuited to use by ground troops. The Navy seemed disinterested and budgets were limited.

Northern Ireland

Armour, Body, Fragmentation, Protective and Vest, Fragmentation

The period after the Korean War saw limited research into the development of body armour, mainly for specialist roles. No new infantry armour was issued. However, the M1952A vests were used in a number of small operations throughout the crumbling empire, including Borneo, Cyprus and Aden. The greatest threat to British soldiers was to come in 1969, however, closer to home in Northern Ireland, when political and religious issues turned into violent sectarian clashes between catholic and protestant communities, and the Royal Ulster Constabulary (RUC) was unable to maintain order. Sparked by minority groups, the violence soon saw mass rioting by certain parts of the two communities, at first against each other, but increasingly against the RUC, which soon called upon the Army for assistance in maintaining public order. Operation *Banner* began on 14 August 1969, with the arrival of troops from the Prince of Wales' Own Regiment of Yorkshire. While initial threats were from rocks and petrol bombs, firearms and IEDs became an increasing problem. To protect them from the numerous nail and blast bombs being employed by the rioters, the troops in Ulster were soon issued body armour. The body armour also provided some protection against the impact of rocks and other hand thrown missiles. It was enhanced by leg protection, helmets with visors and hand-held shields. The armour also provided some protection from roadside IEDs, which grew in size and complexity as the conflict wore on, and an Irish Republican Army (IRA) favourite, improvized mortars. The first armour issued to British troops was the American M1952A, from stocks that had originally been acquired from the Americans during the Korean War, and the identical Chemring vests.

In late 1969 a special purchase of 1,000 Armor, Body, Fragmentation, Protective with Collar was made from the US under NATO agreements. The vests were received in May 1970. Three hundred and fifty were sent straight to Ulster and seventy were used in the production of specialist EOD suits; a further 500 were held as an operational reserve, for spearhead battalions. Period documents refer to this armour as the 'M1964'. Body armour saw a rough time in Ulster, the urban environment and the nature of the conflict causing lots of damage to fabric covers. In February 1970, Headquarters Northern Ireland (HQNI) reported that 322 vests were then awaiting repair and that a future expectation was an average of 50 vest requiring repair each month.

In June 1970 a request for the purchase of another 1,000 vests from the USA was made, the cost of the newly made vests was to be £16.00 each. The following month an urgent operational request was made for an additional 3,000 vests 'at any cost' from the US Army, or any commercial sources. By the end of June 1970 the MOD's stock of body armour was only 10,103 of various patterns, including experimental and commercial items, and material then on order. The Americans immediately lent 1,000 vests, the stock to be repaid from the order already

Great Britain

The first vests issued to troops in Ulster were American Armor, Body, Fragmentation, Protective, Upper Torso, M1952A, a quantity of which was originally procured during the 1950s. These were soon supplemented by American Armor, Body, Fragmentation Protective, with Collar. The US vest fillers were sewn into the covers, which were not replaceable at unit level. The vests, termed Armour, Body, Fragmentation, Protective in UK service, saw hard use with British troops, particularly in hot spots such as Belfast, Londonderry and the 'bandit country' of the borders, and many covers soon required replacement. The first British made cover for the Armour, Body, Fragmentation, Protective, With Collar produced in 1971 was of a similar design to the US original, but allowed easy removal of the filler via a Velcro closure. The cover was modified in 1973 by the addition of a single rubber rifle butt patch on the right shoulder and straight-top rectangular pockets. No grenade loops were fitted and the front fastening relied only on Velcro, as with the American Armor, Body, Fragmentation Protective, with Collar (M69). (John Bodsworth)

The third pattern British made cover used with the Armour, Body, Fragmentation, Protective was almost identical to the second pattern, but had an added rubber rifle butt pad on the left shoulder to allow for ambidextrous use of the weapon dependant upon available cover. The use of the additional pad also offered ease of use by left-handed riflemen. In September 1979, requests had been made to replace the nylon side adjustment cord with an elastic substitute, which soon became standard. (John Bodsworth)

Great Britain

placed in the US. By mid-July, 7,000 vests were in Ulster. In May 1971 a further purchase of vests was made from the US, 5,362 Armor, Body, Fragmentation Protective with Collar (M69) were bought at a cost of $174,299.

The requirement for body armour in Ulster had reawakened the need for a serious appraisal of available armour. During 1972, the Stores and Clothing Research and Development Establishment (SCRDE) ballistic section, which had been formed in 1969, undertook a series of tests on body armour, including products made by Rolls-Royce; Zune, a Belgian company; and American Noroc vests. The Rolls vest were found to be heavy at 10lb 8oz (4.76kg), gave 30 per cent less coverage than the standard US Armor, Body, Fragmentation Protective with Collar and cost considerably more at £24.00. Both the Noroc and Zune vests were apparently well received, but were excessively expensive. Overall it was felt that the US vest provided sufficient protection. During 1973 every effort was made to force the Army to adopt the Rolls vest, by then called the 'BCM' vest (Bristol Composite Materials had bought out Rolls-Royce's armour production). The issue was raised in the House of Commons and the press, and letters were passed between company directors and ministers in an effort to sway the decision, but the Army remained resolute. That same year SCRDE also began work with Galt Glass Laminates, looking at the value of ceramics in body armour, their ability to stop high velocity rounds, and possible employment in Ulster.

The BCM 'Bristol Type 3' flexible body armour made in 1978. This item is typical of the style of armour being produced in Europe during the 1970s. It has built-in abdominal protection and two utility/magazine pouches at the front, as well as grenade loops on the chest. The shoulder sections have prominent ridges to assist in weapon support when firing from the shoulder. Manufactured in the UK, this particular item was exported to Yugoslavia, where the design was later copied and manufactured by the Yugoslav state's Federal Directorate of Supply as the 'Type 3' bullet resistant jacket. The vest weighs 5lb 10oz (2.54kg).

The BCM Bristol Type 3 used a separate front and rear filler. The plastic cover of the side to be worn against the body was coloured black, the opposite face was coloured red to avoid any confusion as to orientation. The Velcro tabs at the shoulder sections aided in securing the filler within the outer cover. The label shows that the filler was capable of stopping a variety of fragmentation and ammunition types, including .45in ACP and .38in Special. The lower label provides adequate warning that this side must be worn against the body. Incorrectly orientated armour could provide less protection because of the incorrect layering and positioning of the individual ballistic fabric layers and backing fabrics.

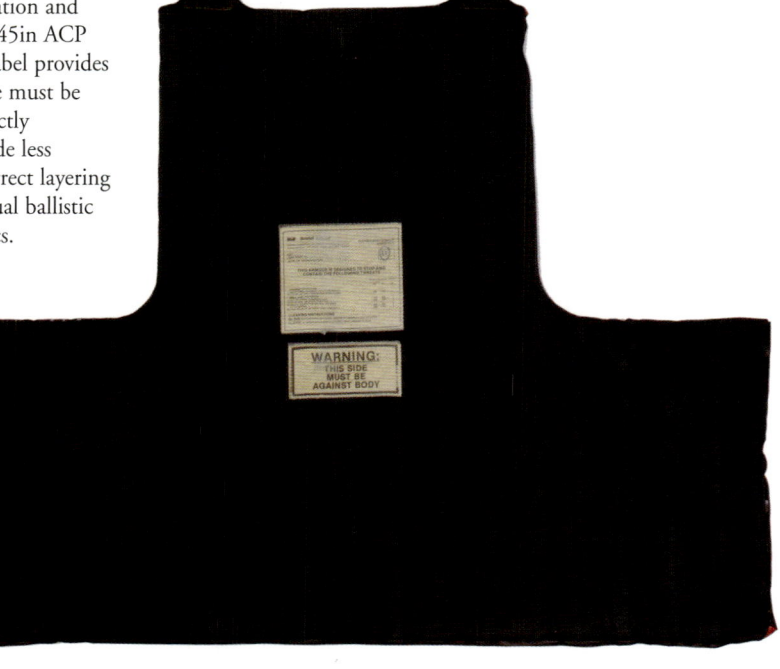

Troopers of the Royal Hussars on foot patrol on the streets of Belfast, around 1979. These men typify the appearance of 'Brits' serving in Ulster during the 1970s, armed with the 7.62mm SLR and wearing body armour and basic equipment in the form of a 58-pattern webbing belt and water bottle carrier. ('Horsepower' KRH Museum)

Great Britain

In March 1971 a user trial commenced for a replaceable cover for body armour. The experimental cover (for the M1952A vest) had grenade loops and small pockets. It was unsatisfactory and it was recommended that the grenade loops were removed and the pockets enlarged to hold a grenade. In April a request for 1,100 replaceable covers for the M69 was made at a cost of £5.75 each. The requirement was for 225 small, 500 medium, 225 large and 50 extra large covers. A further requirement was made for 100 covers for the M1952A. In April 1973 a request was made to modify the covers with the addition of rifle patches. At this time, 7,000 new covers were in stock and were to be modified by the addition of a single rifle patch at the right shoulder before issue. Some 6,000 covers, pending orders from manufacturers, were to be made incorporating the modification. The covers were later modified again, by the addition of a second rifle patch at the left shoulder allowing the rifle to be held securely at either shoulder while still providing cover on left- or right-facing street corners (rather than for the benefit of left handed users). The original covers were replaced by the 'Cover Replaceable, 1979 Pattern' that improved upon the US originals and the early British patterns. The cover underwent some development, having rubber shoulder pads with prominent rifle butt-stops to support the rifle (adequately supporting a rifle at the shoulder has always been an issue with body armour). It was soon provided with a personal 'radio phone' pocket at the lower left front and a field-dressing pocket at the left shoulder. The original American white nylon ballistic filler was supplemented by British made fillers. A copy of the US pattern, it had a green fabric filler beneath a clear plastic cover. Some examples of the M69 were modified by the addition of the 1979-pattern vest's rubber-pattern shoulder pad sections.

The Armor, Body, Fragmentation, Protective, Upper Torso, M1952A and the Armor, Body, Fragmentation Protective with Collar, M69 were both generally referred to as 'Armour, Body, Fragmentation, Protective' or just 'Vest, Fragmentation' in British Service, although the troops wearing them usually referred to any body armour vests generically as 'Flak Jackets', a term also found in official nomenclature.

The Cover Replaceable, 1979 Pattern used on the Armour, Body, Fragmentation, Protective. It was purpose made and incorporated modifications based on the experience of soldiers using armour. The vest had rifle pads at each shoulder, each having prominent integral butt-stops to hold the rifle firmly at the shoulder, always a difficult practice when wearing bulky body armour. This pattern of cover and vest saw limited use with Royal Navy ratings during the Falklands campaign, usually by gunners exposed to enemy fire on the upper decks of warships.

Variant of the Cover Replaceable, 1979 Pattern. This pattern cover, used on the Armour, Body, Fragmentation, Protective, improved the vest's functionality by adding a first field dressing (FFD) pocket at the left shoulder. The left pocket was also modified so that it could carry a personal radio, such as the Pye Pocketfone or Clansman PRC 349. To hold the radio securely, the width of the pocket could be reduced (using two snaps) and the radio was further held in place in the pocket by a strip of Velcro. When the radio was in the pocket the top flap could not be fastened. Two Velcro tabs at the back of the neck held the radio cable.

Great Britain

British made ballistic filler fitted into the second version of the Cover Replaceable, 1979 Pattern with FFD pocket. The Filler, Ballistic, Body Armour, Fragmentation Protective and the cover together, made up the Armour, Body, Fragmentation, Protective. The British filler was made from OG fabric, rather than the white of the original US filler.

A further production variant of the Cover Replaceable, 1979 Pattern used on the Armour, Body, Fragmentation, Protective. This pattern has modified shoulder pads, the upper inner edges have been cut-away, allowing a marginally greater degree of arm movement when compared to the square-section butt pads. As with the other pattern variations, this cover remained listed as Cover Replaceable, 1979 Pattern with no change in designation despite the modifications.

Later production runs of the Cover Replaceable, 1979 Pattern had the FFD pocket located at the upper left shoulder. The pocket was fastened by a single press snap and carried the standard issue 20 × 19cm (8 × 7.5in camouflaged first field dressing. Also visible in this image, between the dressing pocket and the collar, is a small Velcro tab. This was one of two tabs used to secure the personal radio microphone/speaker cable to the vest.

Troopers of the Royal Hussars, clearing their weapons following a foot patrol in Belfast, around 1979. All wear body armour with the variant of the Cover Replaceable, 1979 Pattern having cut-away rifle patches. ('Horsepower' KRH Museum)

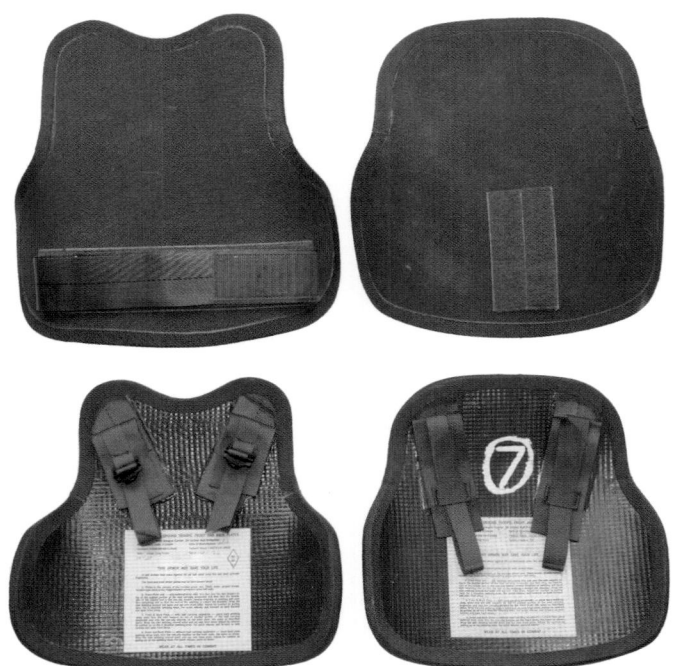

This is the American Body Armor, Ground Troops, Variable Type, Small Arms, Fragmentation Protective. A British made cover was used to encase this US issue armour. The original US vest was modified by having both waist straps and the right shoulder strap cut away, before being inserted into the British cover. Of a similar design to the US original, the lower edge of the cover had two flap-top pockets. These were of a size suited to holding the 20-round 7.62mm SLR magazine, each pocket holding one magazine. The VBA was in service from the mid-70s to the 1990s. The armour was of such a weight that it was generally only worn on static VCP or similar immobile duties.

The ballistic SAPI Body Armour, Ground Troops, Front and Back Plates used with the Body Armour, Ground Troops, Variable Type, Small Arms, Fragmentation Protective. Above left is the outer face of the front plate, at top right is the outer face of the rear plate. Below are the rear faces of the front and back plates, respectively. The rear views show the shoulder strap system that allowed the inserts to be worn independently of the outer cover. These are unmodified US-issue plates. (John Bodsworth)

Body Armour, Ground Troops, Variable Type, Small Arms, Fragmentation Protective (US) or Variable Body Armour

By August 1969 the British were showing a major interest in purchasing a variety of US armoured vests, prompted by the situation in Ulster. In September an official request was sent to the US Army for the loan of six sets of Body Armor, Ground Troops, Variable Type, Small Arms. Follow-up requests were made in February and March 1970, bringing a promise of delivery of the six sets of VBA by April. An urgent request was sent to the Americans again, in early July, requesting an update. This time the reply was more positive, since the vests had finally been despatched by sea on 28 May. The VBA vests were eventually received by SCRDE on 15 July 1970, provided by the US Army on a one-year non-returnable loan. Little is know of the progress made with the VBA, but official communications from early 1973 suggest that its usefulness was still being reviewed and that it was being shown to interested military parties. One set was displayed at an HQNI meeting held on 26 June 1973. A few days later, on 2 July, HQNI raised an urgent signal to the MoD in London requesting that a further 25 sets of VBA be acquired for user reaction assessment, since the six sets previously procured had only been held for review. It was added that an expected order for a minimum of 400 sets would follow. The request was approved by the MoD on 4 July, at an expected cost of £200 per unit. On 17 July an urgent air freight request was made to the US Army for the loan of 25 sets of VBA, 15 large-regular, three medium-regular, four large-long and three medium-long, to be delivered to SCRDE by 20 August 1973. By the end of June it had been made clear that the requested Standardisation Loan could not be effected by US authorities and thus the 25 sets of VBA would have to be purchased at a cost of $130 per set. The six medium vests were despatched on 25 August, with the 19 others being sent on the 29th.

By the end of September, SCRDE had carried out ballistic testing of the VBA, confirming that the ceramic SAPI would indeed withstand the impact of 30-calibre ball ammunition, and vests were already with units in Ulster undergoing assessment. Results of the user trials were expected to be available by November, at which time issue of the VBA would be authorized.

The VBA was issued as the Body Armor, Ground Troops, Variable Type, Small Arms-Fragmentation Protective (US). It was later provided with a replacement cover. Similar to the US pattern, the cover used a simplified Velcro fitting at the right shoulder and included two pockets at each lower side. The pockets, with Velcro-closed flaps, were each able to accommodate a single 20-round, 7.62mm SLR (L1A1 self-loading rifle) box magazine. Like the US cover it had pockets at the front and rear for the insertion of the heavy boron carbide ceramic plates that provided additional protection up to 30-calibre ball ammunition (therefore affording protection from the standard NATO 7.62mm and 5.56mm rounds). The Variable Body Armour was not intended for general issue, but was restricted for those on static duties, such as troops manning permanent vehicle check points (PVCPs). Such use meant that the weight and restrictive nature of the vest was less of an issue; it was also at such locations that troops were most easily targeted. When standardized, the VBA vest was supplied only in one size, large-long, weighing 22lb 8oz (10.20kg). It had been found that the large-long size could be comfortably used by most troops, whereas smaller sizes tended to remain in storage.

Great Britain

Body Armour, Mark 2 or Improved Northern Ireland Body Armour (INIBA)

The replacement for the M1952A and M69 armours was the 'Body Armour, Mark 2' or 'Improved Northern Ireland Body Armour' (INIBA), first issued during 1981. The INIBA introduced a new concept in standard issue military armour, that of armour worn beneath the outer clothing. In an effort to support its 'hearts and minds' objectives, the British Army had limited the use of combat helmets, preferring soft headwear, such as berets, whenever operational circumstances allowed; the use of camouflage cream was banned and the wearing of the new INIBA armour beneath the combat jacket provided a less aggressive image for soldiers patrolling the busy towns and villages of the province. The INIBA was worn over an issue shirt or the specially produced 'Vest, PBA' (Personal Body Armour).

The old US-type Armour, Body, Fragmentation Protective that had previously been used in Ulster was superseded in 1983 by the improved Body Armour, Mark 2. The new armour was frequently called the Improved Northern Ireland Body Armour, or INIBA for short. As well as the standard ballistic filler providing fragmentation protection, the INIBA had front and rear pockets for removable ballistic SAPI plates that offered protection against rifle-calibre impacts up to 7.62mm, but not without the disadvantage of increased weight. This vest is fitted with the second pattern of contoured SAPI with rounded edges.

BELOW: The early pattern Protective Plate, Armour, Body, Mk 2 (with squared edges) fitted into the pockets on the INIBA vest. They were clearly marked to indicate how each plate should be fitted to the armour cover. At left is the outer face and at right the inner face of the plate. The plates were manufactured by Galt Glass Laminates. (John Bodsworth)

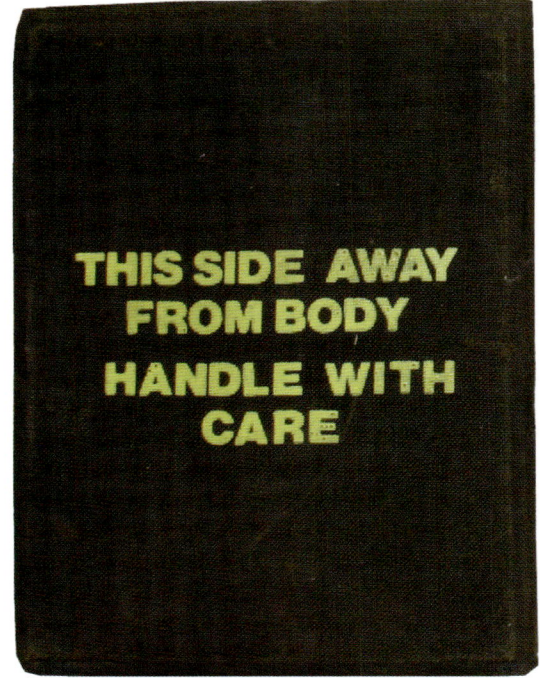

Great Britain

The filler of the INIBA used twenty-two layers of ballistic nylon in the main body and twelve layers over the shoulders. The SAPI ceramic plates fitted in the front and rear pockets resisted penetration by 7.62mm rifle calibre rounds over the vulnerable heart area. The plates were fabricated from composite aluminium oxide ceramic and an aramid fibre, and were a product of SCRDE's work with Galt Glass Laminates. Early issue 'Protective Plate, Armour, Body, Mk 2' were quite flat and had squared edges, which were vulnerable to impact damage, since ceramics are quite brittle. This was remedied by the issue of a modified pattern of plate, the 'Protective Plate, Contoured, Armour, Body Mk 2', which was contoured and had rounded edges. INIBA was well received, but the ceramic plates meant that it was markedly heavier than the older armours, since each SAPI plate weighed 2lb 7oz (1.10kg). The INIBA was supplied in four sizes, small, medium, large and extra large, the vests weighing 10lb 9oz (4.80kg) for the small size, 11lb (5.00kg) for the medium and 11lb 11oz (5.30kg) for the large.

INIBA formed the basis of the 'Suit, Body Armour, Searcher's'. The Searcher's armour used the basic INIBA body armour with an added high collar at the neck and aprons fitted to the lower front and rear of the vest. The Searcher's suit was for use by Royal Engineers and other personnel engaged in searching for IEDs and explosives, rather than Explosive Ordnance Disposal and Ammunition Technical Officers. It provided greater protection than standard armour, such as the INIBA, but somewhat less than the armour worn by EOD units. It was provided in three sizes, small, medium and large. The medium size suit weighed 13lb 11oz (6.20kg).

Suit, Body Armour, Searcher's. This armour was a modification of the standard INIBA, created to provide increased protection to personnel engaged in searching for IEDs and explosives, but not for those involved in the disarming and disposal of them. (John Bodsworth)

Vest, PBA. This polo-style shirt was designed to be worn under the INIBA body armour. Lightweight and breathable, it had short sleeves and a collar. The neck opening was closed with two Velcro patches. (John Bodsworth)

Carrier, Small Arms Protective Body Armour
INIBA's ceramic plate offered protection from the bulk of small arms likely to have been encountered in use with terrorist organisations in Ulster. Popular terrorist weapons included the Armalite AR15, the M16 and variants of the AK47 and AKM. However, in 1985 a new weapon appeared in the IRA arsenal. The Barrett 50-calibre (12.7mm × 99 NATO) M82 long-range sniper rifle. In August 1992, an 18-year old British soldier was shot dead at a vehicle check point (VCP) on the outskirts of Crossmaglen. He was the first victim of the Barrett. In response to the major threat posed by the use of this weapon against British troops by IRA volunteers, the 'Carrier, Small Arms Protective, Body Armour' was developed. The heavy boron carbide SAPI plates fitted onto the front and rear of the disruptive pattern material (DPM) carrier, along with blunt-trauma packs to absorb the high impact energy and provide standoff. Together the ceramic plates and trauma packs provided the best available protection from high-energy impacts. Nevertheless, the degree of blunt-trauma injury from a 50-calibre strike would undoubtedly have been quite severe considering the high kinetic energy value associated with this ammunition. A 660-grain (1.5oz; 42.8g) projectile fired at 2,799fps (853m/s) muzzle velocity would undoubtedly have caused highly incapacitating, if not fatal blunt-trauma if insufficient standoff was allowed between the plates and torso. This item was still listed in the 1999 stores catalogue, but it was not in the 2003 listings.

The last British soldier to die during Operation *Banner* was a 23-year old who was shot while manning a VCP in Bessbrook. He was killed by a single round fired from a .50 Barrett sniper rifle.

In response to the increasing threat presented by IRA weaponry, the Carriage, Ballistic Protection, 12.7mm, DPM, IRR (also listed as the Carrier, Small Arms Protective, Body Armour) was introduced to provide protection from the 50-cal (12.7mm) ammunition of the Barrett sniper rifle. The large and correspondingly heavy SAPI plates fitted onto the front and rear of the carrier, along with blunt-trauma packs. Together these provided the best available protection from high-energy impacts. At left is the front view showing the side opening contoured front SAPI plate pocket (to allow for shouldering a rifle) and at right is the rear view with top opening SAPI pocket. The plate carrier is one size. This example was made in 1995.

Great Britain

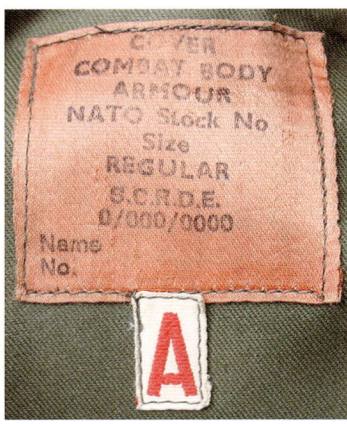

Combat Body Armour. This is the trials Pattern A armour produced in 1987 by SCRDE, using Kevlar filler sections for the first time in British armour (previous armour filler had been nylon based). Pattern A was based on the design of the American PASGT-type vest, but without the front pockets. The interior was marked 'User Trial Prototype March 87'.

Below is the text of the integral label from the Type A armour.

COVER
COMBAT BODY
ARMOUR
NATO Stock No
Size
REGULAR
S.C.R.D.E.
0/000/000
Name
No

(John Bodsworth)

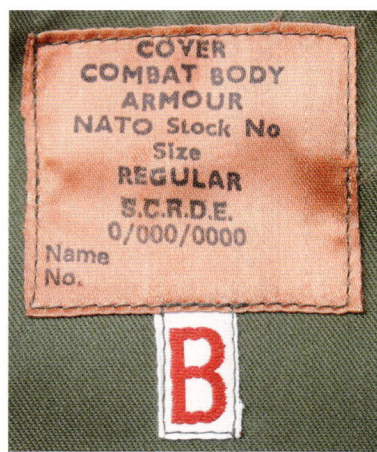

Combat Body Armour. This is the trials Pattern B armour, also produced in 1987. Unlike the Type A armour with its multiple armour filler sections, this pattern used a single-piece filler and was of a simpler design, not having the shoulder sections of the Type A armour. Although this design was not adopted, the filler was later used with the Combat Body Armour L/W Mk 1 that was standardized for general issue. This armour was made by SCRDE and bore an identical label to the Type A armour, the different armours only being differentiated by the white letter positioned below the main label. (John Bodsworth)

The Falklands War

While the British had developed body armour for use in Ulster, a standard infantry body armour had not been produced at the time of the Falklands War, although the requirement had been promulgated. Troops deploying for Operation *Corporate*, the liberation of the islands, were not supplied with armour. Considering the nature of the short conflict, the burden of armour would have been excessive for heavily laden troops 'yomping' great distances over very inhospitable terrain. Interestingly, the greatest percentage of infantry casualties were from small arms fire, rather than fragmentation. It could, therefore, be argued that the INIBA should have been used, but it would have greatly reduced the combat effectiveness of already tired and cold troops. It would possibly have led to British forces suffering greater casualties due to increased fatigue and restricted mobility. While the ground troops were not provided with armour, the American Noroc I armour system, from the Norton Company of Massachusetts, was supplied for use by helicopter crews. Using heavy boron carbide plates, Noroc I saw only very limited use. By contrast, naval upper deck crewmen such as those manning weapon systems or gun direction observers, were provided with Armour, Body, Fragmentation, with 1979-pattern covers. The armour was perfect for the navy, since fatigue was less of an issue in static positions and, other than fire, fragmentation injuries were generally the greatest threat to any crewmen.

Iraq and Afghanistan

Combat Body Armour

As early as July 1971, an SCRDE stores clothing and development requirement was issued for the production of a DPM combat body armour. It was stated that a prototype was required for acceptance by January 1974, with an anticipated in-service date of September 1976. The requirement also stated that there was no need for individual armour for AFV crews. It would seem that little action was taken on this requirement.

The mid-1980s saw extensive efforts to improve the body armour available to British troops. The old INIBA had been adequate for the relatively static duties required of service in Ulster, but it was bulky, awkward in wear and unsuited to use in the tiring, extended duration effort and environments of actual combat. By the mid-1980s calls were being made in parliament for a similar armour to the INIBA to be issued to all British troops and a programme of development was put underway with an expectation that a general issue armour for all arms would be in service by 1989. By 1987, two prototype 'Combat Body Armour' (CBA) vests had been designed, Prototype 'A' and Prototype 'B'. Prototype 'A' was a simple design not dissimilar to the US PASGT vest, with large shoulder pads. Prototype 'B' was of a similar, yet simple vest style, omitting the shoulder pads. The inner vest used the new Kevlar fabric. Development of CBA continued using the Prototype 'B' vest as a base design. From this, an almost identical 'Combat Body Armour L/W' was developed. The new

Great Britain

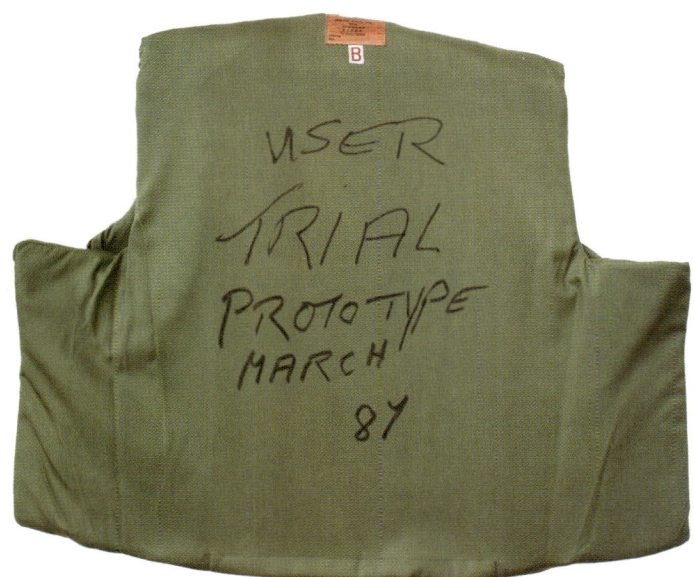

Inner rear face of the Combat Body Armour Pattern B showing the marking 'User Trial Prototype March 87'. The filler was inserted via an opening on the lower rear edge. (John Bodsworth)

lightweight (L/W) vest was produced using the inner vest of Prototype 'B'. It was this lightweight vest, with plain green cover, that was to form the basis of CBA development and eventual issue throughout the 1990s.

It was Iraq's invasion of Kuwait in 1990 that brought about an immediate and urgent requirement for CBA to be provided for troops deploying to expel Iraqi forces from Kuwait. The Combat Body Armour L/W now became the 'Combat Body Armour L/W Mk 1' vest, provided with a newly designed two-colour brown and tan desert disruptive pattern material (DDPM) cover. The cover had two chest pockets, a large pocket on the left breast and a smaller pocket on the right breast. The flap top pockets were closed with Velcro and had elasticated upper edges to help prevent the loss of any contents. At each side of the CBA L/W vest cover were two Velcro-fastened webbing straps that allowed for individual size adjustment within the six issued size ranges. An adjustable vertical strap was fitted to the lower back of the cover. The lower end of the strap attached to the personal load carrying equipment (PLCE) webbing belt to help support the weight of the belt equipment. When fitted, the strap could be quickly separated from the belt using the integral 'Fastex' clip. The filler of the Combat Body Armour L/W Mk 1 was aramid and nylon woven to MoD specifications for ballistic materials. The filler's waterproof cover was made of PVC; it prevented ingress of moisture into the ballistic filler. The outer protective camouflage cover was of a polyester and cotton twill.

An issue of the new CBA began in earnest during 1990. Subsequent experience during the Gulf War highlighted inadequacies in the armour as issued. It provided protection from fragmentation, but unlike the heavy and uncomfortable INIBA, it left the heart and chest vulnerable to small arms fire. Balancing the requirement for a light armour and increased individual protection was not an easy task. British soldiers had not used armour during the Falklands war, since mobility had been paramount, but the desert war, with its increased mobility and vehicle-mounted operations, allowed for the issue of a heavier armour – despite the heat of Iraq. An improved armour was

A development of the trials Combat Body Armour Type B was the Combat Body Armour L/W. Similar to the B-type armour, the L/W type had a modified neck opening and fitting of the filler was achieved via an opening in the inner upper face of the rear section. The Kevlar filler was of the type previously used in the Type B armour. The cover of this Combat Body Armour L/W was made by Chelsea Quilt Company (CQC). It was to form the basis of the Combat Body Armour L/W Mk 1.

Great Britain

developed in 1992. It used the basic Combat Body Armour L/W filler and cover as a base design. The two front pockets were deleted and a large pocket was placed off centre – over the heart – at the back and front of the vest. The two pockets each took an INIBA-type ceramic boron carbide plate to protect the vital heart area. The enhanced armour was officially called 'Combat Body Armour, IS' (IS – Internal Security) or 'ECBA' ('Enhanced Combat Body Armour') for brevity. Issue of the new armour began in 1993 and by December of that year all troops serving in Bosnia, and requiring enhanced protection, had been issued with the new ECBA. The CBA continued in use with troops whose duties placed them under a lesser threat. At that time, a set of ECBA, including plates, cost £156.

LEFT: DPM two-pocket Combat Body Armour L/W Mk 1 Temperate DPM, usually referred to simply as Combat Body Armour or just CBA. It is a simple vest with a front opening secured by a Velcro-closed flap. The front of the vest has a pocket at each side, a small one on the right chest and a larger one on the left side. Two adjustment straps at each side allowed for a degree of personal fit within each of the six individual sizes produced. This pattern of lightweight armour was introduced in 1991. This example was produced in the temperate DPM fabric and destined for use in non-arid areas, such as Europe.

RIGHT: The rear of the Combat Body Armour L/W Mk 1 was fitted with a short adjustable strap and Fastex clip that fitted to the PLCE belt. At left is the component fixed to the armour and at right the removable belt fitting. The Fastex clip allowed the belt and equipment to be removed quickly and easily.

Filler Combat Body Armour L/W Mk 1. This is the pattern of filler used with the Combat Body Armour L/W Mk 1 and early-issue versions of the later Combat Body Armour, IS. The Kevlar inner vest is covered in a heavy-duty plastic that prevents the ingress of moisture that would otherwise increase the garment's weight and reduce the ballistic properties of the filler. The Filler, Combat Body Armour, IS used in the later Combat Body Armour, IS, is of an identical shape to this pattern. This filler was manufactured by Chelsea Quilt Company, but now trading as QCC.

The Filler Combat Body Armour removed from its PVC cover. The filler has hard-wearing green Cordura-type fabric panels on either side of the front sections and on the back. The filler is unmarked.

Great Britain

Author wearing Combat Body Armour L/W Mk 1 Temperate DPM while with 42 Commando, Royal Marines, in Belize. The photograph was taken on a live grenade range where the use of body armour was mandatory. Military body armour is highly effective in protecting against grenade fragments.

This standard Combat Body Armour L/W Mk 1 Temperate has been modified by the addition of a rank strap as used on the later Combat Body Armour, IS and in line with the new positioning of rank slides introduced with the Soldier 95 system.

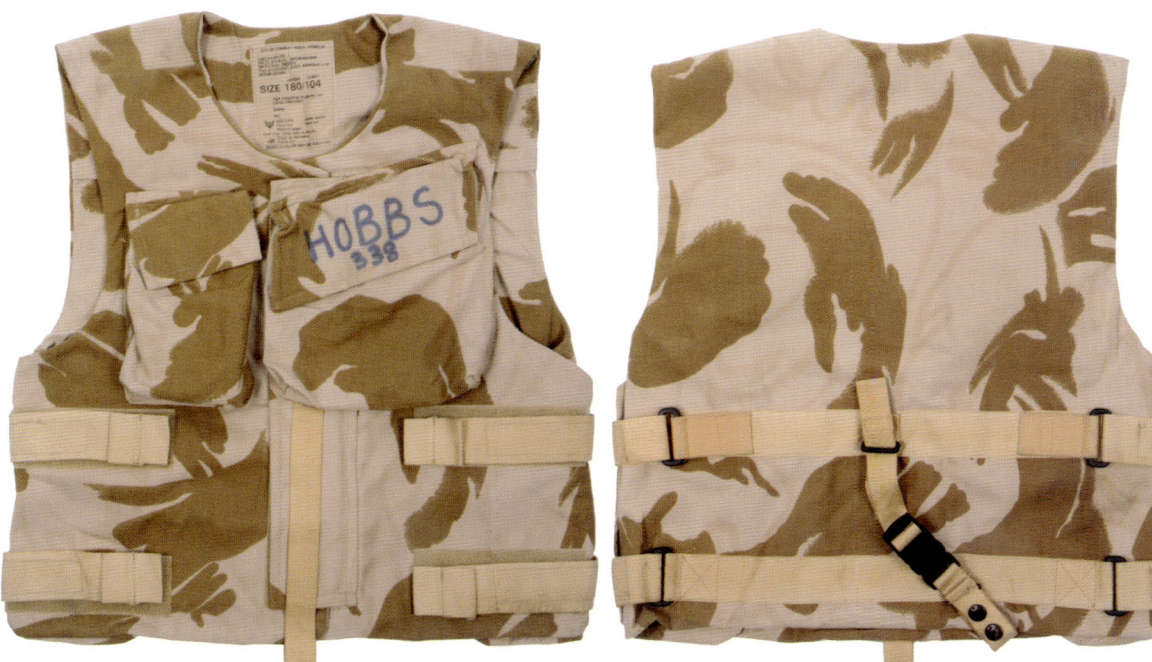

The Combat Body Armour L/W Mk 1, with first pattern DDPM camouflage. This scheme, with its distinctive narrow ghost background print (visible more clearly on the rear of the vest), was used on early production body armour and uniforms. The previously standard four-colour DDPM pattern held by the MoD had also been sold to Iraq, hence it was not practicable to use the scheme for the 1991 conflict and a substitute had to be quickly found.

Great Britain

CBA and ECBA use in Operation Telic

Operation *Telic* was the code name for British forces' operations in Iraq from the spring of 2003, when Coalition forces invaded Iraq in an effort to disarm its military forces under United Nations Security Council Resolutions. It was the UK's biggest military operation since the Gulf War of 1990-91. *Telic* saw the deployment of some 46,000 personnel to the region. The initial Ministry of Defence report on Operation *Telic* highlighted many shortfalls in the equipment needed to maintain a sustained operation in Iraq; among these was a shortage of ballistic body armour. At the planning stage of *Telic*, the standard CBA was envisaged as appropriate, since the primary protection requirement was for protection from fragmentation-type weapons. At a late stage it became apparent that fragmentation protection was inadequate, however, since troops would be fighting in built-up areas (FIBUA) and that rather than standard CBA, ECBA was required. In late October 2002 the decision was made to equip the entire Operation *Telic* force with ECBA. An urgent budget of some £3 million was approved specifically for the purchase of additional ECBA, sufficient to provide sets to equip all personnel in theatre. Within theatre shortages of equipment had arisen because of two main factors. Some equipment had arrived in theatre but could not be located, preventing it being delivered to those troops who needed it. This was a particularly relevant factor in the shortage of body armour. The second factor was the shortfall in operational stock levels. This second factor applied less to ECBA, but it was a problem with regard to civilian-pattern body armour for issue to contractor personnel, the shortage resulting in civilians being issued military camouflage body armour. Prior to *Telic* it had been the policy of the MoD to issue ECBA for peacekeeping operations, such as those concurrently being undertaken in Afghanistan, the Balkans, Northern Ireland and Sierra Leone. ECBA plates had first been issued in 1992, when an initial batch of thirty-two individual plates had been issued – enough to equip only sixteen ECBA vests. By the time of the planning stages of Operation *Telic*, a store of 30,000 ECBA sets had been

The Combat Body Armour L/W Mk 1, with second-pattern DDPM camouflage cover that was standardized as the British desert camouflage during the Gulf War of 1990-91. The DDPM camouflage was rapidly produced so that troops deploying to theatre had a suitable desert camouflage. However, many soldiers were provided with standard DPM camouflage covers as demand outstripped available DDPM armour.

Combat Body Armour L/W Mk 1 in DDPM being worn by men of the Queen's Dragoon Guards during the Gulf War. The troops are test firing their personal weapons, the L2A3 Sterling SMG. This view clearly shows the side fastening and dorsal protection offered by the armour. (US DoD)

Great Britain

stockpiled. The stock included six hundred and ninety DDPM covers, which were soon enhanced by an additional 49,000 full sets of ECBA with a further 31,000 sets procured to maintain sustainability of replacements. At this time, 16,000 pairs of SAPI plates were in service. These were insufficient to provide for warfighting needs and a further 23,700 pairs of SAPI plates were ordered from contractors. The total cost of supplying each soldier with a para-aramid filler ECBA vest, camouflage cover and two SAPI inserts was a mere £167.70 (an increase from £156 in 1993), with a total expenditure of some £2,954,300 pounds for providing body armour for Operation *Telic* (these figures do not include additional spending for Operation *Telic* 2, the post-war sustaining operation). The MoD had stipulated a delivery deadline of 4 April 2003 for the additional armour and accessories. By 24 March, 21,759 body armour covers and 32,581 pairs of SAPI plates had been issued into the supply system. At this time the MoD's Defence Clothing Integrated Project Team gave notice that since the 1999 campaign in Kososvo, approximately 200,000 sets of body armour had been issued, but had apparently disappeared. Indeed, despite the best efforts of all involved, the issue of body armour in-theatre was never sufficient to meet the demands of combat and support troops, the shortfall leading to otherwise avoidable casualties.

In February 2007 the MoD released figures for ECBA issue. A total of 704,205 components had been released. This included ballistic fillers, SAPI plates, DPM, DDPM, civilian blue and UN covers. Of this figure, 165,000 items represented SAPI plates, enough to equip 84,250 individuals, although a number were issued to replace damaged items. At this time all personnel deploying to Iraq or Afghanistan were provided with a personal issue of body armour prior to leaving the UK. However, during the early stages of *Telic* there had been shortages of ECBA and issue had been allocated on the basis of role, with priority going to infantry, followed by soldiers mounted in un-armoured vehicles. Mounted armoured soldiers were considered as the lowest risk. By June 2007 there were more than 14,000 sets of all patterns of body armour in the Iraqi theatre of operations.

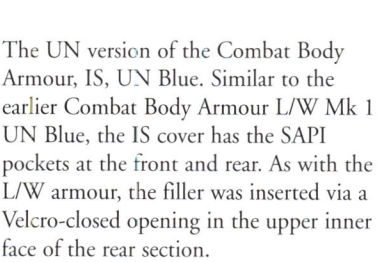

The UN version of the Combat Body Armour, IS, UN Blue. Similar to the earlier Combat Body Armour L/W Mk 1 UN Blue, the IS cover has the SAPI pockets at the front and rear. As with the L/W armour, the filler was inserted via a Velcro-closed opening in the upper inner face of the rear section.

Combat Body Armour, IS, Temperate DPM, better known as the Enhanced Combat Body Armour; the IS in the designation is for Internal Security. This was a modification of the Combat Body Armour L/W Mk 1 with a large SAPI plate pocket added at the front and rear of the cover. This 1992 modification allowed the fitting of ceramic plates to protect the vital heart area at the front chest and the wearer's back. The additional weight of the SAPI plate on the front of the vest required a snap fastener at the top of the Velcro closure to prevent it being pulled open.

Great Britain

Combat Body Armour, IS, Desert DPM. This is a post-1995 vest with an added rank strap at the front. Prior to 1995, rank had been worn on the sleeve for NCOs or at the shoulders for officers (and Royal Navy and RAF ranks). The Soldier 95 uniform placed the rank on a strap positioned centrally on shirt fronts and combat jackets. This vest reflects the change of policy in the display of rank badges.

A Fusilier from the Second Fusiliers (2nd Battalion, Royal Regiment of Fusiliers) watches over the Shatt Al Arab waterway from a Sangar, his 7.62mm GPMG at the ready. Photographed in Iraq in 2005, he wears the Combat Body Armour, IS, Desert DPM, this view clearly showing the rear SAPI plate pocket and the absence of the PLCE strap, which was frequently cut away. (Martin J. Brayley)

A Royal Navy Leading Aircrewman from an 845 Naval Air Squadron Sea King helicopter, wears the Combat Body Armour, IS, Desert DPM during operations in southern Iraq in 2005 (Martin J. Brayley)

Combat Body Armour, IS, Temperate DPM. This is the post-1995 cover with fitted rank strap (badged to a Colour or Staff Sergeant). It is identical to the Cover, Combat Body Armour, IS, Desert DPM shown previously. At right is the rear view of the Combat Body Armour, IS, Temperate DPM, showing the rear SAPI plate pocket and PLCE strap. The term 'temperate' in the designation is used to differentiate between the standard woodland DPM and desert DDPM.

Great Britain

Side fastening and adjustment of the Combat Body Armour, IS, Temperate DPM. The webbing strap arrangement is the same on all patterns of CBA and ECBA armour. This is the right side of the armour and shows the two adjustable webbing straps that are pulled to the front (right of image) and secured with Velcro. The upper strap on each side has an elastic section to aid in comfort and body movement.

Combat Body Armour, IS, Desert DPM. This is the second pattern of ECBA, with a modified cover. It has reinforced corners to the SAPI pockets, rank tab to the front, and an improved opening for the fitting of the filler. The narrow Velcro opening of earlier patterns has been replaced by a full circumference zip opening that runs around the neck opening. The zip made the previously tedious and difficult task of inserting the filler somewhat easier. Despite the modifications, the cover retains the same designation as the earlier pattern, but has a new NATO stock number (NSN). The tape across the SAPI pocket is standard for operationally-issued armour vests and shows the wearer's 'zap' number, BA7161, and blood group, 0 positive. At right is the rear of the second pattern of ECBA Combat Body Armour, IS, Desert DPM. This was fitted with a removable PLCE belt strap attached using a press snap, and usually discarded. Note that the two lower corners of the SAPI plate pocket have a webbing reinforcement.

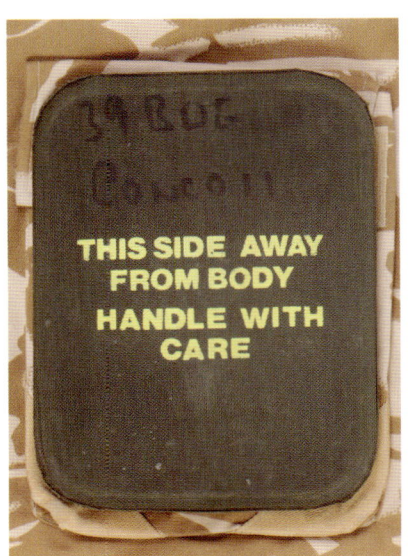

FAR LEFT: Protective Plate, Contoured, Armour, Body Mk 2. This plate is similar to the INIBA's original Protective Plate, Armour, Body, Mk 2, but differs in having rounded corners. Like the INIBA plate illustrated previously, this plate was made by Galt Glass Laminates.

LEFT: Second-pattern Combat Body Armour, IS, Desert DPM, in use with a member of 3 Para, 16 Air Assault Brigade, serving in Iraq.

Great Britain

A Royal Marine on field exercises wearing the Combat Body Armour IS with temperate DPM cover matching the camouflage of his uniform and equipment. (US DoD)

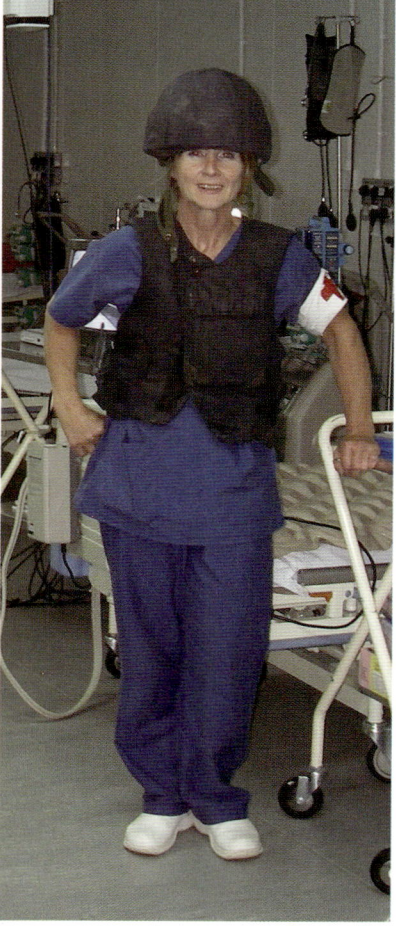

Body Armour, CS being worn by a civilian nurse serving in Afghanistan during 2009. (Surg. Lt Cdr B Tamayo, RN)

The temperate DPM version of the Combat Body Armour, IS, DPM, with second-pattern zip-closure cover. Made to a special contract, this oversize vest does not have the elastic sections on the upper adjustment straps and the rank strap is fastened using Velcro rather than the usual button. It is also without the lower front grab strap found on combat body armour.

Body Armour, CS, with a second-pattern cover in civilian-services non-combatant dark blue. The cover has the web reinforcements at the lower corners of the SAPI plate pocket. The civilian-services blue armour was worn by non-combatant government agency employees such as Ministry of Defence and Overseas Development Agency civilians. (Paul Kearslake)

Body Armour, IS, Navy Blue. Otherwise similar to the Body Armour, CS, the Body Armour, IS, Navy Blue has a rank tab and lower drag strap.

Great Britain

Although EOD armour is outside of the scope of this work, the prototype Body Armour, Light Weight, Combat, EOD Suit used the standard ECBA armour as a base garment, with added shoulder guards that fitted at each side of the vest using Velcro and five press fasteners. The rank strap is fitted centrally and the filler is fitted via a zipper opening. The armour underwent trials in 2000, but was not adopted in this form.

Rear view of the Body Armour, Light Weight, Combat, EOD Suit with the right side shoulder guard removed to show the inner face and the fitting points, Velcro and five press fasteners. The short zip section allowed removal of the Kevlar filler for laundering. The cover has a zip at the inner shoulder for the fitting of the main filler. This vest was made by the Defence Clothing and Textiles Agency (DCTA), in April 2000.

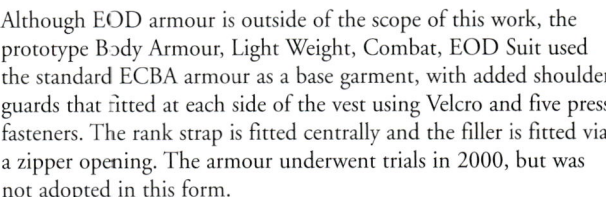

Undergarment, Body Armour. This short-sleeved polo-style shirt has a short front zip allowing it to be pulled on over the head. As the designation suggests, it is worn under the CBA and ECBA body armour. It is manufactured from 'Coolmax' fabric using specially engineered polyester fibres, designed to wick moisture away from the skin. This aids in keeping the skin surface dryer and cooler by drawing moisture away from the body and allowing it to evaporate more easily, keeping the wearer more comfortable. An issue garment, this item has been personalized, at unit level, by the addition of an embroidered unit insignia, that of the Royal Irish Regiment engaged on Operation *Telic* 6 in Iraq.

A trials pattern of DPM camouflage ballistic vest with integral groin plate, believed to date to the 1990s. Many variants of body armour are produced commercially and for military trials or testing. Only a few are accepted for issue or enter mass production. This trials pattern armour, released from Bicester army stores depot, did not enter British military service. The label states that the vest is a prototype and that it is not recommended for operational use.

Great Britain

Detail of the aperture for the fitting of the ballistic filler in the two variants of Combat Body Armour, IS, Desert DPM. Above is the first pattern of cover with the fitting aperture in the upper rear of the vest. This narrow aperture has a Velcro closure and required some persistence if the filler was to be inserted correctly and wrinkle free. The second pattern of IS cover (below) has a full-length zipper closure that runs the circumference of the neck and allows relatively easy fitting of the filler.

Bristol-type DDPM armoured vest issued to the SAS during Operation *Granby*, the 1991 Gulf War. Fitted with the standard Bristol-pattern body armour filler it has large side-opening SAPI pockets at both front and rear. An oblong pocket is fitted vertically over the rear SAPI pocket. The left and right shoulders have integral rifle butt stops fitted at the outer edges and there is a Velcro strip at the lower front edge for the fitting of a groin protector. At left is the front aspect and at right the rear of the vest.

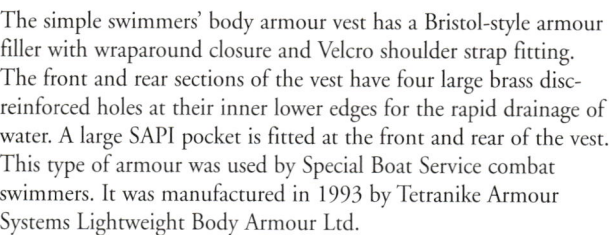

The simple swimmers' body armour vest has a Bristol-style armour filler with wraparound closure and Velcro shoulder strap fitting. The front and rear sections of the vest have four large brass disc-reinforced holes at their inner lower edges for the rapid drainage of water. A large SAPI pocket is fitted at the front and rear of the vest. This type of armour was used by Special Boat Service combat swimmers. It was manufactured in 1993 by Tetranike Armour Systems Lightweight Body Armour Ltd.

The Body Armour RN was similar to the CBA, but with a different pocket arrangement. The Royal Navy's armour cover had a clear plastic window pocket on the upper left chest. Below this was a pen pocket with four divides. The filler was the standard L/W Mk 1, fitted via a Velcro-closed aperture in the upper rear of the vest. Side adjustment was the typical four-strap arrangement, two to each waist, with the upper straps having an elastic section at the rear.

Great Britain

Civilian advisors liaise with a sergeant from the Staffordshire Regiment, in Basrah during 2005. The sergeant wears the ECBA, Combat Body Armour IS, the two civilian advisors wear commercial armour fitted with large SAPI plates. The armour is of unknown origin, but typical of the many variations encountered among such operatives who choose their own equipment, including body armour and weapons. (Martin J. Brayley)

Commercial body armour and helmet worn by the author while working in Iraq during 2005. It has SAPI plates in large front and rear pockets and removable throat protection that is Velcro attached. The tab at the lower front is for the drop-down groin protection panel stored inside the front of the cover. The armour vest is in the standard non-combatant royal blue, as worn by all civilian advisors and press in war zones.

The flame retardant DPM camouflage Beaufort aircrew vest, 'Armour Capable Life Preserver Mk 60'. Designed for non fast jet fixed- and rotary-wing aircrew, this combined equipment carrier, life preserver and body armour vest came in two standard patterns, Mk 60 and Mk 61. Both provided survival and evasion equipment stowage, and ballistic protection. The Mk 60 was designed for rear compartment aircrew (such as helicopter winchmen) who required an additional rear armour pocket and safety strop attachment. The 'Mk 61' was for 'front crew' (such as pilots); it was not fitted with a safety strop and was only provided with a front armour pocket (dorsal protection normally being provided by aircrew seating). A combination of soft and ceramic armour provided combined protection from 7.62mm armour piercing rounds. The separate detachable life preserver was fitted at the neck and shoulder, but is not fitted in this image. At right is the rear view of the Armour Capable Life Preserver Mk 60, showing the pocket for the ceramic ballistic plate that provides protection from 7.62mm AP rounds. This example has been modified to 'Mk 62' standard by the MoD (Beaufort does not actually manufacture a Mk 62 variant, this being solely a service-modified Mk 60).

Great Britain

Waistcoat, AFV Crewman

The fire retardant 'Waistcoat, AFV Crewman' combined load bearing equipment, water carriage and body armour in a single vest. Ballistic protection came from the standard 'Filler, Combat Body Armour L/W Mk 1' as used with CBA. The individual pouches and compartments were all fitted at the front of the vest, on the right and left sides and each covered by a large zip-closed fabric flap. The flap prevented snagging of the pouches inside an AFV and kept them concealed until the contents were required for use, generally when the user was dismounted from the vehicle and operating in the ground role, such as if the AFV had been disabled. When dismounted, the flaps could be unzipped and rolled at each side of the vest, being held in place by Velcro straps.

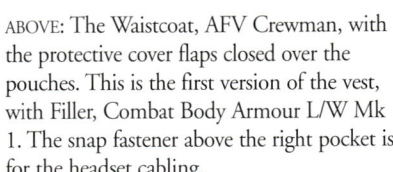

ABOVE: The Waistcoat, AFV Crewman, with the protective cover flaps closed over the pouches. This is the first version of the vest, with Filler, Combat Body Armour L/W Mk 1. The snap fastener above the right pocket is for the headset cabling.

LEFT: The second pattern of the Waistcoat, AFV Crewman with the protective cover flaps opened showing the internal pockets and pouches. As viewed, at left are two utility pouches, top right is the small multi-tool (Leatherman) pouch, alongside the FFD pocket, which had an integral cord-attached ID holder. Mounted below this on the large Velcro patch is a double magazine pocket for two single SA80 magazines. Behind the pouches on both sides is a large internal pocket, that on the right for maps or miscellaneous items and that on the left holding a 2-litre Camelbak. Positioned centrally on the front is a rank strap, visible with the cover flaps closed or open. This second pattern of vest uses the Filler, Combat Body Armour, IS and has ECBA plate pockets at the front and rear. The first and second patterns are otherwise identical. At right is the rear of the second-pattern Waistcoat, AFV Crewman with visible stitch marks showing the positioning of the internal pocket for SAPI plate. Also shown are the side adjustment straps and the Velcro straps that secure the cover flaps when they are folded back. Across the shoulders is a full-width grab strap. This could be used to assist in extricating a wounded or incapacitated crewman from an AFV.

ABOVE: The lower front left of the Waistcoat, AFV Crewman (as worn) had a large Velcro section with nine press fasteners. This allowed the attachment of one of two interchangeable pads, either a two-pocket SA80 magazine carrier or a pistol holster. Shown here are the pistol holster, with 9mm Browning, and two pistol magazine pockets; reverse of the SA80 magazine pad, the holster reverse was identical; and the two-pocket SA80 magazine pad. (John Bodsworth)

Enhanced Personnel Protection Equipment 'Kestrel'
The pace of operations in Iraq and Afghanistan required many vehicle-borne operations. As protection from RPG fire and ambushes, vehicles required a 'top cover' sentry to provide the 'eyes and ears'. Top cover sentries were particularly vulnerable, especially to IEDs and required more protection than was offered by the standard ECBA. The issue of 'Merlin' armour to provide this protection was an interim measure, and somewhat short lived. Essentially Merlin was similar to ECBA with a high, protective collar. It was rapidly replaced by the 'Improved Ballistic Protection Ensemble' (IBPE) (sometimes referred to as the 'Enhanced Personnel Protection Equipment' (EPPE)), but better known as 'Kestrel'.

Introduced in 2006, a total of 4,600 sets of Kestrel body armour had been procured and delivered to operational theatres by January 2007. Of these 3,500 sets were sent to Iraq and 1,100 were sent to Afghanistan. The Kestrel system utilized technology derived from the Mk V EOD suit (that used flexible plate armour), with its lightweight and flexible articulated aramid armour. The first pattern of Kestrel armour was similar to the short-lived Merlin, being an oversize vest with added collar and short sleeves. The high collar gave rise to the armour being nicknamed the 'Elvis outfit' by those using it. The armour filler was a single piece unit that provided protection to the torso, neck and upper arms. It was supplemented by standard SAPI plates front and rear, as used with the ECBA and a removable suede leather patch was fitted to the right shoulder to assist in supporting the rifle butt. However, users reported that wearing the bulky Kestrel armour made it difficult to use any weapon sights. A major re-design of British body armour then saw the introduction of Osprey and the second pattern of Kestrel, which incorporated all of the design features of Osprey in the basic vest. The second-pattern Kestrel was fitted with horizontal PALS loops, for the attachment of equipment, and a large pocket at the front and rear for carriage of the large Osprey SAPI plate. Smaller pockets within the large ones allowed the ECBA's SAPI plates to be used as a lighter alternative to the heavyweight Osprey SAPI.

Kestrel has been superseded by Osprey, since the additional neck ('Full Collar, Osprey DPM Desert') and shoulder components ('Brassard & Shoulder Pad, Osprey, DPM Desert') of the Osprey armour offered similar protection and coverage to that provided by Kestrel, but were considerably less restrictive in wear. Kestrel was issued to top-cover sentries, vehicle drivers and commanders, but was not considered suitable for use by dismounted troops, who were issued the ECBA and Osprey armour.

Body Armour, Improved Ballistic Protection Ensemble best known as Kestrel armour. This shows the first pattern of cover, designed specifically for top-cover sentries who were vulnerable to both IEDs and sniper fire in their exposed positions in the upper hull of vehicles. At left is the front of the armour and at right is the rear. The cover has pockets front and rear for the standard ECBA SAPI plates and has a removable sued leather section at the right shoulder to assist in weapon positioning. Users of the Kestrel armour reported great difficulty in sighting the SA80 rifle when wearing it. The side adjustment straps are actually integral with the filler and are threaded through the cover and fitted to the Velcro side sections. (John Bodsworth)

Great Britain

Interior view of the Kestrel armour showing the front two pockets for ice packs. Ice packs could be inserted into three pockets, one at the rear and one each side at the front, to assist in cooling the wearer in excessive heat, particularly the high temperatures associated with armoured vehicles operating in arid regions such as Afghanistan and Iraq. Two sets of ice packs and an insulated carrier were a part of each issued set.

The second pattern of Kestrel armour used the original pattern as a base, but added the plate carrier pockets and PALS loops designed for the Osprey armour. At left is the front of the armour. The design retained the front opening, the front plate pocket overlapping the opening and the front of the chest. At right is a rear view showing the four Fastex clips used for attaching the issue Camelbak water carrier. Other details are as for the Osprey armour. (John Bodsworth)

Osprey body armour

The urgent need for an improved armour that would reduce casualties in Iraq and Afghanistan brought about the introduction of Osprey 'Improved Performance Body Armour'. Both Osprey and Kestrel were procured under the Urgent Operational Requirement process in 2005 and rapidly brought into service.

The development of the 'Body Armour, Osprey, DPM Desert' cost in the region of £16 million. Some 15,500 sets of the new armour had been sent to Iraq and Afghanistan by December 2006, with the delivery of an additional 5,000 sets, which were for pre-deployment training and maintenance stocks, to have been completed by January 2007. This gave a total contracted order quantity of 20,550 sets of Osprey armour as of January 2007. When first issued the armour received mixed feedback from troops in theatre. Many thought it was a great improvement on the ECBA and would save many lives, but others felt it was too heavy and cumbersome, and would reduce the fighting performance of troops using it. The correct balance between the risk to an individual and the effect upon capability when providing adequate protection against various levels of threat, is difficult to achieve to the satisfaction of all equipment users. The maximum marching load for a fit soldier is considered to be 45 per cent of his body weight. The average British soldier weighs 156lb (71kg) giving a marching load of 71lb (32kg). On operations in Afghanistan, infantrymen routinely carried loads of between 176 and 220lb (80 and 100kg), and often considerably more; back pain is a health issue prevalent among troops.

The Body Armour, Osprey, DPM Desert consisted of a front and rear panel joined at the shoulder and waist by Velcro, with additional security straps and snap fasteners at the shoulder to prevent the load-bearing shoulder Velcro becoming unfastened. A large zip-closed pocket was fitted at the front and rear of the vest. The large ceramic Osprey SAPI plates ('Protective Plate, Osprey, Front' and 'Protective Plate, Osprey, Rear') fitted into these pockets. Within each of the large pockets was a smaller open-top pocket; situated over the heart area, these smaller pockets were able to accommodate the lighter ceramic plates used with the ECBA armour. The large Osprey SAPI was capable of resisting three 7.62mm hits within a 0.6in (15mm) radius.

Load-carrying PALS loops were fitted on the front and sides of the vest to enable carriage of ammunition and other essential pouches. The early issue pouches had short attachment straps. With the PALS system it is essential that the weight of any pouch is distributed evenly over as many loop sections as possible, to prevent undue strain on individual loops. The short straps and weight of the ammunition pouches with fully loaded magazines led to many PALS loops tearing free, before the problem was rectified by producing pouches with full-length rear straps. The snap fasteners used on the Body Armour, Osprey, DPM Desert were omnidirectional, breaking open when sufficient force was applied in any direction. The exceptions were the two snaps, fitted either side of the rear shoulder, used to position the shoulder pad. These were unidirectional, since the movement of the arm would otherwise have led to frequent unfastening of the snaps. Four small Fastex clips

The ECBA had been deemed inadequate for the close-quarter fighting and roadside IEDs typical of the conflicts in Iraq and Afghanistan. The Body Armour, Osprey, DPM Desert was developed specifically to meet the needs of troops in these theatres, by the Defence Clothing Integrated Project Team with input from body armour and equipment manufacturers, as well as troops on the ground. Osprey was originally procured in 2005, with first issues to troops being undertaken in 2006. The main body had an aramid filler, while the pockets at the front and rear of the vest fitted a large Osprey ceramic plate. Smaller pockets within the larger ones allowed the use of the ECBA plate as a lighter alternative, although the larger Osprey plates were standard. Fastex clips at the lower left edge are for the attachment of the respirator haversack or similar items.

The Body Armour, Osprey, DPM Desert consists of a front (shown at right) and rear section (shown at left). The two sections are connected at the shoulder and at each side of the waist. As shown here, the sections are joined only at the right side (as worn). Issued in a range of sizes, Osprey's Velcro side closures allow a small degree of individual size adjustment.

Body Armour, Osprey, DPM Desert fitted with the Half Collar, Osprey DPM Desert that provided protection to the neck area, and the Brassard & Shoulder Pad, Osprey, DPM Desert that covered the vulnerable deltoid and axillary area (note the infra-red beacon pocket on the right and Union flag on the left brassard).

Great Britain

Detail of the left shoulder of the full Osprey ensemble, showing the first pattern Brassard & Shoulder Pad, Osprey, DPM Desert. This is a two-part assembly of the brassard (with Union flag) and the shoulder pad that protected the rear of the shoulder, an area exposed by forward movement of the arms, such as when shouldering a rifle.

Filler, Osprey Mk I. At left is the rear filler and at right the front filler, the two sections being joined at the shoulders using Velcro. (Rifles Museum)

A 3-litre second pattern Camelbak fitted to the rear of an Osprey Mk I vest. The first pattern of Camelbak used by British forces could only be carried using the integral shoulder harness. Obtained from US sources, it was issued in the US tricolour DCU camouflage. The Mk III Camelbak has a larger filler cap covered by a fabric flap. The larger filler cap easily allows ice to be placed into the bladder to keep the contents cool.

were positioned on the rear panel of the vest, two at the top edge and two at the lower edge. These clips allowed the standard Bergen pouches or a Camelbak water carrier to be attached. Two larger clips at the left waist fitted the respirator haversack. A rank strap was positioned at the lower left front of the vest.

Additional protection was afforded by two different sizes of ballistic collar that could be fitted at the neck opening of the Osprey vest. The 'Full Collar, Osprey' was for use by top-cover sentries, vehicle drivers and commanders and the 'Half Collar, Osprey' was for use by dismounted troops. Each collar consisted of two halves, left and right sections, which joined at the rear to provide all-round protection. They were provided with a short Velcro strap at the front that allowed the collar to be secured upright or dropped down against the shoulder when unfastened. The axillary region was given additional protection by the 'Cover Brassard & Shoulder Pad, Osprey' that could be fitted as required. Both the collar and brassard were generally only issued to personnel on static or exposed duties and were not usually to be seen in use with the already heavily burdened infantry.

The range of sizes available for Osprey armour had been increased from the basic six sizes of the older CBA and ECBA to a new range of eight sizes: 170/100, 170/112, 180/104, 180/116, 190/108, 190/120, 200/116, 200/124. As well as these regular sizes, a special measure was also available to specific order. By comparison, the issue desert shirt was available in 21 different sizes.

The Defence Clothing Integrated Project Team (DCIPT) took a great interest in the suitability of Osprey for combat use. Team members toured operational units gaining first hand accounts of the issues affecting Osprey armour from the troops using it. Additionally, wherever possible, armour struck by projectiles or otherwise damaged was recovered and returned to the Porton Down research establishment for assessment. The findings of the DCIPT

Body Armour, Osprey, DPM Desert Mk II. Similar to the first pattern, Mk II modifications included new fittings for the collar and brassard sections and a cummerbund waist strap that improved fit and comfort. The Mk II version of Osprey first saw issue in 2007. At the right shoulder of the armour is a Fastex clip for the attachment of the SA80 butt strap, a short section of webbing that supports the weapon from the shoulder and used in lieu of the standard sling.

The Body Armour, Osprey, DPM Desert Mk II was similar to the earlier Body Armour, Osprey, DPM Desert and also consisted of a front (at right) and rear (at left) section, connected at the shoulder and the waist. Here the sections are joined at the right side and open at the left. The main difference between the original vest and the Mk II was the cummerbund, fitted on the inside of the lower rear and fastening at the wearer's front (inset below). The snap fasteners on the Mk II were all of the unidirectional pattern that were less likely to unfasten, and additional snap fasteners were fitted centrally on the shoulder section for improved retention of the Mk II brassard.

research led to a number of modifications to the Osprey system and the introduction of the 'Body Armour, Osprey, DPM Desert, Mk II' along with the 'Cover Brassard & Shoulder Pad, Osprey, Mk II'; 'Full Collar, Osprey, Mk II'; and the 'Half Collar, Osprey, Mk II'. Manufacture of the Osprey Mk II was underway by the end of 2006 and it was introduced into operational service during 2007. It included several changes that had been suggested by users in theatre in Iraq and Afghanistan. The modifications included a Velcro-fastened waist strap (cummerbund), slightly modified 'Cover Brassard & Shoulder Pad, Full Collar, Osprey' and the Half Collar, Osprey and their fitting arrangement, and the positioning of a short strap and Fastex clip, at the right shoulder, for the attachment of a short butt-strap sling allowing the SA80 rifle to be supported from the vest. The changes to the collars were hardly noticeable. The original collar opening that allowed insertion of the ballistic filler was on the inner face, and set

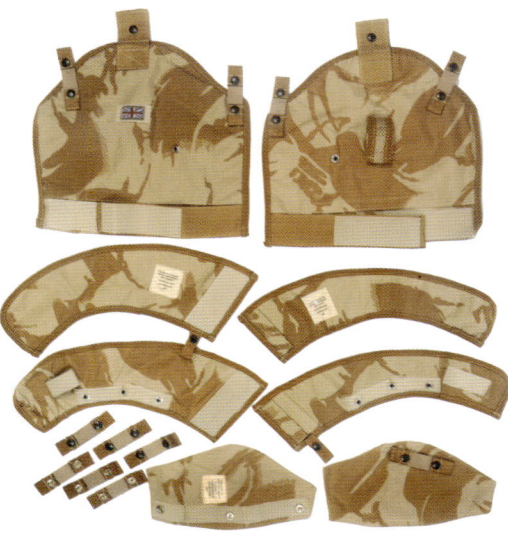

Body Armour, Osprey, DPM Desert Mk II additional components. Top to bottom: Brassard, Osprey Mk II; at left Full Collar, Osprey, MK II; at right, Half Collar, Osprey, MK II; and the Shoulder Pad, Osprey Mk II. Also shown are the elastic snaps for fitting the brassard and shoulder pads to the armour. The replaceable elastic straps have a snap fastener at each end; a spare set is included with each armour ensemble.

Rear of the Osprey Mk II cover, with the SAPI plate compartment unzipped to show the additional small pocket with ECBA plate inserted. The option of using the small ECBA or large Osprey SAPI plates enhances the flexibility of the vest, the large and somewhat heavy plates can be used in static positions or where maximum protection is required, and the smaller plates can be fitted when weight or mobility are an issue. The Fastex clips at the upper and lower edges of the rear of the vest are for the attachment of the Camelbak hydration system or the Bergen side pouches.

Great Britain

A lance corporal of the 2nd Battalion, Royal Anglian Regiment, photographed in Basra, in October 2008, wearing the Osprey Mk II vest with Half Collar. Numerous pouches are attached directly to the front of the vest using the PALS loops, it being standard practice to fit pouches directly to the vest in preference to using the DDPM Vest, Tactical, Load Carrying. The SA80 bayonet has no provision for carriage on the Osprey vest so when carried it is usually inserted directly into the PALS loops without the use of a scabbard, as shown here. This soldier also wears the Under Body Armour Combat Shirt. (US DoD)

Troops from 4th Battalion Yorkshire Regiment conduct vehicle-mounted security patrols in Kabul. The soldiers wear the Osprey Mk II vest with full collar and shoulder brassard protection fitted (without the rear pad). The brassard is of the second pattern, with replaceable elastic fitting straps having press fasteners at both ends. The kneeling soldier has the Camelbak hydration system fitted at the rear of his vest. (ISAF)

slightly inward from the broad end where the two sections joined. On the Mk II, the opening was moved to the end of the collar, on the outer face of the right section and on the inner face of the left section. Additionally, all the fastening snaps were of the unidirectional pattern. The brassard and pad had elastic straps with press fasteners at one end that joined the two items and attached them to the Osprey vest. The elastic tended to perish in high temperatures, thus on the modified Mk II version of the brassard and pad, new elastic straps were introduced, having press fasteners at both ends and thus allowing for easy replacement of the straps if the elastic failed. Additionally, the shoulder pad was fitted using three snaps rather than the previous two.

The apparent increase in incidences of bullet strikes upon the upper arm and axillary region of soldiers injured in Iraq indicated that by 2007, insurgent forces had become more than aware of the excellent ballistic properties of the Osprey armour and the vulnerability of wearers to lateral strikes in the axillary region. However, by this time the initial reluctance of some troops to accept the Osprey armour had changed to one of general acceptance and faith in its protective abilities. This confidence had been brought about by the increasing number of troops who, struck in the thorax by high-velocity rifle rounds or fragmentation, were able to walk away with minor or no injuries, from what would previously have been a non-survivable encounter.

By 2009, Osprey was standard issue for all units in Iraq. ECBA was usually issued in the UK for units proceeding to theatre and then exchanged for Osprey upon arrival. Although Osprey was standard for all troops, the collar and brassards were only issued to persons requiring them for operational or other reasons.

In January 2009, Quentin Davies, the Parliamentary Under-Secretary, announced that the MoD had recently introduced further modifications to the Osprey armour and that more changes were planned. The enhancements had improved the fit and increased the manoeuvrability of wearers, and the new Mk III pattern would be in theatre by the summer of 2009. The 'Osprey Mk III' incorporated a number of refinements over the preceding patterns. The SAPI pocket had no zip, but now had a Velcro fastened flap on the lower edge of the pocket. This made for much quicker and easier removal of the plate. Axillary protection was improved and small pockets were incorporated for ESBI plates. Adjustable quick release straps were fitted at each waist and a rubber anti-slip pad was fitted to the right shoulder to improve butt retention when aiming. A butt stop pad could also be fitted at the outer edge of either shoulder, using a Velcro strip fitted to the inner edge of the arm opening. The fittings for the collar and brassard were

Body Armour, Osprey, Mk III Modified Ensemble. This vest is similar to the Body Armour, Osprey, Mk III but has been modified to include additional snaps at the bottom edge of the SAPI pocket flaps and two side tensioning/adjustment straps at each side.

retained. The 'Body Armour, Osprey, Mk III' and 'Body Armour, Osprey, Mk III Modified Ensemble' differ in detail, the Mk III Modified Ensemble includes additional snaps at the bottom edge of the SAPI pocket, and side tensioning straps, neither of which were used on the standard Mk III.

Osprey has been produced in quantity in DDPM. It has also been produced in limited numbers in civilian blue, police black (the blue civilian version of the armour cover and that issued to MoD police do not have the PALS loop system of the military vests) and standard temperate DPM. The 'Body Armour, Osprey, Hybrid Mk III' was made in the four-colour Hybrid intermediate DPM designed for Afghanistan, with trials patterns also being made in a three- and four-colour DDPM. The next generation of Osprey body armour to be issued to British troops is the 'Body Armour, Osprey, Mk IV'. It is better fitting, has improved rubber pads on both shoulders, designed to improve weapon retention when on aim and to prevent equipment from slipping off the user's shoulders.

The upgraded SAPI plate is carried in a pocket inside the vest (as with the Osprey assault vest), making it less bulky and improving movement. It was to be issued to troops of 16 Air Assault Brigade, who were due to deploy to Afghanistan in October 2010. A total of twenty-three pouches are available for the new vest, issued as follows: three SA80 single-magazine pouches, four SA80 double-magazine pouches, three single SA80 magazine pouches with elastic pull-cord, two smoke grenade pouches, two anti-personnel grenade pouches, one sharpshooter magazine pouch, one utility pouch, one water bottle pouch, one light machine-gun magazine pouch (100 rounds), one first aid kit pouch, one 9mm pistol magazine pouch, underslung grenade-launcher ammunition pouch (eight round) and commander's pouch.

Body Armour, Osprey, Hybrid Mk III. This was a limited procurement item, just 1,200 of these vests being procured during 2008, in the four-colour hybrid DPM intermediate camouflage, for field trials. It would appear that although some were tested by Army units, the majority ended up with the Royal Navy and Royal Marines. However, the introduction of the new Multi Terrain Pattern camouflage in 2010 soon saw troops in Afghanistan wearing the MTP with Hybrid camouflage Osprey armour. The vest was similar to the Mk II, but the most noticeable features were the synthetic rubber (Hypalon) butt stop, fitted at the right shoulder, and the new bottom opening to the SAPI plate pockets. (Loz Moynihan, RM)

Great Britain

Four-colour Body Armour, Osprey, Hybrid Mk III worn by Royal Marines of the Fleet protection Group undertaking maritime interdiction operations in the Gulf. (Loz Moynihan, RM)

PECOC Body Armour, Osprey, DPM Desert Mk III Ensemble. This Mk III armour was made by CQC in 2008 in a tri-colour DDPM camouflage used for camouflage trials. It has no NSN, but is annotated NSN: N.I.V. (Not In Vocab), a label usually applied to limited production trials items that have not been given standard NSNs. A variant tricolour Mk III-type DDPM vest with ambidextrous shoulder patches was also produced for PECOC trials.

The standard DDPM Body Armour, Osprey, Mk III Modified Ensemble in use with members of Task Force Helmand, Marjah, Afghanistan, February 2010. This image clearly shows the rear of the vest, with large SAPI pocket and grab handle at the top edge. The waist fastening flaps are at the end of their useable adjustment range and the side tensioning straps have also been left unfastened on this example, since it is undoubtedly too large for the user. Incorrect sizing of body armour is a frequently reported problem. (US Marine Corps)

Great Britain

Osprey Assault Armour

In June 2009 it was announced that a new pattern of armour, the 'Osprey Assault Armour' was to be issued to British troops, along with a new Mk 7 helmet, with some 10,000 sets being placed under contract at a cost of around £16 million. The first 5,000 would be in theatre before the end of 2009 and the second batch of 5,000 during early 2010. The new Osprey Assault Armour was quite different than the standard Osprey system, which it was to be used alongside. It retained the ballistic performance while being closer fitting, was less bulky and provided less hindrance to movement. The outer covers were made by Solo International Ltd, based in Hereford. Initial batches were made in desert tan and later in two-colour DDPM, but in early 2010 the colour was changed to the newly approved 'Multi Terrain Pattern' (MTP) camouflage for all future orders. A new SAPI plate was introduced with the Osprey Assault Armour. Being thinner, it was also lighter and thus offered improved freedom of movement. Unfortunately, problems with the lightweight SAPI were soon reported, with large numbers failing testing. While no defective SAPI were sent to theatre, the test failures did result in a shortage of plates being available to issue with the vests. In Afghanistan, troops issued the Osprey Assault Armour vests resorted to fitting the standard Osprey SAPI plate into the armour, but this could not be fitted without first removing the protective rubber edge. The armour was destined for use by infantry, engineers and medical staff, with others retaining the standard Osprey armour. The Osprey Assault Armour was first fielded in Afghanistan in the late autumn of 2009.

Manufacturer's marketing picture of the Body Armour, Osprey Assault, Mk II. This shows the basic armour, void of pouches, clearly illustrating the front fastening and PALS loops system. The new armour has the ambidextrous rifle shoulder patches absent from the standard Osprey vest, which was designed for right-handed use (the SA80 rifle's bullpup design requiring right-handed use). The 'D' rings below the patches allow for the attachment of the SA80 butt strap. (Solo International)

A mix of armour types is shown in this image taken in Afghanistan, during February 2010. At left is the Body Armour, Osprey Assault worn by a Lieutenant Colonel of the Grenadier Guards, at centre is the Body Armour, Osprey, Mk III, and at right the USMC scaleable plate carrier. (US Marine Corps)

Great Britain

PECOC trials

A variety of experimental conceptual clothing items, helmets, body armour and load-bearing equipment were developed under the Army's Personal Equipment Common Operational Clothing (PECOC) project launched in 2004 and concluded in 2010. The merits of the equipment and camouflage were tested between 2007 and 2009 in the UK, Cyprus, Kenya, and Afghanistan. The Hybrid, intermediate four-colour DPM came close to being adopted, along with the three-colour DDPM, indeed many had believed that this was a *fait accompli*, but the Hybrid camouflage was ousted by the last minute adoption of Crye's Multi Terrain Pattern (MTP) camouflage. MTP uniforms were in use in Afghanistan by the late summer of 2010. A selection of PECOC trials-pattern armour and load-carrying vests, designed for wear over armour, are illustrated.

RIGHT: Variant concept demonstrator PECOC body armour Tabard, better known as a plate carrier. Manufactured in temperate DPM camouflage, the front and rear panels have a large top opening for the SAPI plate. A small 16 × 16cm (6.3 × 6.3in) pocket at either waist holds ESBI. The front section has a rank strap and a zip-opening access to an internal pocket. The narrow shoulder straps each have a small and inadequate pad to help distribute the weight of the SAPI plates. PALS loops are fitted front and rear.

LEFT: Variant of the DPM Tabard, manufactured in the trials-pattern tricolour DDPM camouflage. Identical to the preceding DPM pattern tabard, this example is not fitted with the side-mounted ESBI pockets.

RIGHT: Variant concept demonstrator PECOC body armour Tabard plate carrier. This test garment was produced in temperate DPM camouflage. It is a simple carrier that holds two large SAPI plates, with no axillary protection. It is fitted with PALS loops front and rear.

Great Britain

Variant of the preceding temperate DPM Tabard plate carrier. This Tabard was produced in the four-colour Hybrid DPM intermediate camouflage, but is otherwise identical to the temperate DPM variant.

Variant concept demonstrator PECOC body armour Fragmentation Vest, in Hybrid camouflage. The vest has Hypalon patches at each shoulder, extended down at the right side. Ballistic protection consists of filler panels with front, rear and side SAPI plates inserted through external zippered openings.

Variant PECOC body armour. This vest uses the four-colour hybrid DPM intermediate camouflage. The basic label shows the designation Fragmentation Vest, the size 170/104, and a space for name and number. The vest has Hypalon patches at each shoulder, with ballistic protection consisting of filler panels with front and rear SAPI plates. The plates are inserted into internal pockets via an opening at the lower front and rear edges.

PECOC four-colour hybrid DPM intermediate camouflage Tactical Vest and pouches. As with the Osprey Vest, Tactical, Load Carrying and Osprey armours, the pouches could be worn on the Tactical Vest or the Fragmentation Vest. However, many of the low-profile body armour patterns produced for PECOC trials were better suited to having the pouches worn on a tactical vest. The use of a separate vest allows the heavy ammunition and equipment to be easily discarded.

Great Britain

PECOC variant body armour. This vest is quite an elaborate affair compared to many of the PECOC trials patterns, which were often quite simple and of poor quality. It is a waistcoat-type, front-fastening vest with a large SAPI pocket fitted over the front. The SAPI pocket has a fabric hinge at the front right and a side zip at left (as worn) allowing it to be opened to allow access to the full length front zip that closes the vest in wear. The rear SAPI pocket is supplemented by two smaller, side mounted ESBI pockets. The vest has provision for the attachment of shoulder brassards using large Fastex clips (visible at each shoulder) and a neck protector. This example is marked simply 'Fragmentation Vest' and P3T0008.

PECOC Body Armour, Vest, Osprey, DPM Temperate Mk IV Ensemble. This armour bears only a passing resemblance to preceding Osprey patterns. The Mk IV features a front-opening mesh vest, it has provision for soft armour fillers, two front sections and a single rear section (not fitted in this image) and there is no integral provision for SAPI plates. The vest has provision for the attachment of additional shoulder and neck protection. Shoulder sections are secured by snap fasteners, allowing the yoke or Bergen straps to be held securely beneath. Made by CQC in 2008.

Front left and right filler sections for the PECOC Body Armour, Vest, Osprey, DPM Temperate Mk IV Ensemble shown above, manufactured by NP Aerospace. The right panel is marked 'SPACE MODEL ONLY' and 'PECOC CD2'.

Great Britain

DDPM Plate Carrier

In January 2009, the Parliamentary Under-Secretary announced that ballistic plate carriers had been introduced for operations in Afghanistan. The carriers allowed the Osprey SAPI plates to be used independently of the Osprey soft armour and cover. The plate carrier system was for issue to troops requiring extra mobility or operating in confined spaces. Trials were limited and among the units receiving the carriers was 3 Para, which was issued the carriers for trials during late March 2008, while engaged on Operation *Herrick* 8 (*Herrick* being the code name for ongoing operations in Afghanistan). Prior to this issue, members of 3 Para had been buying their own plate carriers, but had been advised that they were not to use them, since their insurance would be void if they wore private-purchase body armour. The new plate carriers were produced by Blackhawk to a commercial design, but using the DDPM camouflage scheme. The Paras found that the carrier was: '…a hell of a lot lighter than the Osprey'. It also allowed good ventilation at the sides, was easily adjusted and one size fitted all users. It used the PALS equipment fitting system, which allowed the use of Osprey or other commercial pouches, and most importantly, it allowed a great degree of freedom of movement and, '…didn't make fire positions as stressful'.

However, while the increased ventilation was welcomed by the troops, the first 'contacts' brought home the shortcomings of the carrier. Shayne Coyne, a section commander with 3 Para in Afghanistan commented:

…it provided limited protection against fragmentation from grenades, mortars and RPGs. Your sides were open, therefore when in contact you had little protection whilst lying prone, easy prey for sharp shooters who knew about its weakness. Overall many preferred the plate carrier, we mostly used it on strike ops and initial insertion ops with our Osprey in our Bergens, which would follow us up after 24 hours. We were given the choice to either wear Osprey or plate carriers, but when the shit hit the fan the blokes with the plate carriers tended to keep that little bit lower and were reluctant to fire back, knowing that their sides were exposed.

The weight distribution of the plate carrier was not ideal and when loaded with a basic eight magazines and two grenades, compensatory weight had to be placed on the rear to prevent the SAPI sitting low and exposing the upper chest. It was also found that the shoulder straps were inadequate and troops stripped the padding from the inside of ammunition tins and taped it to the shoulder straps to prevent them digging in and cutting through the skin.

On the whole the plate carrier was quite well received, but it was felt that it needed some refinement. However, at the end of its *Herrick* 8 tour, 3 Para was advised that the use of plate carriers in theatre was to be discontinued and troops were either to return their carriers to the quartermaster (QM), or keep them if they so wished. Despite the

Typical plate carrier-type armour vest. The plate carriers provide less coverage than standard vests, but allow greatly increased freedom of movement, making them popular with special forces and reconnaissance units. This plate carrier was retailed in the Afghan theatre by Black Ops Corporation of Kandahar. Fitted with Osprey SAPI plates, the vest was used by a member of 'C' Company, Second Battalion, Royal Regiment of Fusiliers (2 RRF) in the Sangin Valley, Afghanistan, during deployment on Operation *Herrick* 6 in March–June 2007. The British owner was attached to the 82nd Airborne Division, US Army.

Black Ops' plate carrier fitted with typical basic operational accessories: A radio pouch, three ammunition pouches (each holding two 30-round 5.56mm magazines) and a medical pouch.

Great Britain

increased manoeuvrability, reduced weight and improved ventilation, the markedly reduced protection offered by the plate carrier, especially to the axillary areas, made it a short-lived item on the British body armour inventory. However, after the British had discarded the plate carrier, US forces undertook extensive evaluation of plate carriers under the PEO Soldier programme and a number of variants were issued in Afghanistan.

At the time of writing (December 2010), current British armour has no provision for any groin or lower back protection, with ballistic cover ending at the waist. It is recognized that groin injuries can be seriously debilitating psychologically, even if rarely posing a risk of fatality. While most nations provide groin protection as standard, many also offer additional lower back protection. The British are notable for their persistence in not providing such protection on body armour.

Blackhawk plate carrier. This DDPM carrier was worn by Shane Coyne of 3 Para, during Operation *Herrick* 8 in the summer of 2008. The shoulder straps were inadequate in supporting the weight of the vest and equipment, and in use were covered in additional padding, taken from ammunition boxes, and masking tape to improve comfort. This pattern was provided to the Paras for field trials, but it was not adopted for widespread issue.

Paratrooper Shane Coyne photographed in Afghanistan during Operation *Herrick* 8. Shane wears a Blackhawk plate carrier fitted with numerous Osprey-pattern pouches. (Shane Coyne)

Great Britain

Under Body Armour Combat Shirt

The 'Under Body Armour Combat Shirt' (UBACS) was not a new concept in under-armour garments; moisture wicking clothing had previously been produced for use with the INIBA and CBA. However, the UBACS was designed specifically for use with the Osprey armour and incorporated a number of developments not previously seen on British issue clothing. The Coolmax body fabric of the shirt readily absorbs sweat, while the arms and shoulders were produced from a hard-wearing, infra-red reflective (IRR) DDPM fabric with integral padding at the elbows and forearms. A large pocket was fitted on each upper arm. The faces of the pockets were covered in Velcro for the fitting of insignia. Special forces (SF) units tested the original trials garments during 2006 and the standardized UBACS entered service in 2007. It was well received by the troops using it and was vastly superior to the outer garments previously issued in hot climates. However, it was only of use in hot, dry, desert environments. In most arid regions the difference between day and night temperatures can be quite marked. For troops operating in mountainous regions the extremes of temperature can be even greater, from the baking heat of the day to the sub-zero nights, with rain and even snow to contend with. In these situations the UBACS was unsuitable. It could not be worn as an outer layer over insulating under layers and was unsuited for wear beneath other garments because of (removable) padding which made it unduly bulky. Equally, the bulk of insulation required in cold weather or environments, often required the Osprey vest to be worn beneath the camouflage smock, making the carriage of equipment on the vest impossible and requiring the use of an outer load-carrying vest to support magazines and essential equipment.

The Under Body Armour Combat Shirt was specifically designed to be worn beneath body armour. Manufactured from Coolmax fabric, it wicks away moisture from the skin surface, aids in keeping the user cool and improves general comfort when wearing body armour. Made in both DDPM and DPM, its fabric is IRR. Large pockets are fitted on each upper arm, with Velcro sections for the fitting of insignia.

UBACS being worn by Surgeon Lt Cdr Brando Tamayo, during service in Afghanistan. The pouches contain medical equipment, with the SA80 rifle being for self, and patient, defence. Dr Tamayo wears the naval ensign insignia on the right sleeve of his UBACS. Of note is the SA80 butt strap fitted to the right shoulder of the Osprey armour. (Surg. Lt Cdr B. Tamayo, RN)

Great Britain

Vest, Tactical, Load Carrying
Designed to be worn with the Osprey armour the 'Vest, Tactical, Load Carrying' was introduced in 2007. It could be worn directly over the Osprey armour, or outermost when the smock or other bulky clothing was worn over the armour. The size adjustment made it easy to wear the vest over the armour alone, or armour and insulating clothing. It was supplied with the following pouches as issued, as standard components: three utility pouches, one small utility pouch, one water bottle pouch, one medical pouch, one knife/torch pouch, two 40mm grenade pouches, two SA80 ammunition pouches, two AP grenade pouches and one helmet bag pouch. All are attached using the PALS strap-and-loop system. The two ammunition pouches supplied with the vest were sufficient to hold only four of the six magazines issued to frontline infantry units. Fastex clips on the rear allowed carriage of the Camelbak reservoir, or rucksack pouches. A number of variants of PALS-system 'Ops Waistcoats' and 'Tactical Vests' in a variety of camouflage patterns (as well as regular yoke- and belt-based webbing sets) were tested during PECOC trials. At the time of writing development into body armour and ancillary items continues apace.

Osprey Mk II body armour vest. Worn over the armour is the Vest, Tactical, Load Carrying designed to be worn with the Osprey vest and introduced in 2007. The load-carrying vest is most often used when cold weather clothing is worn over the Osprey armour, such as in the high mountainous areas of Afghanistan, where temperatures can be quite low. However, it was intended to be the principal method of carrying equipment pouches, fitting them directly to the vest being a secondary alternative, although undoubtedly the most popular method.

Variant concept demonstrator PECOC trials-pattern Ops Waistcoat. This is almost identical to the Vest, Tactical, Load Carrying illustrated previously, but has been produced in tricolour DDPM. It also has a Hypalon rifle patch at the left shoulder. This item is marked 'PECOC PLCE Ops Waistcoat' and dated 2008.

Variant concept demonstrator PECOC trials-pattern Tactical Vest. Similar to the preceding Vest, Tactical, Load Carrying and the PECOC Ops Waistcoat, this trials item was produced in the tricolour DDPM. Both shoulders have Hypalon rifle patches with added outer ridges to provide a better support to the rifle butt.

Great Britain

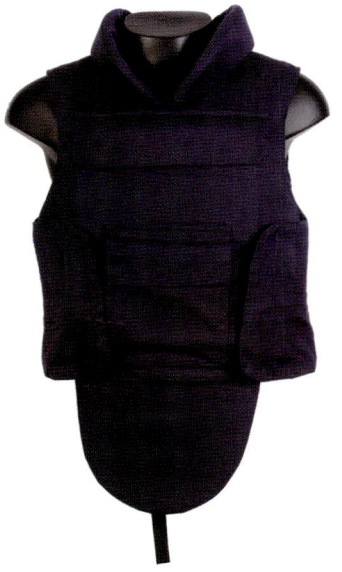

The number of companies that produce body armour has expanded greatly over the last two decades. Operations in Iraq, the Balkans and Afghanistan, to name but a few, have seen the growth of a major worldwide market for personal armour and associated materiel. The variety of commercial armour is far too extensive to cover in this work, but an illustration of a few of the now mainly obsolete patterns marketed by RBR Armour Ltd during the 1990s will give an idea of the types produced. RBR provided armour to a number of users, including the Netherlands armed forces. This vest is the civilian version of the 'RBR 305' and dates to 1992. It has large SAPI plates at the front and rear, as well as a groin protector and a high neck guard. This vest provided superior protection and coverage compared to the armour available to both British and US troops at the time it was produced. However, it weighs 21lb (9.53kg) with the two SAPI plates.

Military DPM camouflage version of the RBR 305 ballistic vest, showing front and rear aspects. When not in use, the groin protector was stowed inside the front of the vest.

A DPM camouflage 'RBR 201' ballistic vest dated October 1995. This is a simple vest with Velcro waist adjustment and large SAPI pockets at front and rear. (Armour courtesy Sabre Sales)

DPM camouflage 'RBR 3053' vest. This was an upgraded version of the RBR 305 model. It had two large pockets beneath large flaps on the front, shown at left. The RBR 3053's groin protector was detachable, fitting to a Velcro strip beneath the flap visible at the lower edge of the front of the vest. Velcro waist and shoulder fastenings allowed for rapid removal of the vest if required. At right is the rear aspect of the 'RBR 3053'.

Great Britain

A view of police-type vests, showing typical patterns compared to military vests, is warranted. Shown here is a police ballistic vest of the type used during the 1990s for firearms and related tasks. The vest did not have SAPI plates and was not stab proof. It weighed 9lb (4.08kg). Dated 1995, this vest was manufactured by Armour Shield.

Current-issue pattern of police body armour, as used by Hampshire Constabulary, but typical of the types in use with UK police forces. The vest provides dual stab and ballistic protection. The plastic clips allow fitting of an Airwave personal radio or other equipment.

Police firearms officer's ballistic vest. The vest issued to armed officers has standard stab/ballistic inserts, but also has additional SAPI plates fitted. A two-part ensemble, shown at left is the inner ballistic vest and at right the outer cover, which has multiple pockets for items such as handcuffs, CS spray, ASP baton and a Taser.

Rear panels from a police body armour vest. At left are the quilted ballistic panels and at right the stab-proof panels. The stab panels are inserted in a Pertex cover, then placed inside a second cover along with the ballistic panels.

Great Britain

In a quiet part of urban England, uniformed and plain-clothes firearms officers attend the scene of an incident involving firearms. A suspect is detained while a Tactical Firearms Team officer looks on. The plain-clothes officers wear covert body armour, just visible beneath the grey shirt of the officer at the centre of the picture. (Martin J. Brayley)

A Hampshire Constabulary Tactical Firearms Team (TFT) officer armed with an HK G36 rifle. This female officer wears the pattern of ballistic vest shown opposite. (Martin J. Brayley)

Members of Surrey Police TFT photographed during a training exercise. The image of modern policing has changed dramatically in recent years. (Martin J. Brayley)

Chapter 3 Other Nations – A Visual Summary

Belgium

Belgian 'Jigsaw' pattern camouflage 'Veston Pare-Eclats' worn by Belgian forces during the 1990s. This armour is similar to the pattern worn by Dutch forces and was made by Seyntex-Wittock in 1996.

A UN blue body armour vest manufactured by 'Highmark' of Dromara, Northern Ireland, and made in the standard PASGT-style configuration with additional shoulder and neck protection. This vest was used by Belgian soldiers serving the UN. (Ed Storey)

Detail of the United Nations logo on the Highmark vest. (Ed Storey)

The Highmark vest worn by a Belgian airman, Sgt Filip Annaert, serving in Kosovo with the UN. (Ed Storey)

Other Nations – A Visual Summary

A Belgian soldier, serving with the UN in Somalia in support of Operation *Continue Hope* during 1996, gives bottled water to Somali farmers in Kismayo. The soldier wears British-issue DDPM camouflage CBA. (US DoD)

Belgian Quick Reaction Force soldier chats with a local Afghan Nation Army (ANA) officer in Kabul. The Belgian wears a plain OD armour vest of a pattern used by the majority of Belgian troops serving in support of International Security Assistance Force (ISAF) operations in Afghanistan. (NATO)

Canada

Canadian-issue 'Body Armour Fragmentation Protective, Vest Style' introduced in 1994. Being a bilingual nation, Canada also has a French nomenclature for this vest: 'Veston Pare-Eclats'. It has large blocks fitted to each side of the upper chest to act as rifle butt supports, and a webbing tape at each shoulder to prevent load bearing equipment slipping. This vest was probably inspired by the 1980s' French 'Gilet de protection pare-éclats modèle commun'.

Canadian Body Armour Ltd vest manufactured in 1994. This pattern of vest, with groin plate, saw only limited use. (Ed Storey)

SNC Industries' body armour produced in 1991. The filler was marked as being made from Kevlar treated with Zepel D. The cover was ballistic nylon. The vest saw only limited issue. (Ed Storey)

Other Nations – A Visual Summary

Rank strap, positioned centrally on the front of the vest, bearing the rank slide of a WO1.

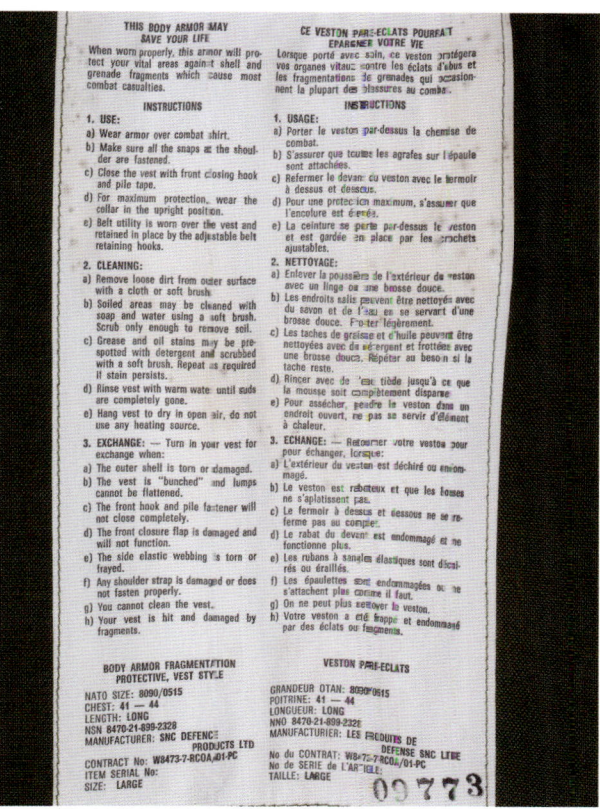

Bilingual instruction label from the Canadian Body Armour Fragmentation Protective, Vest Style. The left-hand side is in English and the right side in French. All details, including stock numbers and contract numbers, are duplicated. The vest was made by SNC Defence Products Ltd.

Staff Sergeant Ed Storey, Royal Canadian Engineers, photographed wearing the Body Armour Fragmentation Protective, Vest Style in Bosnia. (Ed Storey)

Vest, Tactical, Load Bearing showing the internal pocket that held the front SAPI plate. (Ed Storey)

Other Nations – A Visual Summary

A Canadian CV90-40C crewman wears the 'Carrier, Small Arms, Frag, Temperate' (CADPAT) personal body armour during an exercise held in California with US troops. While the armour and Bergen are in temperate camouflage, the field uniform is in arid finish. The armour has the collar fitted, but the shoulder pads have been removed. (US DoD)

The Vest, Tactical, Load Bearing, being used in conjunction with the US-issue PASGT vest and helmet. The PASGT provided fragmentation protection, but had no SAPI plate. The use of the PASGT and vest with SAPI provided maximum ballistic protection. It is worn here by PO Dave Maxim. (Ed Storey)

Wearing the desert-issue personal body armour 'Carrier, Small Arms, Frag, Arid' Sgt Maranda Robertson patrols Kandahar, Afghanistan, in August 2008. The armour has the collar and shoulder pads fitted. The Canadian personal body armour is made by Pacific Safety Products. (ISAF)

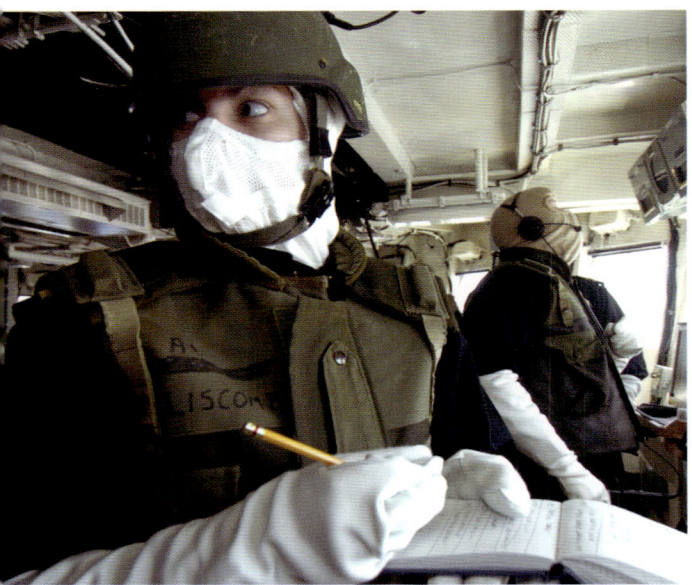

On the bridge of HMCS Algonquin during July 2006, watch officers wear a variant of the Armour Fragmentation Protective, Vest Style during a live missile firing. (US DoD)

'Vest, Tactical, Load Bearing' ('Veste, porteur d'equipment tactique'). This equipment vest was in use from about 1993 to 2003. It has pockets for magazines, bayonet and ancillary equipment. It also had internal pockets to allow the fitting of SAPI plates. At left is the front aspect and to the right, the rear of the vest. This example is dated 1997. (Ed Storey)

Denmark

Danish 'Fragmentationsvest' body armour, introduced in the early 1990s. This pattern is very similar to the German 'Splitterschutzweste'. However, it is produced in the Danish M84 camouflage and has two side-mounted magazine pouches and a front rank strap. (Armour courtesy Julian Attwood)

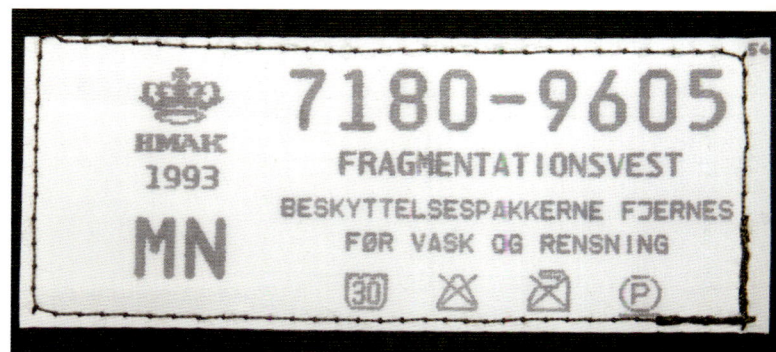

Manufacturer's label from the Danish Fragmentationsvest showing that it was manufactured in 1993. (Armour courtesy Julian Attwood)

The Fragmentationsvest, in M99 desert camouflage, is worn by this soldier patrolling in Helmand Province, Afghanistan, during January 2009. Although similar to the preceding vest pattern, here the magazine pouches have been moved to the front. (ISAF)

A Danish Konstabel serving with the UN Headquarters, Zagreb, Croatia. Photographed in February 1994, this soldier wears the M84 camouflage Fragmentationsvest with M75 (G3) bayonet fitted to the front and a UN patch on the right shoulder. (Ed Storey)

A second shot of the desert Fragmentationsvest in use in Afghanistan. It is worn with a temperate M84 camouflage tactical vest. In 2010 the Danish army introduced a new UBACS for wear with body armour. Similar to the British pattern, it was produced in the M99 desert camouflage. (ISAF)

Detail of the 'DANMARK' title fitted at the shoulder of the Fragmentationsvest. (Armour courtesy Julian Attwood)

France

The 'Gilet, Type Air V' ('Aircrew Armour Vest Mk V') was a composite (polyester glass) and nylon vest that consisted of a back and two front panels, joined by quick release fasteners at the shoulder and waist, allowing the vest to be rapidly discarded. Period images show this type of armour being used in Algeria by T-6 pilots. It was usually worn over the parachute harness, with a US M1952A vest worn beneath for additional protection and to defeat any spall. The large ballistic plates make the vest bulky and uncomfortable in wear.

Label from the Gilet, Type Air V, showing that it was made by Gallec.

This 'Gilet, de protection' was manufactured in France during the 1960s. It was considered for adoption by Canada and efforts were made at marketing it elsewhere. It was made from polyester glass ballistic plates with a nylon cover. It weighed a little over 12lb (5.44kg).

French Gilet, de protection. Similar to the US M1955 vest in basic design, it has two front pockets with snap closures, and a zipper and snap-closure front flap. A short strap and snap at each waist provided support for the equipment belt. (Armour courtesy Eastwestrading)

1 - Désignation de l'article	1 - Designation of item
GILET DE PROTECTION	**ARMOURED VEST**
2 - Présentation	2 - Description
Le gilet affecte la forme d'une chasuble sans manches, s'enfilant par une ouverture formant encolure et l'ajustage à la taille s'effectue par un système de sangles avec boucle, assurant la fermeture du gilet sur la partie ventrale. Deux poches à soufflets sont plaquées sur le devant.	The vest looks like a non sleeved chasuble that can be slipped on by an opening that serves as a collar ; the adjustment of the vest is realized by a buckle and strap system insuring closure at the front part. Two extensible pockets are plated at the front.
La protection est constituée :	Protecting consists of :
a) sur les épaules et à la bavette centrale par plusieurs épaisseurs de tissu nylon haute ténacité,	a) several layers of highly stiffened nylon cloth on shoulders and bib,
b) sur le devant et le dos, par des plaquettes amovibles introduites dans des alvéoles possédant deux volets latéraux en tissu élastique qui maintiennent en place la plaquette.	b) detachable plates, at the front and at the back inserted in elastic cloth alveoles provided with two side flaps maintaining the plate.
3 - Matières utilisées	3 - Used materials
— Tissu nylon 215 kaki foncé imperméabilisé.	— Dark khaki nylon cloth 215, waterproofed,
— Tissu nylon 415 (pour épaulière et bavette).	— Nylon cloth 415 (for shoulder strap and bib),
— Plaquette en matière plastique stratifiée (verre polyester).	— Stratified plastic plate (polyester glass).
— Sangle en lin pour bordage.	— Linen strap rimmed.
— Sangle en nylon pour système de serrage.	— Fastening by means of nylon strap.
— Sangle élastique pour maintien des plaquettes.	— Plates held in position by means of elastic strap.
— Boucle à axe mobile.	— Buckle with movable shaft.
— Bouton pression.	— Snap-fasteners.
4 - Nombre de tailles : 4	4 - Number of sizes : 4
5 - Poids moyen unitaire : 5,500 kg	5 - Average weight per item : 5,500 kg
6 - Remarque :	6 - Remark :
Cet article a été breveté par la Société ARIEL, 39, avenue de Friedland à Paris, mais cette Société a cédé à l'Administration le droit de reproduction. Cette cession ne vaut pas pour un pays étranger.	This item was patented by the ARIEL Company, 39, avenue de Friedland Paris, but this company has transferred the copyrights to the Government. This transfer is not available for foreign countries.

Descriptive document accompanying the original photograph of the Gilet, de protection, showing that it was made by the Ariel company in Paris. It was available in four sizes.

Other Nations – A Visual Summary

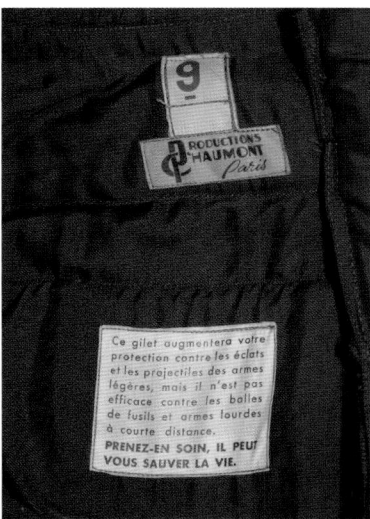

Interior of the Gilet, showing that this example was made by Productions Chaumont of Paris. The large black and white printed label indicates that the vest provides protection from fragmentation and 'light arms', but not rifle or heavy weapons fire. The last line states 'TAKE CARE, IT CAN SAVE YOUR LIFE'. (Armour courtesy Eastwestrading)

'Gilet de protection pare-éclats modèle commun' manufactured by Nebon-Carle of Lyon, in 1986.

Gilet de protection pare-éclats modèle commun.

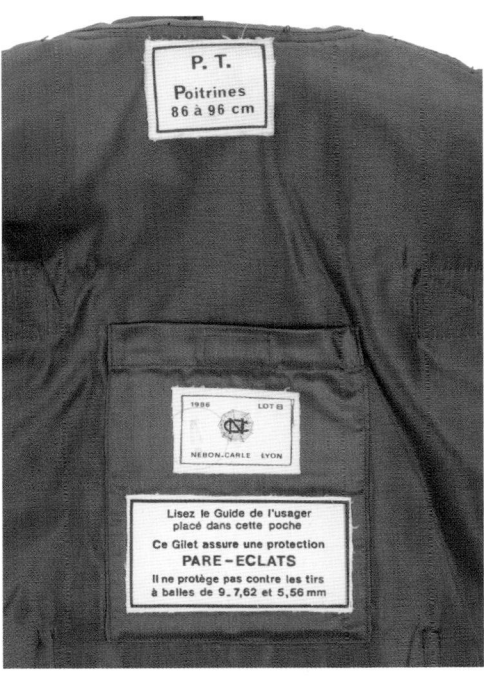

Rear interior of the Gilet de protection pare-éclats modèle commun, showing the size, maker and protection labels. The latter two are stitched to a small pocket that contains the user guide. The lower label advises the reading of the user guide and notes that the vest protects against fragmentation, but not 9mm, 7.62mm or 5.56mm rounds.

The subdued field rank badge for a Caporal, fitted to the 1980s' Gilet de protection pare-éclats modèle commun.

Other Nations – A Visual Summary

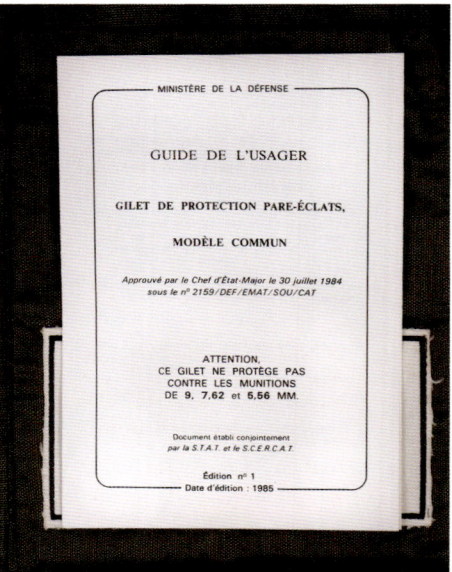

User guide for the Gilet de protection pare-éclats modèle commun, stored in the internal rear pocket.

Gilet de protection pare-éclats, similar to the German Splitterschutzweste. The vest front bears the rank insignia of a Sous-lieutenant. The vest has provision for the carriage of SAPI plates, inserted via a zippered opening. A small ridge at each shoulder aids in retention of field equipment straps or a rifle sling.

Interior label of a 1990-production Gilet de protection pare-éclats. As with the preceding example, this vest was made by Nebon-Carle of Lyon. The lower label advises the reading of the user guide and notes that the vest protects only against fragmentation.

Operation *Eagle*, Afghanistan 2008. A French soldier wears Central European camouflage 'Gilet pare-balles série 3', with full equipment load, during operations against insurgents in the Sarobi Mountains. This aramid vest weighs around 23lb 2oz (10.50kg) and is issued complete with a carriage bag, user guide and a small blade used for cutting away the vest in an emergency. A small transparent pocket on the front contains a blood group indicator. (ISAF)

Kabul, April 2009. This soldier wears a tan-camouflaged lightweight plate carrier during urban patrol operations. (ISAF)

Germany

The model 1916 Sappenpanzer (trench armour), also called the 'Infanterie Panzer' (infantry armour). The four-panel articulated Sappenpanzer was a silicon-nickel steel armour designed for static positions. It was supported on the shoulder and could be worn at the front of the body or on the back. Troops in the prone position or standing against a parapet, often used the armour reversed. The Sappenpanzer was manufactured in three sizes, marked in paint on the inside of the breastplate. (John Bodsworth)

The Sappenpanzer in use by a German soldier, who also wears the 'M1916 Stahlhelm' with the 'Stirnpanzer' (forehead armour) front plate.

The improved 'M1917 Sappenpanzer'. This armour (also referred to as the 'M1918') incorporates modifications set out in official documents dated 1917. These included a rifle butt stop at the right shoulder, a hook positioned at each lower edge of the breast plate (for the carriage of equipment) and a strap to help prevent the armour from falling off during movement. (John Bodsworth)

Detail of the articulated panels on an M1917 Sappenpanzer. The webbing strap linked the four armour panels, while felt pads provided a buffer between each. (John Bodsworth)

Other Nations – A Visual Summary

An undated image shows German troops in a frontline position. M1916 Sappenpanzer and Stirnpanzer are stored in a pile at the lower right edge of the image – ready for immediate use as required. Sappenpanzer reached German troops in quite large numbers as production was rapidly increased. In June 1917 the scale of issue was two sets of Sappenpanzer per rifle and MG company, but by 1918 entire sections were equipped with the armour.

The standard German Bundeswehr-issue 'Splitterschutzweste' (fragmentation vest) of the 1980s. It is a simple garment with high collar and additional shoulder protection. The increased protection offered by the flexible shoulder sections was minimal. There is no provision for additional SAPI plates, the small pocket to the front being a utility pocket.

The filler of the Splitterschutzweste consisted of six sections of aramid, in waterproof nylon covers. Top left is the back section, top right is the front section, bottom left are two neck sections and the two shoulder sections. The main body panels were made by R. G. Walker GmbH, in 1987, while the neck and shoulder sections were made by LBA and Wahler GmbH.

Bristol-manufacture 'Körperpanzerung Aussenweste (body armour vest) Type 18' produced for the Bundeswehr with the standard British DPM camouflage fabric cover and manufactured in 1985. This view shows the detachable groin protector, worn fixed in the 'up' position. This allowed greater freedom of movement or comfort when seated, as well as increasing the protection over the chest. The vest is fitted with a large collar and has flock-covered anti-slip shoulder pads with ridges, to assist in weapon support, at the shoulder (the flock is heavily worn on this example).

The Körperpanzerung Aussenweste Type 18, with the groin protector in position.

The Körperpanzerung Aussenweste Type 18 in use by a Bundeswehr Panzer Grenadier at Prizren, Kosovo, in December 2000. (KFOR)

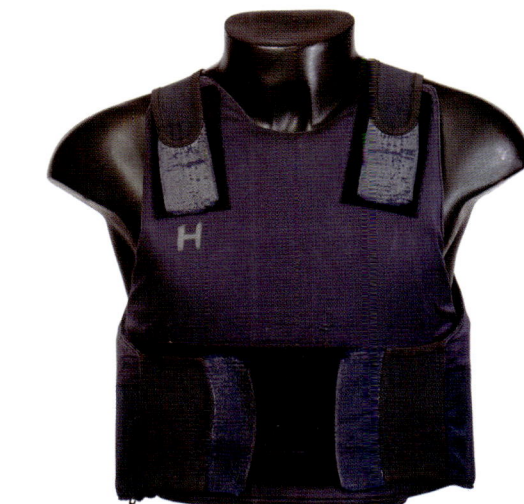

RIGHT: Covert police body armour vest of a pattern produced by Enforcer GMBH during the 1990s. It weighs 5lb 8oz (2.49kg) and is listed as Schutzclasse I (protection from pistol-calibre ammunition). It is a simple vest-type garment, with Velcro shoulder and waist adjustment.

A heavy (30lb; 13.61kg) armour produced by TIG of Koln, during the 1980s. The armour used large overlapping plates. It was secured using quick release clips at each shoulder and a double waist strap. The waist strap uses a British P1919-type buckle, easily released when discarding the armour.

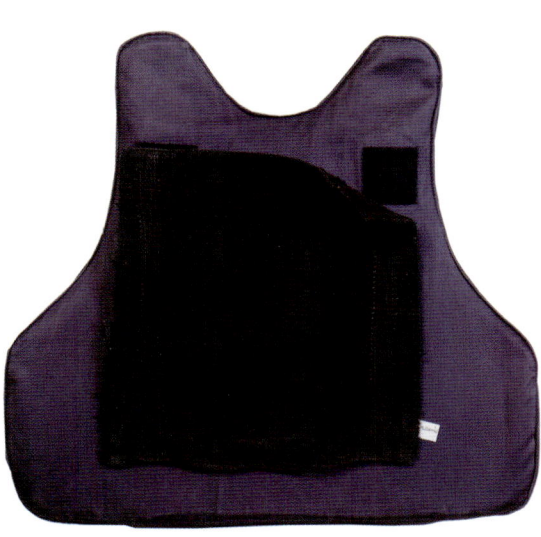

The inner faces of the police armour have a Velcro-fitted towelling section for the absorption of sweat. It is removable for easy laundering. The towelling section is little more than a commercially available face flannel with added Velcro, but it serves its purpose well.

An early production 'Mehler ST' armour vest. The Mehler ST had three ammunition pockets, for HK G36 rifle magazines, fitted to its front. A modular equipment fitting was attached at the front of each shoulder, allowing for attachment of ancillary items. SAPI plates could be fitted to large pockets at the front and rear of the vest. The early vest had a large Cordura collar with green edge binding; the heavy duty fabric caused chaffing around the neck and face. A groin protector could be attached at the lower edge, but is not fitted in this image. Fastex clips were originally installed at the bottom edge of the two outer ammunition pockets, but they have been removed from this vest. The first pattern vest was soon modified by the addition of modular equipment fittings at the lower edge to each side. Each fitting allowed the attachment of two equipment items, such as an entrenching tool, canteen, or ancillary pouches.

Other Nations – A Visual Summary

The early production Mehler ST armour vest in use with German troops of the 2nd Reinforced Infantry Company, serving in Bosnia and Herzegovina (BiH).

At left is the third pattern Mehler ST vest with the groin plate fitted, but secured up over the abdomen, typically worn in this manner when vehicle mounted or when the plate would impede movement. At right is the rear of the Mehler ST vest, showing the equipment pouch fitted over the SAPI pocket. This example has a strip of reflective tape fitted below the pocket.

The large collar of the early Mehler ST vest was modified to a slightly smaller pattern, with a cotton fabric face. The cotton fabric provided a less abrasive surface in contact with the face and neck, but it was also less hard wearing. This third pattern vest has the groin protection fitted. The Mehler ST was first fielded in Kosovo in 2000.

LEFT: The Mehler ST ballistic plate laid over the rear SAPI pocket. The pocket opens at the right and is secured using Velcro and a press snap.

RIGHT: Third pattern Mehler ST vest manufactured for use in Afghanistan and produced using 'Wustentarn' camouflage.

138

Other Nations – A Visual Summary

Rear view of the third pattern Wustentarn Mehler ST vest.

The ballistic filler used in the Mehler ST vest. It offers protection in Schutzklasse 1. This level is resistant to 8 grain 9mm ammunition fired at a velocity of 1,560fps (475m/s), with a back face deformation of 22mm (0.87in). This image shows the front and rear panels, and the groin panel. The two collar components are not removable.

Bundeswehr soldiers deliver humanitarian goods to a children's home in Kosovo, in 2000. The soldier in the truck wears the then newly introduced Mehler ST vest, while the soldier receiving the package has the Körperpanzerung Aussenweste Type 18. (KFOR)

German Major General Bruno Kasdorf, Chief of Staff, NATO forces in Afghanistan, wears the body armour vest associated with AFV crews, in Afghanistan during 2007. Of note are the large grab straps at each shoulder and the metal loops for attachment of communications equipment. (USAF)

Other Nations – A Visual Summary

German Panzergrenadiers patrol the Kosovan city of Prizen in December 2004, following extensive unrest. The armour worn by the Grenadiers dates to the early 1990s and is of a pattern used by police and army personnel on public order duties (note the baton carried on the armour of the soldier at right). (ISAF)

RIGHT: The 'Mehler MI-275-949' tactical infantry vest, often referred to as the 'IdZ Mehler Armour Vest'. IdZ (Infanterist der Zukunft; infantryman of the future) was an integrated equipment project, the armour being but a single component of the system. The IdZ vest uses a framework of webbing loops, similar to the PALS attachment concept, and has a removable neck and shoulder yoke that can be worn independently by AFV crews. The vest incorporates a hidden grab strap and is available in sizes medium, large, x-large and xx-large. (Thomas Kuehnlein, Mehler Vario System GmbH)

The Mehler MI-275-949 tactical infantry vest in Wustentarn camouflage finish. (Thomas Kuehnlein, Mehler Vario System GmbH)

An early image of the 'Flecktarn'-camouflage IdZ Mehler Vest in use by a Bundesweher Panzer Grenadier at an OP observation post in the Kosovan city of Prizen, during December 2004. (KFOR)

Iraq

A member of the Iraqi Police TSU (Tactical Support Unit, or SWAT team), photographed in Basra during 2005. He wears a simple blue ballistic vest with 'POLICE' written on the front in English and Arabic. (Martin J. Brayley)

A pattern of vest manufactured in the UK in 2004 and exported to a number of buyers, including Iraq. The vest has two integral pouches on the front waistband fastening and one larger magazine pocket at the right side. As well as ballistic filler there is provision for a SAPI plate to be worn front and rear.

Iraq, 2008 and soldiers wear a pattern of vest that saw widespread use among Iraqi police and military forces, but which has progressively been replaced by camouflage patterns. Uniform is ex-American 'choc-chip' camouflage DBDU. (US DoD)

Other Nations – A Visual Summary

Iraqi police officers patrol in the Meshra al Bawi area of Baghdad in 2007. A variety of armour types is in use, with no two men wearing the same pattern. A DBDU plate carrier and a DCU OTV vest can be identified at the far right of the group. (US DoD)

Iraqi soldiers manning an IVCP (Improvized Vehicle Check Point) in Sa'ada, on 7 July 2008, wear DCU uniforms and DBDU camouflage plate carriers with PALS loops. (US DoD)

An Iraqi Air Force crewman dons body armour at Joint Base Balad, 2008. The armour provides very basic cover to the chest and lower abdomen, with considerably less area of protection than standard aircrew armour patterns. (USAF)

Israel

Israeli body armour manufactured during the late 1970s. The vest is missing a flap-top pocket from the lower right front. It has a waterproof cover, with non-slip fabric surface at each shoulder for weapon retention. Israel's position in world politics has meant that the production of military equipment has been a priority for the small nation. Body armour has been produced by Israel for many years, although US patterns were used to some extent during the 1970s.

Israel Defence Forces (IDF) body armour based on the US M69 vest. It has a few minor differences from the US original: There are no grenade loops, it has an elasticized section at the back of the neck, and a small hanging loop is also fitted, visible at the top of the picture.

Label from the IDF M69-type vest showing IDF 'Zahal' property stamp at top right and the year of manufacture, 1984.

An Israeli soldier photographed in Lebanon during 2006. He wears body armour and a load carrying vest. (Dor Posner)

Italy

World War I Italian 'Ansaldo' body armour. This was a heavy plate armour that weighed 21lb (9.53kg). It was effective, but cumbersome. As well as being used as a body armour, the plate could be ground-mounted, two legs (visible as a ridge, at either side of the plate in this image) could be swung out and back to support it. A small firing slit – visible on the lower left side of the plate above the ammunition pouches – allowed a rifle to be fired from behind prone cover.

During a 2003 exercise, Carabinieri worked alongside USAF personnel at Aviano Air Base in Italy. These Carabinieri are wearing US PASGT armour and PASGT helmets. (US DoD)

Italian body armour in desert camouflage, believed to have been used by the San Marco Regiment in Somalia. Showing influence of the PASGT vest, it has shoulder pads, grenade loops, two lower pockets and a rank tab. (Armour courtesy Eastwestrading)

An Italian Capitano of the 'Death Company' (shock troops), wears a heavy steel 'Farina' helmet, and body armour with chest and shoulder protection, during December 1917.

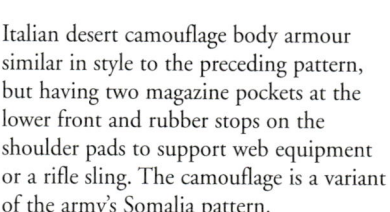

Italian desert camouflage body armour similar in style to the preceding pattern, but having two magazine pockets at the lower front and rubber stops on the shoulder pads to support web equipment or a rifle sling. The camouflage is a variant of the army's Somalia pattern.

144

Other Nations – A Visual Summary

Improved Italian woodland camouflage body armour, with SAPI plates and removable groin protection. The vest also has two grenade pockets and quick release Fastex-style fastenings.

An Italian soldier searches a civilian man suspected of setting fires, in the town of Gorbavice, a suburb of Sarajevo, prior to the town being returned to Bosnian control. He wears a woodland version of the body armour shown previously. The shoulder pad stops can be clearly seen. (US DoD)

Blue police armour being worn by a member of the Carabinieri serving in Basra during 2005. The armour has pockets for large SAPI at front and rear, and a detachable groin plate – not worn in this image. (Martin J. Brayley)

Italian soldiers on patrol during an exercise in Afghanistan, during 2008. They wear woodland body armour and tactical vests. Many nations rely on secondary equipment carriage systems rather than carrying equipment on the armour. The benefit of this is that in an emergency, ordnance can be jettisoned with the tactical vest, yet the armour can be retained – essential during casualty evacuation. (ISAF)

Italian army engineers work on a bridge at Forward Operating Base (FOB) Bala Murghab, Afghanistan, in 2008. This engineer wears woodland camouflage body armour with SAPI plate. (ISAF)

Japan

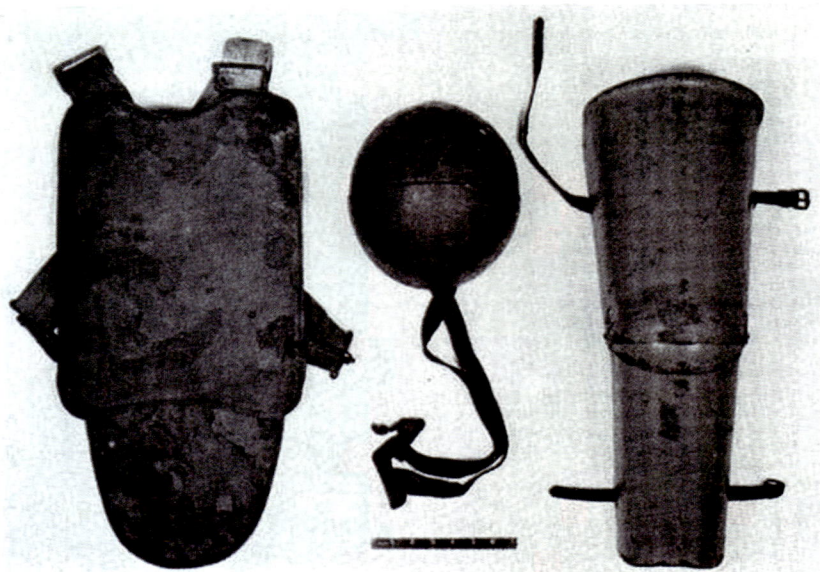

During World War II, the Japanese made extensive studies of body armour and deployed a number of patterns of armour into frontline service. These armour patterns included basic fragmentation vests and more extensive ensembles that included groin and leg protection. Shown here is the 'Type 111' armour with helmet and leg shield.

Lieutenant Colonel Ridgeway Trimble, photographed wearing a Japanese armoured vest. Lt Col Trimble was at the forefront of US armour development during World War II and made extensive studies of captured Japanese body armour.

A Japan Air Self-Defense Force Staff Sergeant photographed during 2007. He wears a US-issue PASGT vest during an air defence exercise. (US DoD)

A Japan Ground Self-Defense Force (JGSDF) Leading Private wears the distinctive JGSDF camouflage uniform with camouflage body armour vest. (US DoD)

Netherlands

This Kogelwerend Vest is based on the British commercial RBR 305 vest. It is believed that initial contracts for this pattern of vest were placed with RBR, but that manufacture was soon taken up in the Netherlands. An improvement over the preceding vest, this one has pockets for SAPI at front and rear.

Dutch 'Kogelwerend Vest' (bulletproof vest) in British DPM material. This was the standard vest in use with the Koninklijke Landmacht during the 1990s. Web sections at the inner and outer edge of each shoulder aid in preventing equipment straps slipping off the shoulder. The two rows of loops along the front of the vest allow the attachment of equipment using US-style ALICE (All purpose Lightweight Individual Load Carrying Equipment) clips.

The RBR 305-type Kogelwerend Vest in use in Afghanistan by members of the 42nd Bataljon Limburgse Jagers, undertaking a search for weapons and explosives caches. (ISAF)

A Dutch soldier from Task Force Uruzgan patrols in the green zone of Afghanistan. The RBR 305-type vest is worn with a tactical vest to carry the soldier's equipment. The vest's loop system allowed limited carriage of only basic equipment. While Dutch troops wear DPM equipment, clothing is usually predominantly US DCU pattern camouflage, with some DPM clothing worn. (ISAF)

Norway

Polish, US and Norwegian soldiers of the HQ, 16th Airborne, North Poland Brigade (NORDPOL), photographed in Bosnia-Herzegovina during 1996. The Norwegian soldier wears OD uniform and body armour, although the field jacket would have been in 'M80' camouflage. (IFOR)

A soldier of the Norwegian Hans Majestet Kongens Garde (His Majesty the King's Guards), wears M80 camouflage pattern field jacket and body armour in 1998. (Norwegian Army)

Norwegian body armour of the 1990s, produced in the tricolour M80 camouflage. The vest has two magazine pockets for AG3 rifle magazines and loops to hold an equipment belt. (Armour courtesy Eastwestrading)

A Norwegian soldier, wearing M2000 desert camouflage uniform with plate carrier armour. This picture shows the dramatic change in uniform and equipment that has taken place in those forces committed to Afghanistan as the operational needs of that theatre dictate weapons and equipment requirements. (ISAF)

Mazar-e-Sharif, Afghanistan 2009. Norwegian soldiers wear M80 camouflage uniforms with M80 and (at right) 'M2000' desert camouflage plate carriers, fitted with PALS loops and used with tactical vests for equipment carriage. (ISAF)

Russia

During the early 1950s, Soviet authorities had been experimenting with new body armour patterns. In 1957 the '6B1' body armour was adopted. Using a wrap over 'Lancer'-type front, fastened across the chest with three buttons, the body enclosed multiple overlapping aluminium armour plates and ballistic nylon filler. It is believed that fewer than 1,500 of the 6B1 were ever made. Photographs from the later conflict, show that the armour was in limited use in Afghanistan. (www.soviet.com.pl)

The Soviet Army issued a variety of armour types to its troops during the Great Patriotic War. They were typified by the use of heavy steel plates not dissimilar to the World War I German Infanterie Panzer. Trials patterns were produced as the 'SN38', 'SN39' and 'SN40'. The standard wartime production model was 'SN42', the 'SN' being the Romanisation of the Cyrillic 'C' and 'H' (Es and En), the 'SN' translating as 'Stalynoi Nagrudnik' (steel breastplate). Weighing some 7lb 11oz (3.49kg), the armour was issued to motorized infantry and armoured infantry units. This image shows captured SN42 armour modelled by a German Obergefreiter. The armour was made of a large breastplate and a smaller abdominal plate; the breastplate on this example has two large-calibre holes to the front.

An experimental armour, first field tested in Afghanistan in 1979, was adopted as the '6B2' in 1981. The 6B2 was the primary armour of Russian ground forces during the conflict in Afghanistan. It was a very basic vest, relying on multiple overlapping 1.25mm thick titanium plates for armour protection. It had Velcro-secured shoulder sections and side straps, with additional straps secured by 'D' rings taking the weight of the vest at the shoulder. This vest has a green nylon cover, but earlier examples used tan canvas. Production was probably no more than 4,000.

The 'BZH 1 Pilot's personal armour system' vest was issued to aircrew. The armour resembled the World War II American Armor, Flyer's, Vest M1 and incorporated a similar quick release system. The BZH 1 incorporated shoulder and neck protection not found on the US vest. This illustration from a period Soviet manual shows the BZH 1 worn with a harness over the vest, concealing the quick release shoulder straps.

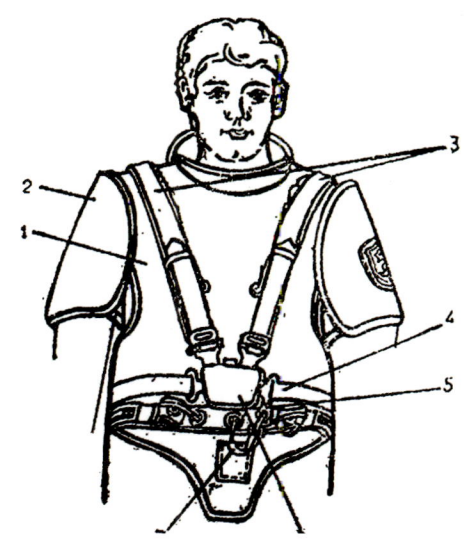

Other Nations – A Visual Summary

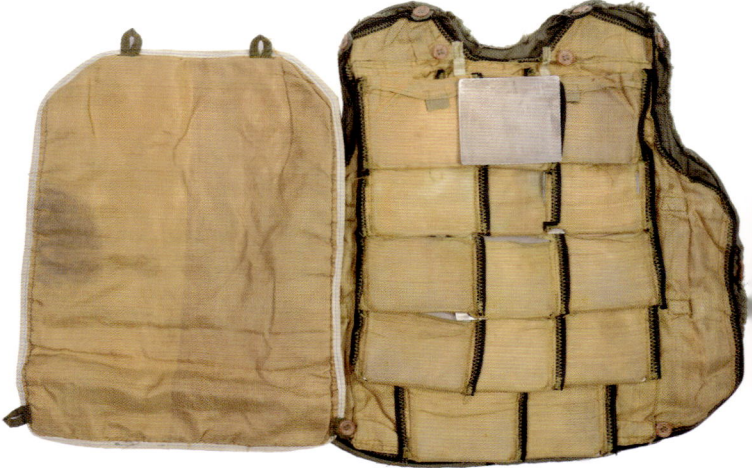

Interior of the front section of the 6B3 vest showing the nylon panel holding fourteen titanium plates, each in an individual pocket. The panel was buttoned into the vest at the shoulder and bottom edge. Four additional buttons allowed the attachment of the backing pad shown at left. With the exception of the top three, which had small Velcro tabs, the pockets were open topped. As can be seen in this example, the metal plates easily wore through the pockets.

The '6B3' armour was adopted in 1985 as the replacement for the 6B2 and saw use during the closing stages of the conflict in Afghanistan. It had four magazine pockets on the lower front, each holding a single 30-round AK magazine, and a central chest-mounted utility/plate pocket. A large equipment/plate pocket was fitted to the upper back, with two grenade pockets at each side of the lower back. The vest was secured using Velcro shoulder flaps with web security straps, and two web-adjustment straps at each waist. Original 6B3 covers were drab brown, but green was soon the predominant colour. A cover in dark blue was issued to naval infantry. The armour was still in use during 2008, but with a cover in 'Flora' camouflage. Two rifle/equipment pads and large anti-slip rubberized panels were fitted at each shoulder. The pads provided a stop for the rifle butt and prevented web equipment from slipping from the shoulders.

LEFT: The ballistic panel insert of the 6B3 vest, worn without the outer cover. The front and rear panels could be fastened together independently of the cover, since the fitting straps were a component of the panels and not the cover. While this was not a common practice, period images show that some soldiers wore the armour in this manner. The panels are worn with the 'RD-54' webbing set.

ABOVE: Adopted in 1986, the '6B4' was an improved version of the 6B3 armour, with a Velcro-fastened waist cummerbund in lieu of the side straps of its predecessor. It also had improved lower body protection, with a drop-down groin section holding four ceramic plates (shown worn buttoned-up in this image). Frontal ballistic protection was from ceramic plates, while rear protection was from titanium plates.

Other Nations – A Visual Summary

The ballistic plate pockets of the 6B4 vest were fixed to the cover at the shoulder and were not removable. Shown here at left is the front panel, which held 26 heavy ceramic plates, each in an individual pocket with a small Velcro strap top closure to the open pocket top. The thick plates required a suitable padding to provide some comfort in wear and the 6B4 vest used two large foam-backed panels, shown at right. The rear ballistic section of the vest used titanium plates and a nylon pad like that used with the 6B3.

Russian ballistic plates. Above is the 90mm square 13.5mm thick B4C boron carbide ceramic plate that provided level III protection. Below is the 1.5 × 120 × 115mm titanium plate that provided level II protection. An alternative 7mm titanium plate (not shown) also provided level III protection.

The '6B5' resembled the 6B3, but with an added collar section. While the Kevlar pads were attached with buttons, the heavy ballistic panels were fixed using carbine clips and buttons, better supporting the weight of the heavy panel. The 6B5 was used in large numbers during the Chechnya conflicts, with production believed to have been stopped in 1998. The 6B5 can be found with covers in a variety of camouflage schemes. It incorporated several minor improvements over the 6B3 and 6B4, including a short protective collar and large rifle 'butt-stops' similar to those that had been used on the 6B3.

A 6B5 armoured vest with 'KLMK'-pattern camouflage in use by a Ukrainian soldier serving with the UN in Sarajevo, during 1994. (Ed Storey)

Other Nations – A Visual Summary

Russian paratroopers serving with SFOR, photographed at Tuzla Air Base, Bosnia-Herzegovina, during 1997. They wear the 6B5 vest with drab green cover. Of note is the belt fitted through the belt loops that were provided on the 6B5 cover. (US DoD)

The '6B11', '6B12' and '6B13' armour were similar in design. They were basic vests with no pouches, requiring a web system or assault vest for the carriage of magazines and ancillary equipment. Introduced in 2003, the '6B15' armour was specifically for armoured vehicle crewmen, with a pocket arrangement suited to their specific user requirements. The 6B13 body armour shown here was used by airborne forces, marines and special units of the Russian forces. This armour shows a marked improvement in quality of product when compared to earlier Russian armour patterns. The shaped steel SAPI plate provides good coverage and will stop a 7.62mm Dragunov round. The armour is cut well at the shoulders, allowing good freedom of movement when using a weapon. The new millennium saw the introduction of the '6B23' body armour as a component of the 'Barmitsa' soldier system (from the Russian term for medieval chain mail armour, also known as 'Barmica') as a replacement for the older 6B12 and 6B13 armour. (Private collection)

Rear of the 6B13 body armour showing SAPI plate pocket and the typically oversized 'stops' fitted to prevent equipment straps or rifle slings slipping from the shoulder. (Private collection)

Serbia

DPM camouflage 'Type 3' body armour produced by Borovo in Yugoslavia under a Federal Directorate of Supply contract. The vest offers Level III protection and is a copy of the Bristol Type 3 armour. Pockets at the front and rear allowed the fitting of SAPI plates, there are two large magazine/general purpose pouches on the lower front chest and non-slip rifle patches at each shoulder. This pattern saw use during the Yugoslavian civil war. At right is a rear view of the Type 3 armour. The large SAPI pocket is clearly defined and has a Velcro-closed opening on the right. (Ljubisa Kovacevic)

Yugoslavian 'Type S/VK-P' ballistic vest produced by Borovo during the 1980s. This pattern also saw use during the Yugoslavian civil war, often with police units. It has a single rifle patch at the right shoulder and two chest pouches. Unusually, it has an external waist strap that fastens at the front with carbine clips. At right is the rear of the armour. This example was made in 1990. (Ljubisa Kovacevic)

ABOVE: 'Point Blank Hi Lite IIIA' Kevlar/Spectra ballistic vest imported into Yugoslavia during 1992. The US 'M81' camouflage vest has four small pockets imposed over the large frontal SAPI pocket and broad elastic side closure sections. Velcro closures at each shoulder allow for easy donning, or rapid removal in an emergency. (Ljubisa Kovacevic)

RIGHT: Interior rear view of the PZB M98A vest showing the rear drop-down panel that protected the posterior. The panels were held in the 'up' position by Velcro strips when not required. Few manufacturers offer a protective butt panel on body armour, and even fewer are in use with military forces. This vest was made in 1999, by Mile Dragic.

ABOVE: Serbian- (Mile Dragic) made 'PZB M98A' ballistic vest. It has large pockets at front and rear for SAPI plates and the lower front is fitted with four detachable pockets for 7.62mm M70 rifle magazines. At right is a rear view of the vest showing the large pocket for the SAPI plate. The vest has drop-down groin and butt panels that can be secured internally when not in use. Butt panels are rarely encountered on body armour. A similar pattern of vest is retailed commercially by Mile Dragic as the 'Paragon'.

Other Nations – A Visual Summary

Serbian-made 'OMZ M98' vest as issued to combat engineers. The four front pockets are fitted directly over the large SAPI pocket. Unlike the PZB M98A, the OMZ M98 is not fitted with integral groin and posterior panels, but does have increased axillary coverage and can be fitted with additional deltoid protection, as well as anterior and posterior groin panels. At right is the rear aspect of the OMZ. The flap at the lower edge allows a posterior groin protector to be fitted using Velcro sections. A similar flap is positioned on the lower front of the vest. Manufactured by Mile Dragic in December 2000. (Private collection)

Serbian 'M99' plate carrier. This simple two-pocket carrier allows ballistic panels to be worn over the back and chest to protect the vital upper torso organs. It provides only a limited area of coverage, with no axillary protection whatsoever.

The M98A ballistic plates used with this M99 carrier are made from lightweight polyethylene, with an integral high-density foam anti-trauma backing, which helps make them buoyant. They provide NIJ Level III protection.

Although the M99 carrier can be worn alone, it provides no means of equipment carriage, which is provided by the 'M99 tactical vest'. The M99 tactical vest is worn over the M99 plate carrier, as used here by Serbian troops liaising with Swedish KFOR soldiers monitoring the Serbia/Kosovo border during 2007. (NATO KFOR)

Serbian-made 'PBB M99' ballistic vest. This vest offers Level IIIA protection. As with other Serbian vests, there are two large pockets for the SAPI plates fitted at the front and rear of the vest. Additionally, the PBB M99 has a grab strap across the rear shoulders, allowing a casualty to be dragged to cover if required. Essentially the PBB M99 is a simplified version of the PZB M98A. At right is the rear of the PBB M99 vest, showing the rear SAPI pocket and the nylon webbing grab strap. The cover is manufactured in Serbian 'M89' woodland camouflage. Made by Mile Dragic in August 2002. (Private collection)

Slovenia

Croatian made 'Zastitni Prsluk' (protective vest) manufactured by Borovo in 1994. This vest was used by Slovenian forces in the mid-1990s. Rubber ridges at each shoulder prevent slipping of load bearing equipment. A single rubberized rifle patch is fitted at the right shoulder. The groin protector is shown fitted, but worn up for ease of movement. At right is the rear view of the Slovenian Zastitni Prsluk, showing the large SAPI pocket.

Zastitni Prsluk, with the groin protector worn down. The groin protector is fitted using four Velcro straps and is easily removed.

One of the two heavy SAPI plates issued with the armour. The plates each weigh 7lb 11oz (3.49kg), bringing the total armour weight to 25lb 8oz (11.57kg).

Chapter 4 Conclusion – The Future of Individual Body Armour

The development of improved body armour continues apace at the time of closing this tome. Ultimately no great advances have been made recently in weight reduction without a resulting significant loss in protective coverage of soft armour. Much of the improvement has been cosmetic or in striking the correct balance between weight and protection to suit specific roles. Compared to the overall burden of soldiers in the field, the difference in weight between a full body armour vest, such as the MTV, and the reduced weight of the SPC is actually quite minimal, but the reduction in protective coverage is marked. It is unlikely that any major changes can be made to the currently available soft armour, but a reduction in the weight of SAPI plates would provide a major breakthrough.

The use of liquid armour, currently being researched by BAE Systems, could offer a major improvement to the soft armour filler. Liquid armour utilizes shear thickening fluids (STF) and used in conjunction with Kevlar it can reduce the thickness of ballistic fabric required. In BAE Systems' testing, ten layers of Kevlar with STF provided greater protection than thirty-one layers of dry Kevlar. The reduction in Kevlar improves freedom of movement in any Kevlar/STF vest, but weight reduction would again be minimal. The greatest barrier to improved ballistic protection remains the weight of the equipment borne by the average combat soldier.

This is the US Army prototype combat uniform from the Objective Force Warrior Program being researched and developed at the US Army Soldier Systems Centre during 2002. The prototype helmet incorporated infra-red thermal day/night video cameras, chemical-biological sensors, a global positioning system, broadcast heads-up display and ballistic protection. The torso garment incorporated body armour and included physiological status monitors that allowed the individual soldier, as well as medics on the battlefield, to know exactly what the individual soldier's physical condition was at any given time. Although only a concept, the reality of such equipment being in frontline use is rapidly approaching. (US DoD)

Glossary

Aramid: Abbreviation of aromatic polyamide, a high strength fibre similar to Kevlar. Para-aramid fibre is produced commercially as Kevlar and Twaron

Abdomen The area between the thorax and the pelvis (not including the back), often called the belly

ACP Automatic Colt Pistol (a type of cartridge)

Anterior thorax Front of the thorax (see thorax)

Axillary Pertaining to the axilla, the armpit region

BuAer US Navy Bureau of Aeronautics

Back face deformation, or back face signature The deformation effect of a non-penetrating projectile on the rear face of body armour. The NIJ standards allow 44mm of indentation. Excessive back face deformation causes blunt-trauma injury

Blunt-trauma injury Compression or shock injury caused by a non-penetrating impact, such as when a projectile is stopped by body armour and resulting from back face deformation

CBA (UK) Combat Body Armour

CBA (US) Concealable Body Armor

CBRN Chemical, Biological, Radiological and Nuclear (warfare)

Composite Ballistic protection made up from a mix of materials, such as Kevlar and ceramic, usually to give the best weight to protection ratios

CPE (US) Cupola Protective Ensemble

CQB Close Quarter Battle

DAPS Deltoid Axillary Protection Systems

Deltoid Deltoid muscle. Situated across the shoulder and used to raise the arm

Doron A woven glass-fibre fabric laminated with plastic. Named after Lieutenant Colonel Georges Doriot, US Army

DDPM Desert Disruptive Pattern Material (camouflage)

Dyneema A high strength synthetic polyethylene fibre, having a strength to weight ratio some 40 per cent greater than aramid

ECBA Enhanced Combat Body Armour

EOD Explosive Ordnance Disposal

EPPE Enhanced Personnel Protection Equipment

ESAPI Enhanced Small Arms Protective Insert. Protects against 7.62mm AP

ESBI Enhanced Side Ballistic Insert

ETO European Theatre of Operations

FSN Federal Stock Number

IBA Interceptor Body Armour

IBPE Improved Ballistic Protection Ensemble, or Kestrel armour

ICPE Improved Cupola Protective Ensemble

IED Improvized Explosive Device. A home-made bomb associated with terrorists

Inguinal Pertaining to the groin

IPBA Improved Performance Body Armour, or Osprey body armour

IRR Infra-red reflective

IOTV Improved Outer Tactical Vest

Kevlar Trade name for a synthetic para-aramid fibre developed by DuPont in the 1960s

LBE Load Bearing Equipment (US). Web equipment, or webbing in UK service

LR Long Rifle (a type of cartridge)

LTD fastener 'Lift The Dot' fastener. A quick-release closure used in various military applications

MOLLE MOdular Lightweight Load Carrying Equipment. MOLLE is an integrated, modular load-carrying system designed for a variety of configurations, allowing soldiers to tailor kit to meet individual or tactical requirements. The MOLLE system uses a flexible arrangement of loops and straps called PALS

MRC Medical Research Council

Nape The back of the neck

Glossary

NIJ National Institute of Justice

NSN NATO Stock Number

Nylon A synthetic polymer (polyamide) fibre developed by DuPont in 1935. Synonymous with 'nylons' (stockings), the fabric was further developed during World War II as a replacement for silk and other fabrics in military use. Originally called 'No-Run' the term was unjustified since the fabric did indeed run (ladder). Nylon was coined as an arbitrary name and is not a compounding of other words

OG Olive Green

Operation *Banner* Code name for British military operations in Ulster (Northern Ireland) between August 1969 and July 2007

OTV Outer Tactical Vest

OQMG Office of the Quartermaster General

PALS Pouch Attachment Ladder System. An arrangement of webbing loops that form a grid to which pouches and equipment can be fitted using semi-rigid straps. PALS is used with the MOLLE load-bearing system and is often erroneously called MOLLE loop. The PALS system is standard with US and British forces and is being adopted by many forces worldwide

PASGT Personnel Armour System Ground Troops

PECOC Personal Equipment Common Operational Clothing project

PEO Program Executive Office, or PEO Soldier

Posterior thorax Back of the thorax (chest)

PLCE Personal Load Carrying Equipment

PVCP Permanent Vehicle Check Point. A protected permanent structure, usually situated at military installations or other vulnerable locations (see VCP).

QMC Quartermaster Corps

SAPI Small Arms Protective Insert. Also called Trauma Plate. Protects against 7.62mm

SCRDE Stores and Clothing Research and Development Establishment

SFSG Special Forces Support Group

Spall Particles or fragments ejected from a body due to impact or high stress. The process is called spallation or spalling. Typically used to describe fragments of ceramic SAPI plates broken away by a high-velocity impact, and pieces of the impacting projectile. Spall can be reduced or defeated by a secondary, soft-armour backing to hard-armour SAPI.

SPCS Soldier Plate Carrier System

SPIW Special Purpose Individual Weapon. The SPIW was a developmental rifle that used a flechette-type ammunition. The flechette saw limited use in Vietnam

Standoff The required separation between the wearer's body and armour vest, required to limit or prevent blunt-trauma injury. Armour is usually worn in contact with the body, with little allowance for standoff

Thoracoabdominal Relating to the thorax and abdomen

Thorax The part of the body between the neck and the abdomen; the chest

Twaron Para-aramid aromatic polyamide fibre developed in Holland during the 1970s. Originally known as Arenka it was re-named Twaron in 1984. Similar to Kevlar

UBACS Under Body Armour Combat Shirt

ULW Ultra Lightweight Warrior

USAAF United States Army Air Force. Created on 20 June 1941 by redesignation of US Army Air Corps

USAF United States Air Force. Created as independent air force from the USAAF on 18 September 1947

USMC United States Marine Corps

Velcro Brand name associated with hook-and-loop fastener

VCP Vehicle Check Point (see PVCP).

Bibliography

Bashford, Dean, *Helmets and Body Armor in Modern Warfare* (Yale University Press, 1920)

Brayley, M. J., *Tin Hats to Composite Helmets* (The Crowood Press, 2008)

Brayley, M. J., *USAAF Airman Service and Survival 1941–45* (The Crowood Press, 2007)

Heaton, Lieutenant General Leonard D., *Wound Ballistics* (Medical Department, United States Army Office of The Surgeon General, United States Army)

Judge, Thomas H., *Ballistic and Spall Tests for Aircrew Body Armor* (National Technical Information Service, 1972)

Scheetz, Hayden A., *Human Factors in Evaluation of the USMC M1955 Armored Vest and the Proposed Titanium Nylon Improved Conventional Munitions Protective Armored Vest (48 plate)* (National Technical Information Service, 1973)

'Advance Materials and Process Technology', AMPTIAC Newsletter (Vol. 5, No. 1, Winter 2001)

Armor, Body, Fragmentation Protective, with Collar (Mil-A-12370D US Army, 1963)

Armor, Vest, M1952B (MIL-A 12370A US Army, 1954)

Ballistic Protective Clothing for Operations in Northern Ireland (SCRDE, 1981)

Ballistic Resistance of Body Armor, NIJ Standard-0101.06 (US Department of Justice, 2008)

Body Armor in a Hot and Humid Environment (Bureau of Medicine and Surgery, Navy Department, 1969)

CRS Report for Congress: US Army and Marine Corps Equipment Requirements (Congress Research Service, December 2006)

Defense Logistics (US Government Accountability Office, June 2007)

Final Report – Body Armor (Department of the Army, 1967)

Helmets and Body Armor (Office of the Chief of Ordnance, 1945)

HOSDB Body Armour Standards for UK Police, Parts I, II and III (Home Office, 2007)

Men-at-Arms No. 157: Flak Jackets – 20th Century Military Body Armour (Osprey Publishing, 1984)

Operation Telic – United Kingdom Military Operations in Iraq (National Audit Office, HMSO 2003)

Pattern Recognition Body Armor and Aircrew Assemblies (US Department of Commerce, 1968)

Personnel Armor Handbook (US Naval Weapons Laboratory, 1971)

Purchase Description Body Armor Multiple Threat/Interceptor Improved Outer Tactical Vest (US Army, 2007)

Resume on Programs on Development of Body Armour Undertaken at Watertown Arsenal during World War II (US Army, October 1945)

The Infantry Conference, Report of Committee on Equipment and Supplies (US Army, June 1946)

United States Army Rangers in Somalia: An Analysis of Combat Casualties on an Urban Battlefield (US Army)

Index

6B1 149
6B2 149, 150
6B3 150, 151
6B4 150, 151
6B5 151, 152
6B13 152

ACS (Army Combat Shirt) 70, 71
Air Warrior 68, 69
Armor, Body, Fragmentation Protective, with Collar 40, 42, 46, 84, 85

CBA/ECBA 10, 94, 95, 98, 99, 157
CBA (US Concealable Body Armour) 70
CPE/ICPE 67, 156, 157
Chemico 76, 78, 79
Cover, Replaceable, 1979 Pattern 88, 89, 94
CVC. 50

INIBA 91, 92, 93, 94, 95, 96, 101, 121

Kestrel 107, 108, 109, 157

MARCIRAS 73
Mehler 137, 138, 139, 140
Merlin 107
MRC 18, 80, 81, 82, 83, 157
MTV 61, 62, 63, 156

M1951 30, 31, 32, 33, 34, 37
M1952A 11, 30, 31, 33, 36, 38, 44, 91, 83, 84, 85, 88
M1952 33M1955 36, 37, 132, 159
M1953 30, 32, 33, 35, 37

M1 16, 19, 22, 23, 24, 25, 30, 31, 84
M2 21, 23
M3 18, 20, 21, 22, 23, 24, 25, 26, 30
M4 18, 20, 22, 23, 24, 26
M5 23, 24, 26
M12 27, 28, 29, 30, 33
M69 38, 40, 41, 42, 43, 46, 47, 85, 86, 88, 91, 143
M71-N 43

NFV (Navy Flak Vest) 73, 74

Osprey 9, 10, 107, 108, 109, 110, 111, 112, 113, 114, 115, 117, 118, 119, 120, 121, 122, 157, 159
OTV/IOTV 8, 9, 52, 53, 54, 55, 56, 57, 58, 59, 60, 61, 62, 64, 66, 67, 70, 142, 157

PACA (Protective Apparel Corporation of America) 73
PECOC 114, 116, 117, 118, 122, 158

Sappenpanzer 135, 136
Sentinels armour 16, 17
SPC 62, 63, 156, 158.
SPCS 64, 158

TMBAS (Tactical Maritime Body Armour System) 75

UBACS 121, 131, 158
ULW (BAE Ultra Lightweight Warrior) 65, 158

VBA 39, 90

Wisbrod armour 17